TRANSGRESSOR IN THE TROPICS

TRANSGRESSOR IN THE TROPICS

by Negley Farson

AUTHOR OF "THE WAY OF A TRANSGRESSOR"

Seeing Red

Harcourt, Brace and Company   New York

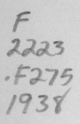

Typography by Robert Josephy

CONTENTS

I. Boat Load   3

II. Exiles   15

III. Tropic Trader   21

IV. "Old Captain Johnny!"   28

V. In the Islands   32

VI. South American Set-Up   39

VII. Colombian Contact   50

VIII. Spanish Main—Bullfight   57

IX. Spanish Main—Sailors Don't Care   65

X. Spanish Main—Shedding Illusions   72

XI. Night in the Cooler   89

XII. Along the Canal (I)   95

XIII. This Rough World   106

XIV. Along the Canal (II)   111

XV. Price of Freedom   121

XVI. Seeing Life   130

XVII. A Single Man's Post   137

XVIII. Lost Souls   143

XIX. Capital in the Clouds   147

XX. How the Strings are Pulled   158

XXI. Enough of Politics!   176

XXII. Two Haciendas   183

XXIII. Man of Letters   188

XXIV. Over the Andes   200

XXV. A Bureaucrat's Heaven   211

XXVI. Military Dictatorship   216

XXVII. The Military Dictator   222

XXVIII. Mutiny in Ecuador   226

XXIX. Cocktails in Quito   231

XXX. Serfs of the Andes   240

XXXI. "White Man's Grave"   248

XXXII. The Man Who Lost His Head   254

XXXIII. A Sailor's Husband   258

XXXIV. Portrait of a Dictator   267

XXXV. Two Exiles   279

XXXVI. A Duck Shoot   284

XXXVII. Chilean Reflections   287

XXXVIII. Landscape with Fish   295

XXXIX. Antonio and Eric   302

TRANSGRESSOR IN THE TROPICS

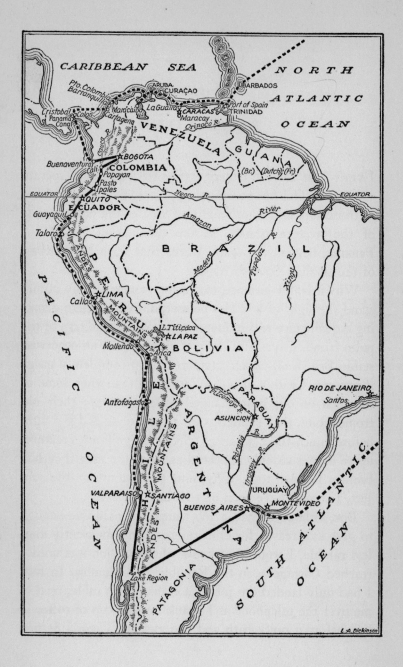

Chapter I

BOAT LOAD

EVERY boat for the tropics carries its quota of desperate characters. This has no sinister application. The answer lies in those soft seas whose night air rustles the palm fronds of the western islands, in the debilitating jungles of Panama, beyond the soapy waves that wash the seacoast of the sizzling Spanish Main.

Why it is, for instance, that some women simply cannot stand the sight of a scarlet poinsettia. Why a mere drinking acquaintance will suddenly tell you that the rasp of the palm fronds drives him crazy at nights. Why an otherwise stable British oil-tanker captain will go completely ga-ga if presented with a cactus. Why it was that when some of the men on our boat changed back again into their old tropic white, they suddenly got disconsolate and got tight before lunch-time, whereas others, insignificant creatures up to date, suddenly appeared as twice the men they had been in London togs. Why, now that we are on the subject, I should have been on that boat myself.

For, although I had a job which was plausible enough to give as a reason for embarking on my apparently aimless ramble, I would not know what that job was until I reached Cartagena, in the Republic of Colombia. In fact, I had only landed the job by a transatlantic cable, read to me over the telephone as I drank my last cup of coffee in bed before a quick bath and taxi rush to Victoria Station

3

three hours before my boat sailed, or was scheduled to sail; for the procrastination, endemic in South America, began that watery sunset in Dover harbor. And while my job would pay for about half my expenses, it was up to me to find the money for the rest of them. In other words, the job was incidental—an aftermath—a tardy excuse and insufficient fund-provider for the experience I felt I must have at that particular junction of my life in order to set things right with myself.

The fact that my job was to involve me in long arguments with military dictators was also unexpected—and most exhilarating.

I had deliberately selected South America because (*a*) I had never been there before; (*b*) in something over twenty years trying out what life was like in other parts of the world, I had always steered clear of South America. I had a strong hunch that that part of the world would bring me bad luck. And in this idea I am not sure even yet that I was not quite right. At any rate, I can speak with feeling when I say that if you want a strictly emotional adventure to test, or reorient, yourself, South America is the right spot to go for it.

✢ ✢ ✢

This secret knowledge, my own reason for being there, warmed me with a feeble glow of romance as I talked with our one and only lady tourist on this autumn Dutch *stoomboot*. She had gray hair and lived in South Kensington; but she had a childish enthusiasm, mixed with apprehension, over this travel adventure occurring so late in her life, that made the mornings seem all they ought to be when you have nothing to do but lounge in a deck-chair and watch the bubbles of your white wake vanish under the soft trade winds.

"My brother," she said, with her air of constant surprise at the family paradox, "is an admiral—and yet I have never been to sea!"

I felt like making the poor joke that I was always at sea and at that particular moment I had never felt so completely adrift. Such confidence would have cheered her immensely. I am sure it was an experience she expected from travel. She was a nice woman. And when she was solicitous about my drinking so many gin-slings with the island traders I bore her no grudge for it, but merely cut down in her presence; and I cheered her all the way through to the semi-finals in deck-tennis. Even lost a shilling on her. The nearest I ever got to a confession was to inform her one night, after a discussion about palm-trees and moonlit atolls, that, if she was setting out to see the world, I, like the very wise Count Keyserling, was merely traveling to see what effect seeing the world would have upon me.

"How beastly egotistical of you!" she said.

And I am sure everyone will agree with her.

❦ ❦ ❦

That ironic moon below the Tropic of Cancer had some surprising revelations. One of these was an obvious tourist, with curly black hair like Epstein's Rima, who cornered me in the smoking-room one night. He announced: "I think sex is wrong, don't you?" Then he giggled: "What I mean is, I think a young man should keep himself to himself, don't you?" I felt like telling him that as long as he did that everything would be quite all right with me. The point was that he sat opposite me at my table, and he poured sugar into his red wine at night. Spoonfuls of it. There was no getting away from him, as he was also going to Cartagena, in the Republic of Colombia. There was no way to demolish him, because he was an athletic youth; he walked around on his hands, with his feet in the air, for his morning constitutional. So he was too tough for me. And even after eighteen days at sea I was not to be liberated. He turned up at dawn my first morning in Cartagena and bedeviled me into going for a swim with him.

Actually, he was a Syrian from Manchester, going out to Medellin, known locally as "The Manchester of the Andes," to resume his business of selling the latest thing in cotton frocks to the local inhabitants. And this, aside from showing you what the South Americans have to put up with, is an example of what you might expect to meet on a tropical boat.   ✐   ✐   ✐

There was a hiatus on Victoria platform while we waited for our train to pull out, nobly filled in by a British magnate who posed as proudly as Mr. Toad for the Press photographers. He, pompous personage, was going out to Barbados, where his family have enjoyed the rich income from sugar plantations since the days of Charles the First. The mere spectacle of his presence among the rest of us, going out on such inauspicious jobs, subdued our whole train. The Press men were such snobs that they would not snap anyone else. It was a pity. We had a Bishop in our carriage whose vintage was "Oxford, my dear sir—of over half a century ago." A famous and satiric Bishop! And when, at the last instant, a red-faced young man was decanted into our laps, who would insist on telling us that this was his third trip round the world, and who couldn't be prevented from relating all the weird places his journalistic profession had led him to, the Bishop scored a lovely bull's-eye with:

"My dear sir, you should have a Boswell for your Johnson."

* * *

I came on the Parrot in the depth of Dover railway station.

"Please," she asked, in seductive sing-song, "where is the telegram?"

As I was looking for that myself I offered to try and find it with her. We had to run for it. I carried her cardboard bag. I was relieved by its lightness; shocked when I was told it was the only luggage she had on board ship. I was rushing to the telegraph office to send a wire; she to get one. And while she was insisting there must be some mistake—"I tell you, dere mus' be one!"—I tried to place her. Her species, I felt sure, was tropic, not English. She was a study in green and scarlet. Red hair (she wore no hat); sullen, scarlet lips; scarlet, and very dirty, fingernails; and the most daring collection of fake jewelry I have ever seen on any girl. Her blouse was bright scarlet and her skirt and coat were the light green of a parrot's wing. Later, I was to learn that she also had scarlet toenails. For the present, the other outstanding thing that I noticed about her—aside from her almost vicious despair—was that she was clasping a bunch of very much wilted chrysanthemums that looked as though they might have been (and I soon came to the conclusion they were) recently plucked from the vase of some cheap Soho restaurant. There was no telegram.

"It will be on the boat," I tried to assure her. "It always is.

"Are you Spanish?" I asked.

"Me! What do you take me for? I am English—born of British parents in the West Indies."

✶   ✶   ✶

On the way out to where the black sides of our ship glistened under its gangway lights in Dover harbor, she announced that she had come to England, only five months before, on this very same boat. "I came first class." Now she was returning third.

Staring at me with her smoky eyes, in which there was no iris in the pupil—none to be distinguished, that is, in all that smoldering—she spoke to me as if I were to blame for it all. "Mister, let me tell you; money is the root of all evil. I *know*."

Encouraged by my emphatic nod, she went on to say that five months before she had come to London to get a job in, of all places, the Post Office. For some reason they had not wanted her there. Then she had tried taxi-dancing in some of the Soho midnight "clubs." Also a flop. That was a thing I could *not* understand; and, when I asked her how such a thing was possible, she again glared at me as if I were to blame for it all and made that profound remark about the root of all evil.

She must have been right. At any rate, her Tottenham Court Road relations must have thought so; for when she could no longer pay them for her board and lodging they told her to pack up and go back to Trinidad.

She produced her purse and showed me her third-class ticket. It was a slick purse: scarlet leather, black onyx clasp, with her initial set in diamonds. Inside it was ten shillings.

"And dat's all I've got!"

Again she stared at me as if it were all my fault. And I suddenly realized that in those resentful eyes I represented all the men she had had to deal with in England— Soho night-clubs not excepted.

✓ ✓ ✓

I waded through the lather of lost bags and passengers round the purser's office to get her telegram. It was there. It read: "AU REVOIR CARLO."

"He didn't even use the nine words," she said.

✓ ✓ ✓

Through the passionate desire of two Dutchmen to room together my berth was changed, and I found that I had drawn the Bishop as a cabin-mate. When I got down he was already going into camp. He was an old campaigner. Out of a canvas hold-all suspended by the washstand peeped, bulged, or dangled every instrument known to a proper old gentleman's toilet. There was even a brush for his felt slippers at night, a chore he never neglected during the twelve days that I bunked with him. And already residing on the washstand was a little tin billy that I learned was for his hot shaving-water.

He had great courtesy. Although the bunk away from the porthole was his by right, he was kind enough to ask me if I minded the other one. "Not in the least," I said. "When we got below the Azores it will be nice to have that porthole open."

"Ummm . . . must be careful of draughts."

✤   ✤   ✤

I might say that at that moment in the convulsive English Channel, and for the next three plunging days, we might as well have been going across the Atlantic in a tunnel as far as any glimpse of the ocean was concerned. The prudent Dutch had lashed in the decks with canvas tarpaulins, and it was only by peeking around them that a sight was obtained of the black mountains of the sea rising one after the other, to crash into their valleys and rise again in unwatched loneliness—a wild, cold loneliness that made the snug campaigning curriculum of the Bishop transform Cabin C 135 into a home from home.

This was his twenty-seventh ocean passage.

The Bishop was the only man in my life whom I've known to rise every day at 6 o'clock to take a bath—and then go back to bed; who drank two cups of tea and ate one biscuit (no less and no more) precisely at 6.30—still sitting up in bed; who hung his two separate pajama pieces up on two separate coat-hangers; and who could shave all round with an old-fashioned razor, using only one hand (his left), without ever touching his face to draw the skin taut or slitting his throat.

He had picked up these habits, he told me, from living twenty-one years in British Guiana.

"Torrid spot," he said.

✶   ✶   ✶

At first I was inclined to resent the Bishop. I did not want to feel that I must always be on my best behavior in my own cabin. Had he but known it, he had as his cabin-mate a brand that was demanding to be plucked from the burning; and, had I enough perception to have grasped it, in this case, where the lion and the lamb were lying down together, the Bishop was the lion.

This truth gradually made itself known to me. Studying his gaunt, gallant face as he shaved it in the mornings, or looking down on his gray visage as he lay asleep, for two hours after every lunch, with a handkerchief tied over his eyes to keep the light out, looking like a blindfolded Justice, it dawned on me that in this figure from which the flame of life was fading I beheld a lesson from the tropics. Here was a man whom the tropics couldn't break. And his safeguard had been his unshakable daily routine.

Later, in the sweating jungle, I was to learn just why he hung up his pajamas on two separate coat-hangers every morning. Why he rose like clockwork at the ungodly hour of six, had his bath and nibble, and had got through most of his day's work before even breakfast-time. (He had a card index system of parishioners, a certain number of whom he ticked off for letters every day.) And in the degenerating climates of Central and South America I was to learn what high price others set upon an invincible man like that down there. He was a standard, something to steer by, a lighthouse among men. Yes, the Bishop was one of those interesting creatures whom the tropics had made!

He was no prig. The first time the Parrot—in emerald shorts this time—appeared in our habitat, the second class, the Bishop looked at the scarlet toe-nails peeping from her sandals and remarked: "I wonder that doesn't rub off." It was the only judgment he expressed on that exotic bird of passage. Yet when the extremely proper and bounding young Dutch bride of a pimply clerk from Curaçao galumphed past on their daily twenty-turns-round-the-deck, the Bishop buried his nose in his book until they swished past.

"Unpleasant couple," he said. "Too healthy."

✦   ✦   ✦

The Parrot, as you might have guessed, did not have an original mind. Yet she was a gorgeous example of what makes the world go round. She kept the third class from thinking about their poor tummies and iron bunks all the way to Trinidad. There was a nice communal spirit down there where there was only one living-eating-and-sitting-room, and the propellers thudded like drums to the continual squeals of the seasick babies. Happy family, with nothing much worth the losing between the lot of them; when the British magnate arose at the captain's table in first to make an infuriatingly condescending speech about the advantages of brotherly love, as exemplified by the British, among the nations of the world, the third class had long since had their grub and were now sitting in a ring round the Parrot while she sang "Knock . . . knock . . ." to the radio. She wore a dress of slinky scarlet that might have been painted on.

They were a mixed lot, the third class. Dutch clerks going back to the gaudy shops of Curaçao or Surinam; Englishmen for the west coast of South America or the oil fields of Lake Maracaibo. Syrians, like a plague of locusts, headed anywhere to sell anything.

"I sell lipsticks," grinned an Egyptian. "Lipsticks that won't come off."

"*You* . . . you're telling *me* about lipsticks!" said the Parrot, putting him where he belonged. With impressive sophistication she named all the well-known brands. "There is no lipstick," she announced, "that won't come off. I know."

"Vell, den, try it."

The Parrot did.

"Now kiss me."

↑   ↑   ↑

It was a request that very nearly produced a riot in the democratic third class.

"I'll bet you that girl isn't a day over eighteen!" gasped a leathery-faced young English sailor who was going out to take over a Brixham trawler at Trinidad. (And how did *that* get there?)

"She's not sixteen!" snarled a Syrian, born in Cairo, but now going out to "work" South America for some "beek" American concerns. "Mister, you be careful! Myself, I make it a point never to have a love-affair on board a boat. It might awaken prejudices."

"Then lay off this one," grinned the trawler-man, inviting the Parrot to join him in a mug of beer.

"You play deck-tennis," advised the Syrian; "we got eighteen days on board this boat."

✦   ✦   ✦

The trawler-man might as well have saved his beer. Lying flat on his back beside the Parrot, usually holding her hand—never sitting upright except to take nourishment—was a type of young gentleman whom the trawler-man would soon come to loathe. He was a beautiful youth, in a sugary, repellent way—a sort of Milk-Chocolate Apollo. And his story, like the Parrot's, was the public property of the chummy third class.

Four months before, his people had sent him to England to join the Army. Presumably they wanted to put some backbone into him. The Army simply snapped at him. But the recruiting sergeant must have been too much for him, for the Milk-Chocolate Apollo fled to London—and here he put up one of the most extraordinary feats of endurance known to man.

He went to three movies daily.

"All told, Ah saw 148 movies," he told me with that charming, worthless smile.

"Fine. What are you going to do when you get back to Barbados?"

"Me? My mummy's goin' look after me; she runs a hotel."

Then he lay down.

Chapter II

EXILES

When you have to sit opposite someone for eighteen days on board a ship, it's highly important who it is. My affliction, as I have mentioned before, was the Manchester-Syrian who put sugar in his red wine. Somewhat taking the curse off him were three British oil-tanker captains. For the first two days, as they never had a word for each other during mealtimes, I had taken them for Dutch; and one of them did have a red, round, hairless face exactly like a cherub, billykin—or Dutchman. On the third night he spoke.

" 'Enry," he said, "the only interesting thing on this menoo is the date."

"Aye, lad, and that's all they change."

From then on I clung to them. Each in his own particular fashion was an example of what a life of monotony and exile can do to, or make of, a man. The three were now returning, after their first leave home in three years, to their boring job of running oil-tankers out of Lake Maracaibo to the Dutch island of Aruba—fifty hours the round trip—out in the Caribbean. A gigantic American oil combine has built one of the largest oil refineries in the world on that god-forsaken rock.

"What's Aruba like?" I asked.

The two eldest oil-tanker captains scratched their jowls

and searched for a word. "Cactus," said one. "Bloody," said the other. The third merely sighed.

Other details given me were that nearly all the water used on Aruba has to be brought down in returning oil-tankers from the United States; that, to grow things, soil has to be brought across from Venezuela, but that the ants that come with it eat everything up; that Aruba is the spot where they grow the bitter aloes for patent medicines; and that it is an island inhabited to a painful extent by men only.

"We're just blawsted tram conductors!" the eldest exclaimed, describing the fifty-hour run they made into Maracaibo and back, a trip they made ten or eleven times every month, and had been making for ten years. "Wonder we sticks it."

"Why do you?"

"Because we ruddy well has to. Captains' jobs ain't to be had for the asking these days—not in the ruddy old British merchant marine. Why, we've got captains serving as mates on our ships!"

When I put the obvious question why a big American oil corporation should be using British ships and not American, they answered in chorus: "Because the Yanks won't stick it. They tried 'em. Maybe the captains might, but the crews just raised hell. So they took 'em off. It's us patient Limeys what does the job."

It was a first-hand example of what I found to be the case all the way through the tropics and down the west coast of South America: the Americans are content to hold the higher positions, but in the lower ones they always feel they can get as good, anyway more comfortable, a job back home. That is why in so many of the big American banks, shipping, and cable company offices in South America, you will find that the minor official you are talking to is an Englishman.

The Chicago steel-workers, said the British tanker captains, who had been brought down to build the big oil tanks, would often chuck up their jobs after a few days' work inside a tank where it was 136 degrees in the shade.

"Ho, boy!" laughed the Cherub, showing how American slang had already corrupted him, "when those Chicago riveters came out of those tanks they nearly tore Aruba up!"

One of those tanker captains, the Cherub, was one of the best-read men on contemporary literature I have ever met. He had plenty of time for it, he told me, and no distractions. And, reading in such solitude, his interest was poignantly vicarious; you could see that he lived himself as one of the characters. His discussion of *Dodsworth* was so contentious that it was like arguing with Dodsworth himself. And of Somerset Maugham he said: "I wonder that chap ever dares go back East after what he has written about those poor blighters out there." Every story was completely real to him . . . as they are to children.

In fact, in the limited horizon of their uneventful lives, where the slightest of incidents looms important, these two elder captains had regained almost a child's capacity for enjoyment. And their talk was all about men; the way other captains ran their ships, the scrapes they got into, the jokes they played on each other. Such as the time when Old Bill, the refinery drunk, lay unconscious after a blind, and they trussed up a young donkey and put it in bed with him. . . . They cut holes and stuck its ears through an old Panama hat.

"Ha!" The two captains reeled in their chairs. "When Old Bill woke up and saw that face on the pillow beside him . . . !"

They would have fallen over backwards if their chairs had not been screwed to the deck. . . . "He woke up and ran three miles . . . jumped right out of the window, he did . . . and we couldn't catch him. . . . That's a fact. Old Bill went T.T. for three months—until some blighter told him."

The young captain with them scarcely ever spoke a word. He just sat there and nodded his head to show that he was listening.

"He's brooding," one of the others told me. "Got married when he was back home. Won't see her again for three years. They're the ones that take it the hardest."

Gastric ulcers and perforated intestines played a dismaying part in their conversation. Drink, quite obviously, was the way some of the more desperate exiles on Aruba tried to kill the monotony and thoughts of home. "And if you come adrift down here," said the tanker captains, "you're done."

Not so the youngest captain. Although not yet thirty, he was already famous. Two magazines had printed stories about him. This was his exploit of taking a burning oil-tanker out from Aruba to save her from blowing up the station. With the bridge ladders burning beneath his feet, this young Sussex lad took command of her—it was not his tanker—and a crew of volunteers worked the ship for him. There was a pet-cock of some sort up forward that had to be turned off without delay if they didn't all want to be blown sky high. They wrapped a man in an overcoat, with wet towels over his face, and played the tanker's hose on him while he crawled forward through the burning oil to turn off the cock. Then they beached the burning tanker on a safe spot on Aruba, jumped overboard, "and swam like hell for shore."

The irony of this story, aside from the fact that the young British captain got no other reward than the publicity, which he hated (he didn't tell me this story), was the fact that he nearly broke his neck diving into the shallow end of the Dutch *stoomboot's* swimming-pool. And the interest he showed in keeping himself fit, the account of his fast football on the baking rock of Aruba, reminded me of the fanatic way the young British officers go in for sport in burning India: underlying motive being the same in both cases (whether recognized and admitted or not): a form of flagellation, to ease the strain of the sexual strait-jacket such careers in exile place upon their minds.

In Lake Maracaibo, where the three biggest oil companies in the world are still fighting it out to see which can get the lion's share of the "black gold" of Venezuela, many of the oil wells are standing out in the open water —some in the 100-foot depth—with pipes going down from 5,000 to 8,000 feet below them to tap the oil. Speaking of their seventy-mile run into Maracaibo and back to Aruba refinery, one tanker captain admitted:

"It fair gives me the willies. . . . Yet it's one of the grandest sights in the world, isn't it, 'Enry, to see those twenty-five steamers coming out, one right after the other,

on the tide? Don't think you'll see a sight like that anywhere else in the world, will you, 'Enry?"

'Enry was not to be moved. "Just so," he said. "Give
me half the money that's in one of 'em—and catch me
looking at that sight again."

"Ah, come on, lad; when you get back you can turn on
the wireless, can't you, and listen to Major Bowes?"

They both hastened to tell me that Aruba is wild about
Major Bowes. He broadcasts every Sunday night. Boon
and blessing is Major Bowes and his "Amateurs." By the
time the two oil-tanker captains had finished telling me
what a treat he was, I suggested they ought to put up a
statue to him. Major Bowes, probably quite unknown to
himself, is prime savior of Aruba's sanity.

✓   ✓   ✓

The big American oil company, following the Y.M.C.A.
tradition of installing Christianity through gymnasiums,
steel lockers, and shower-baths, has built a comfortable
club and model town on the island of Aruba; and the
way the men there now answer the woman-problem is by
marrying all the stenographers that the big company sends
down.

"No girl can miss it," said the oil-tanker captain.

Chapter III

TROPIC TRADER

"ALL FOR belly!" sniggered a Hindu as we watched the crates of whiskey, jam, biscuits, condiments, and what-have-you being slung overside into lighters off Barbados. A horn of plenty, that fairly made my mouth water, being tipped over for the complacent British sahibs on that smug little island. We had reached the first of the western islands. And, after ten days of meaningless sea and vaporous clouds along the horizon, the Hindu was back once again amidst the clatter of deck-winches and drays, swinging cargo-booms, the pungent, profit-promising stink of warehouses; all the familiar hustle and bustle that makes up the life of a trader—the life that was to dominate the action of our ship from now on. It simply made a new man of the Hindu.

"Got shop!" he told me excitedly. "Got biggest shop Curaçao; sell you everything. Come to *my* shop." He forced his card on me. Hitherto he had been just a dark little chestnut in the same corner of the smoking-room, singing quietly to himself as he read in Gujerati. Now, having safely regained the islands where he was obviously a merchant of importance, he was rudely bumptious.

He eyed Barbados malevolently. Whether he was envious of the rich cargo of food being taken ashore—his line was haberdashery—or whether he was at heart a Gandhi-wallah and disliked the British, I'm not sure. On the voyage, I had tried to draw him out on the Gandhi question, even going so far as to tell of my first two-hour talk with the Mahatma while the gray monkeys swung overhead through the branches of his mango-tree, out in Karadi, in "native" India. But this Hindu wasn't having any.

If he was anti-British, I can well understand why the sight of that low, green little island (twenty-one by fourteen miles) should have irritated him. In the first place, with its quilt of rising green fields and hedges, it might have been a chunk of the south English seacoast itself, were it not for those tall palms standing guard over the pink traders' sheds on the waterfront. Then, what other part of the British Empire would dare to dress its Negro harbor police in the straw hats and sailor's uniform of Nelson's day? These rowboat police were standing at salute now as the Governor's pinnace, with a red-tabbed brass hat of a general lolling in its stern, put out to escort our British magnate from the boat to the shore. Brass Hat's spurs jangled martially as he clunked up the ship's ladder and gave a pukka salute to the Personage. Old Service salute, forearm quivering, that wartime Australians turned into travesty. Yes, Barbados was more English than England herself, nowadays, would dare to be. That's the charm of it.

My first sight of it had been through a porthole that morning when the Bishop and I were politely inviting the other to shave first. Clear dawn. Through the porthole I watched the fleet of little "flying-fish" boats studded like butterflies across the green sea.

"Busy little island," said the Bishop, between swipes of

his old-fashioned razor. "Has to be. One thousand people to the square mile. Most densely populated place in the world except Malta, which is full of priests and soldiers, and"—another careless hack at his gray-stubbled jaw—"some parts of China."

"For some reason, Padre," I suddenly heard myself confessing to him, "I feel unreasonably gay today."

"Ought to, my lad, for you're losing me tomorrow. Tomorrow we reach Trinidad."

He put back his false teeth, that he always kept in his trouser pocket while shaving, and eyed me with a smile. He had never had much to say for himself; and what he had was usually sophisticated to the point of being caustic. Whether he knew or not that I had knocked off drinking a few days back I'll never know. Yet I fancied something must have lain behind his next remark.

"I hope," he said, "you will always feel as gay as you say you do this morning. The hot countries are dangerous."

✼   ✼   ✼

When a freshening of the trade winds caused our ship to slew gently on her cable, the patchwork green, masts of sailing-ships, and pink traders' sheds of Bridgetown were framed in the porthole—decorative traders' sheds that were to witness an island tragedy that day.

For there was another man on our ship who was even more anxious than the Bishop to reach Trinidad on the morrow—and he wasn't going to get there. He was one of the men who had simply doubled in size the minute he had changed back into his immaculate tropic white. An island trader. He wasn't the boss of his firm, but he held a good job in it; and, as we neared them, he and his wife began to talk more and more to me about life in the islands. Not a big life, they said; but they had a bungalow out on Mariquipa Road by the sea; they could swim when they wanted; usually after the office they played a few sets of tennis; and before dinner, between seven and eight, at the club, they always drank four gin swizzles. "Much more," he said with surprising modesty, "than a man of my ability could ever hope to get out of life in England."

They were returning to Trinidad after their first home-leave in nine years to England—which they still spoke of as "home." While in London they had seen every show that they could get a ticket for. But there had been nothing outstanding; nothing like when they had been there nine years before and *Desert Song* had been on. Wasn't that a marvelous show! She hummed me the tunes. But the outstanding achievement of this last trip to England had been the toys bought for the children—all born in the islands since the previous visit "home." For a time they had debated whether or not they ought to buy some "remaindered" books and take them back as presents to their friends in Trinidad; but the four children won the day. Result was they had taken a small trunk to Woolworth's and simply filled it with toys. "Quantity," he said to me the night before Barbados; "that's what counts at their age."

"I say," he said suddenly, "you'll understand, won't you, if I don't take you about in Trinidad? You see . . .

it's the kids . . . they'll be down at the dock to meet us tomorrow."

"Of course!" I said.

And there, lying in wait for him in one of those pink traders' sheds, was this telegram:

"TAKE OVER BARBADOS PENDING INSTRUCTIONS."

⚹ ⚹ ⚹

As a matter of fact, it was brought out to him by a brother trader who was full of admiration for my friend's keen judgment in buying, while on leave in England, all the olive oil he could, before Spain's civil war stopped the shipments.

"By Jove! You must've cleared hundreds per cent on that!"

But my little trader friend's face was gray. He heard nothing. Instead he went wearily off to his cabin to unpack some luggage and fill his own bag with clothes for the shore.

"Now listen, mummy," he said, as he lingered at the gangway. "Don't you give Johnny that railway train—*I* want to give him that. I want to show him how it *works*."

"All right," she smiled consolingly. "If only Johnny will wait."

"Well, don't you *tell* him about it then!" he almost screamed.

I went ashore with him in the launch. There would not be another steamer for Trinidad, he told me, for at least a week. "But, by God, I'll get there—I'll get to Trinidad if I have to take a schooner."

⚹ ⚹ ⚹

Not unexpected tragedy, watched in silence by the sympathetic third class, was the spectacle of the Parrot losing her Milk-Chocolate Apollo. He came ashore in the same launch that I did; immediately engaged in telling a slightly darker colored boy friend all about the 148 movies he had seen while in London. He never once looked back. I chanced to do so; and even from the shore I could see her red blouse, just a dot of color at this distance, above the ship's black side. Later, while I was having a "small" breakfast of beer and flying fish on one of those painted and shuttered balconies that overhang narrow Broad Street, I saw him pass below me, following a push-cart with his baggage, and turn into the Negro quarter.

✓   ✓   ✓

There is a statue of Nelson in Bridgetown, Barbados. It stands in Trafalgar Square. He looks as if he had just stepped up there for a moment, gazing at the white cross-trees in the Careenage standing up in the blue sky, listening to the woodpecker sounds of caulking mallets and the planing of topmasts just as they were in his day. Tall palms stand sentinel behind him, and a stand of scarlet poinsettia seems paying homage to the exalted dead.

I was so touched by this that I spoke about it when I came back aboard to an Englishwoman on our ship.

"Yes, it is touching," she said. "This whole place is simply redolent of his day; it's the nearest place to Nelson on this earth. I hope they can keep Barbados out of this rotten world."

"As far as I can remember," I said, "I think this is the first time I have ever seen scarlet poinsettias—at any rate, such beautiful ones."

"Beautiful . . . my . . . God!" She fell back as though exhausted in her chair. "Scarlet poinsettias! Do you know what I'd like to do? I—oh, well, what's the use?"

"What's the matter?" I was alarmed by the emotion I had stirred up. She was biting her lip.

"Well, you live in the tropics for a while. . . . You'll get to hate those damn' flowers . . . and anything vivid or brilliant . . . and those damn' little things that grow on the cactus or cacti or whatever I should call the beastly things. . . . You'll *loathe* them!

"You see," she said when she had cooled off a bit, "I live in Colombia. My husband's a contractor there. I've nothing against Colombia—I loved it when I first went there—but of course we were always thinking in terms of coming back home. We did. He made lots of money. If only he'd taken it out! My God—when you think of it—it would have been so easy. . . ."

She sat up and her voice was hard: "Slump. . . . Lost every stiver we had in England. . . . Tried to get out what we'd left in Colombia . . . couldn't because of these damn' exchange restrictions . . . *et voilà!* My kids are at school in England and I and the Old Man"—her voice changed to mockery—"have a nice—large—stucco house at Barranquilla—that's a sort of sun-scorched Colombian Miami—where, I suppose, we shall end our days. Don't talk to me about scarlet poinsettias. Our garden is rimmed with them."

"I won't," I promised. "Have a drink."

"Yes—and, if you can think of anything stronger than a double whiskey, order that."

Chapter IV

"OLD CAPTAIN JOHNNY!"

If I had had my own way (and it seems silly now to think that, up to then, there was no time when I couldn't have had it) I would have got off at Barbados. I would have taken a room off one of those cool green balconies overhanging Broad Street (not one over the local department stores, where they have gossipy cocktail lounges in the back rooms). I would have refused all efforts of bulging Negro wenches, with wicker baskets on their heads, to sell me oranges, and I would have spent my days over in the Careenage. They still call it that; and sailing-ships are still careened as an everyday performance in it. They are careened by merely hauling over their masts and lashing them down to the shrouds of other sailing-ships. In this position their bottoms, even their keels, are exposed, and gangs of Negroes out on rafts, usually directed by a fluent white man, are scraping, putting on fresh copper, even removing and inserting whole new sections of planks. The air is sweet with tar and oakum, the rattle of caulking mallets, and molasses. Also rum.

In such pleasant surroundings I might have actually done the thing that I merely played with the thought of this day: taken a schooner and sailed in and out among the islands. I would find peace there. The five years as a journalist I had spent watching England ride the world slump, the 800- to 1,000-word cable I used to send on

28

politics, economics, or social reactions every day, all the war clouds now darkening quarreling Europe, would be forgotten in these untroubled seas. It is true that between July and October they are often swept with hurricanes that blow the houses down—witness *High Wind in Jamaica*—but the sailing-ships being overhauled in the Careenage of Barbados, and the men that handle them, are built to expect this sort of thing. With perhaps the exception of the 1,000-odd bugeye and skipjack oyster-boats dredging back and forth across the mouth of the Potomac in Chesapeake Bay, I doubt if there is another such collection of strictly business sailing-craft left in the Seven Seas. And I noticed that two men I watched planing a topmast were treating it with the full consideration that one day it would be tested to its breaking strength.

It was while I was admiring the smooth taper they were giving to it that a young Negro appeared silently beside me and whispered:

"Want a nice sporting girl, captain?"

I shook my head. Then a nice sporting girl came up herself.

"Hel-lo, cap'n!" she grinned, invitingly sticking out her belly and showing her perfect teeth. "Wanta treat Old Mister Johnny? Mus' look after Old Cap'n Johnny. . . ."

This was a new way of putting it. At first I almost asked her who Mr. Johnny was! She was a nice young nigger wench, a bit overdressed, what with her white shoes and purple blouse; but she bore me no malice when I told her to shove off. But from then on my meditations about the peace of cruising the islands were continually interrupted by the approach of "nice sporting girls," and

if by any chance I was neglected for a moment, a young
Negro buck edged past, whispering: "Got to look after
Ole Mister Johnny, cap'n. Don't do let Ole Mister Johnny
get lonely."

The Careenage, in fact, seemed full of pimps.

✦   ✦   ✦

Back aboard ship, I saw the result of what had happened in Barbados from giving Old Mister Johnny a treat.
They were in rowboats all around us. For a coin of any
description they would dive into the water and retrieve
it. They would swim down to enormous depths. For a
shilling they would dive down, swim under the keel, and
come up on the other side of the ship. They were all
shades, from dusky white through to rich *café au lait*.

"There's a beauty!" said one of the British oil-tanker
captains. "That one's had more than a dash of good garrison blood!"

The man they were alluding to had the aspect of tragedy. He could easily have passed for a high-cheeked, hard-
bitten, imperious-nosed Englishman, were it not for the
fact that the color of his skin was a nauseating salmon-
pink.

"What in the old days they used to call a 'Red Leg,'"
explained the tanker captain. "Poor whites. Red Legs, I
suppose, because they used to run around with nothing
much more than singlets on them. Sorry-looking blighter,
isn't he?"

Then we both had to laugh. For the "Red Leg" had
pushed his craft out from the other results of giving Old
Mister Johnny a treat; and it is the only rowboat I have

ever seen which bore a Plimsoll mark. There it was, the black circle and cross line, painted on the side of the "Red Leg's" skiff, which was the same color as himself. And its name was *Mae West*.

Somebody threw him a coin. And, with a lack of dignity that was embarrassing to witness, the old salmon-colored man dived overside and fought a battle under water with the coffee-colored boys. He got the coin.

❧ ❧ ❧

"Although what he'll do with a Belgian franc I don't know," said the Manchester-Syrian.

Chapter V

IN THE ISLANDS

THE CHARM of life in the islands is that the stage is so small that every character feels important—as if the play could not possibly get along without him. Traditions are unjostled by world progress; and the spirit in which the islanders comply with obsolete etiquette bears the date of over half a century ago. My little Trinidad trader friend was well-off enough to have a "yard-boy"; tradition therefore required that he have one. And tradition, apparently, required the yard-boy to do no other work than just hang about the yard—although it was his ambition to have gold teeth and drive the baby Austin. Trinidad, I might say, is only twenty-seven miles long by seven and a half wide.

Every rowboat has its captain. If you come into Port of Spain at sunset you will see these Negro fishing-skiffs sailing in from the sea. A pretty sight. In stiff winds one Negro is always standing up, hanging on to the shrouds as he leans out overside to balance the craft against any sudden puff of wind that might capsize it. This is the crew; the important, pipe-smoking figure at the tiller is the sailing rowboat's captain.

As the high headland of Venezuela is only five miles away across the peculiar moss-green sea, and these hardy Negroes will fish anywhere, even out of sight of land, they have to pass through a form of customs when they sail back at nights to Port of Spain. One night a fishing-skiff arrived after the customs was closed.

"Fro out de anchor!" people on shore heard its captain shout.

"No can fro out de anchor," yelled the other Negro in the bow. "Anchor ain't got no tring."

"Tring or no tring, fro out de anchor! Got to show my authority."

*   *   *

Trinidad is the perfect tropic island. It is claimed that its deeply wooded mountains rising straight from the sea were what Defoe had in his eye when he wrote *Robinson Crusoe*. It might be interesting to know that Chile also makes this claim for Juan Fernandez island; and enterprising tourist steamship companies have now so arranged it that when a boatload of gaping globe-trotters is turned loose on Juan Fernandez, good man Friday himself appears in his ragged skins, with his parrot on his arm, and demands pesos.

Trinidad—save the mark—is marred by no such vulgarity. And for me it will always remain as the last place in the tropics where color did not hurt. For one whole luscious day—and I am not ordinarily a gushing person— I wallowed in the colors of this tropical paradise; the gold saman-tree, large as a royal oak, with flaming candelabra on the tip of every branch. Splashes in the green jungle of mountain rose. The riot of scarlet, purple, orange, and rose bougainvillaea that drapes every yellow wall on the outskirts of Port of Spain. Seen against the pale blues of Trinidad's jungle hills, these colors are intoxicating.

Two days later, on cactus-covered Curaçao, among the goats and Dutchmen, I was already beginning to be fiercely resentful of the vicious brilliance of yellow and scarlet, those two violent tropic colors that were from then on to sear my eyes.

And if Trinidad was the last place where I could stand color without feeling angry, it was to be the first on this trip where I began to think why they call the tropics "the white man's grave." Cause of this was the spectacle of four fat men, presumably planters or prosperous traders —at any rate they were locals—drinking heavily at 11 A.M. in the cool lounge of the Hôtel de Paris. They were engaged in making themselves pleasant to an aristocratic but rather wilted blonde. She, falling in line with the exotic color-scheme of Port of Spain—the painted balconies, the saffron, amethyst, and soft rose-red saris of the Hindu and Mohammedan girls in its colored streets—was wearing a broad sunshade of a hat in bright scarlet. The faces of the four men were about the same hue. And— disturbing physical phenomenon—they all looked as if they had been coated with a thin layer of candle-grease. What their livers must have looked like I hate to think.

✓   ✓   ✓

The lives of several of our boat-load took on another turn at Port of Spain. First, the Bishop; he was having a certain amount of trouble this morning, trying to button a new and officially high clerical collar at the back—eventually achieving this with a buttonhook he peevishly removed from his packed bag. The Parrot also went ashore. So did the trawler-man, in hot pursuit.

Our ocean-going steamer anchored far out in the road-bed, and I went ashore with the Bishop in the second launch. It was a strange sight to see his black figure pass into the colored streets of Port of Spain. "I'll walk," he told some devoted parishioners who were at the dock to meet him. "Pleasant to feel my feet on dry land again." And it was only after he had vanished completely that I realized, after sharing the same cabin with him for eleven days, I did not even know his name!

In the customs shed stood the young British trawler-captain, bewildered and rightly furious.

"Gave me the bird, she did."

"Who?"

"You know, that girl you were always buying beer for."

"Oh—the Parrot?"

"Yus!"

He grinned. "Dammit . . . went through all the trouble of helping her through the customs . . . must say, wasn't much, as the poor little devil only had the one bag. Then I loaned her a couple of bob, so as she could go and telephone. . . . Turned me back—and she was gone!"

I looked at the gaudy crowd that was watching the launches bring passengers from the ships. A Norwegian boat had just dropped anchor beside us in the roads; also a black German flaunting the swastika; and an entirely different assortment of human beings was being brought ashore from these. But none of them, despite the fancy get-ups that tourists will wear, could be mistaken for the tinted faces of Trinidad, whose blood-stream is one-third Hindu and Mohammedan, mingled with Chinese and

Negro love. Background into which the Parrot had flitted unseen.

"Well, it would be hard to pick her out in this lot," I said to the trawler-captain.

"Hell! I'm not looking for her any more. I got to pick up a scratch crew. Mine's just deserted when they heard I was here today. Who the blazes . . ."

Two Negroes who had been gazing down into the incoming launches had just introduced themselves to him. They were fishermen, they said, from the island of Tabago. Their schooner was being repaired at Port of Spain, and if the captain was looking for a couple of good, able-bodied seamen—why, here they were.

They were two very respectable-looking Negroes, dressed in clean khaki and blue shirts. We took them to a near-by pub, where the trawler-man bought a bottle of rum and the deal began. While the captain of the Negroes debated about wage and time of service—"also Ah'd like to know where we's gonna go"—the other one, helped by the rum, told me all about his service during the war with the B.W.I.

"Yessuh—we went to de *Holy* Land. Dese here eyes of mine have seen the Sea of Galilee."

When he smiled, he opened a mouth that could have swallowed the bottle of rum—unopened.

I don't know why that particular scene should have been stamped so indelibly on my mind. Perhaps it was because another Negro who had joined our group walked off, while I was away in the lavatory, with the two bottles of angostura bitters I had just bought. I didn't notice my loss until I was down at the docks again, waiting to go back on shipboard, but by that time the stray robber-Negro had also vanished in Port of Spain's color-scheme.

It is a scheme which pursues you to the end. For even after your ship has got its anchor aboard, and she breasts the fierce tide rips through the Dragon's Mouths, you pass a small island on which are two men who have nothing to do but raise and lower the Union Jack at sunrise and sunset, and:

"For company," says a local guide, "they have green lizards with blue eyes."

As night falls you see the two masthead lights of an oil-tanker sliding along at the foot of Venezuela's headland shore. The light on Trinidad's leper island drops into the sea.

✐   ✐   ✐

Aftermath of Trinidad was the sequel to the Parrot; the reason why she spent several shillings of the poor trawler-man's money indulging in long-distance telephone calls on an island which is only twenty-seven miles long —and she smack in the middle of it. It was given to me by the Cairo-Syrian who was coming out third class to "work South America" for some big American concerns.

"Serves her right," he began sullenly. "She had a boy friend she left in Trinidad when she come to England to try her luck. She wanted to try London instead of them getting married. Now she's trying to get him back—anyway, she wants him to come down and have a long talk.

"But he's living up at the other end of the island—and he says it's too far. Maybe he'll come down tomorrow— if he can find time. She had the idea he would be down there to meet her on the dock. No fear. She was sore as hell when she hung up."

"How do you know all this?" I asked.

"How do you think? I am standing right beside her all the time she was telephoning. I see her touch the English fellow for two bob: we used some of it for a drink. Made me sore like hell, too, to see the way he think that girl was going to fall for him. That's just like the English. He was never one, two, three with that girl."

"What do you think will happen with her and her Trinidad boy friend?"

"I think he'll come back okay. If she can get him in a corner. She is a very hot piece of work."

I don't know how much he understood the import of the American slang he had picked up; but his remarks left me with the disconcerting thought that, despite his protests that he never allowed himself to have a love-affair aboard a boat—"because it might awaken prejudices"—that confounded Cairo-Syrian had been on the inside track with the Parrot all the time.

It made me feel quite sympathetic with the poor South Americans he was coming over to "work."

Chapter VI

SOUTH AMERICAN SET-UP

It was in the tradition that our arrival in South America should have been greeted by bugle-calls. They came from the three warships of the Venezuelan navy lying at anchor in the harbor of La Guaira. "Where," said an Englishman building their breakwater, "they have been at anchor for years and years." They were of an ancient pattern, and about the size of steam yachts.

"Silly old navy," said the Englishman, half affectionately. "Always gives the tourists a laugh. Always strikes them as comic that they are not big blighters, like we have, with fourteen-inch guns. None of them ever stops to think, I suppose, that some of the countries down here just don't *want* a navy. Revolution, of course. Either it comes from the army or it comes from the navy—and, if you ain't got no navy, why, you have halved the risk."

Seen rusting at anchor against the rustling coco-nut palms that fringe the harbor of La Guaira, with the inevitable buzzards wheeling high over the snow-capped foothills of the Sierras, with more bugle-calls from an equally ancient and obsolete fort, the three toy ships gave just the right comic-opera touch to the South American scenario.

It was precisely the scene I had expected to see. And, said the Englishman, if I wrote it in that vein, I would add nothing new to the world's knowledge of the Americas below Panama. I would only infuriate South Americans, humiliate English and American diplomatic officials, to say nothing of the business men who are trying to secure or hold concessions in these Republics—and be completely off the mark. In fact, I would only be doing what too many people had already done.

The way he took it for granted that I had come there merely to play up the comic-opera side of South America —an attitude I encountered frequently from then on— prevented me from telling him that I had been making quite a decent living for the last fourteen years as a foreign newspaper correspondent. That I was tired. Stale. Bored to death both with Europe and myself. And that my trip to South America was too important to me to gush or be comic about things.

✓   ✓   ✓

My first sight of this Sad Continent—and I was to find many reasons for calling it that—was the heat haze obscuring the Venezuelan coast. Then, above it, I became aware of something shining like white clouds in the sky; these were the snows of the high Sierras. Tantalizing sight, for, as I stared up at them from the sweltering ship, my polo shirt clung like a plaster to my back. Then the heat haze blurred everything, and for several hours there was nothing but following waves of soapy green. Down here, where the muddy Magdalena and Orinoco pour in, the Caribbean is no longer a romantic blue. Even off the coast a certain salubrity had gone out of the atmosphere; and

I was conscious that the peace of the islands had been left behind me.

"Most dangerous coastline in the world," grinned the British oil-tanker captains, "sixty miles inland. The Indians are damned clever in there. They don't shoot you; they shoot your native guides—leave it to you to find the way out."

This was in explanation of what a gigantic task it was, even for old Dictator Gomez, to rule such a mountainous and unexplored country; where a person could commit almost any crime in the capital and be practically certain of making an easy get-away. Local officials and remote ranch-owners, as a consequence, were all too prone to take the law into their own hands. Witness the case of one of their brother oil-tanker captains. He had run down a native sailing-ship which was running without lights in the darkness. He was entirely free from blame in this case. In any other part of the world a local court would instantly have acquitted him.

"But not down here. He was jailed the next time he took his ship into Lake Maracaibo to load with oil. He's been in jail ever since. This happened before we went to England, and we've been in England three months. No use appealing to your Consul down here. Those days are over. These people now feel that they can do what they damn' well like."

This, I might add, was a feeling I faced everywhere in South America. The days when British and American warships used to come down here to protect their nationals are over.

One of the three toy warships of the Venezuelan navy

in La Guaira harbor had been troubling my mind. With her thin, twin stacks and ram bow she aroused dusty memories. I felt I ought to know her.

"Why, she's the old *Cuba*," said the Englishman, "sunk in the Spanish-American War. Back in 1898. Raised, reconditioned, and sold to the poor Venezuelans by your Secretary of State, Philander Knox."

Already the South American picture was coming into focus. Philander Knox, American Secretary of State, backer of the U. S. "Dollar Diplomacy" in the Caribbean, Central and South America, believer in the Big Brother Policy, wielder, when these things didn't work, of the Big Stick under a much perverted Monroe Doctrine. Misinterpretation of which brought U. S. Marines to Haiti and Nicaragua to settle their domestic affairs (usually on behalf of the New York banks)—a few of the reasons why, strange as it may seem, the South Americans are still not in love with us. Memories of which, no doubt, contributed to the fact that the United States was able to reach nothing more than sentimental agreements at the recent Buenos Aires Pan-American conference, despite the enthusiastic personal reception that President Roosevelt received, and his popular "Good Neighbor" speech.

"The South Americans are still waiting," said the Englishman building the La Guaira breakwater, "to see what sort of line the U. S. will take after Roosevelt goes out."

"And we," I retaliated, "are probably waiting to see when the South Americans will ever be able to agree on any question of importance among themselves."

There was enough discord brewing in this conversation for the name of Gomez to come up. Gomez always comes up. Even though he has just died, that old man will probably live for ever as the outstanding example of the power of sheer "personalism" in South American politics. And Captain Urbina, the Venezuelan political exile who pulled off the feat of capturing the Dutch fort on the island of Curaçao, in 1929, runs him a close second. Both of them show to what extremes South Americans will go, the chances they will take, in the picaresque way the game of politics is played south of the Rio Grande.

The story of these two men is the ideal introduction to South America.

✶ ✶ ✶

Venezuela, from before 1909 until he died at the end of 1935, was under the hand of the most ruthless, cruel, bull-headed, perhaps brilliant, dictator that the modern world has known. Compared to old General Juan Vicente Gomez—full-blooded Indian, unmarried father of eighty-five children to whom he admitted—Mussolini and Hitler must be classed as amateurs. Had this "Tyrant of the Andes" ruled in Europe, the picture of his swart, hedgehog face would have been on the front page of the world Press for the last thirty years. Ruling, as he did, in far-off, almost unthought-about Venezuela, when he died on December 17th, 1935, no one was excited about it except the thousands of politically exiled Venezuelans living in Havana, New York, London, or Paris—where there was a large colony comprising practically all of Venezuela's intellectuals—these, and the still-alive members of the Opposition, hundreds of whose *confrères* old Gomez had sent to their death in the underwater dungeons of Porto Cabello, where, when the tide rises, it comes up to your neck.

All in all, it is said that old Gomez sent something over 5,000 political critics of his regime to their death. He also had a first-class row with the Vatican. When the Archbishop of Valencia took it upon himself to write an article saying that civil marriage, recognized as legal in Venezuela, was merely a form of "shameful concubinage," old Gomez deported him, together with every other foreign-born Catholic priest or Protestant minister. He never did things by halves.

When Venezuelan "society" plucked up enough courage to refuse to meet his favorite mistress, Gomez brought a famous architect out from France, had him build a palatial dance-hall—and then the old Dictator gave a State ball. At it, his mistress stood by his side to receive the official guests. All the aristocrats and their ladies, together with the Diplomatic Corps, had to bow over her hand.

He was a remarkable man. Of General Juan Vicente Gomez it might be said that until he was nearly fifty he had never seen a road, but as he afterwards sentenced all petty thieves and minor political offenders to public works, Venezuela now has perhaps the finest road system in all South America. While he never married, he supported every one of the small army of children he acknowledged in the style he thought suited to a son or daughter of Venezuela's rich President. One of his own sons tried to assassinate him. But old Gomez, getting wind of the plot, did not take his favorite drive along the sea-road from

La Guaira to the bathing beach of Macuto that night on which he was to have been ambushed. Instead, he deported his son to Paris, where he gave him the income of an Indian rajah and a hundred thousand dollar funeral when he died. Although he feathered his own nest, taking a lion's share out of the profit of every Government and commercial enterprise in the country, with the attendant corruption, he nevertheless refused to let the hysterical Wall Street bankers force their loans on Venezuela during the boom years of 1924-28 (loans which have practically wrecked every other South American Government), so that today Venezuela is probably the only country in the world with not a penny of foreign debt. This was almost a personal, rather than a patriotic, precaution, because, with the way the old Dictator was parceling out the land among his extensive family, Venezuela was on the way to becoming little more than the Gomez family estate.

At the gates of his private country home, outside of Maracay on the high grassy uplands of Venezuela, he had a private zoo. The name of his house was Las Delicias. And studded among the homes of a hippopotamus, giraffe, and a very much distressed polar bear were the Florida-like villas of the old Dictator's mistresses. "Esmeralda, she lived there," says the chauffeur as you pass. He always speaks in the past tense, for, the instant it was known that the old Dictator was dead, every relative or person closely connected with him tried to get out of the country.

Trinidad claims that the day after his death 128 little Gomezes turned up in Port of Spain—like the evacuation of the Spanish children from Bilbao.

He ruled with his army—an army, say his enemies,

which was kept unnaturally efficient and faithful with the money Gomez received from the British and American oil interests exploiting the fabulous oil-fields round Lake Maracaibo.

When I was at La Guaira, the captain of the port was a fairly young regular navy captain named Pacardi. Gomez had imprisoned him for five years in the dungeons of the Rotunda, at Caracas—the Venezuelan Bastille. For the first eighteen months Pacardi lay in a cell which had a flannel flap over its peephole to keep him in utter darkness. There were 60-lb. iron shackles on his legs. He survived that—although his wife died while he was in prison.

There was one man, however, who stood up to Gomez and nearly got away with it.

During the latter days of the good health of the sexy old Dictator, Captain Urbina was residing as a political refugee on the Dutch island of Curaçao, forty miles off the Venezuelan coast. Of how he came to be there stories differ. Some say that he seduced the wife of the Governor of the Province of Falcon; others have it that the Governor, friend of Gomez, seduced Captain Urbina's pretty sister. Some stories say that he was assisted by six hundred Venezuelan refugees in the following escapade; others, more unflattering to the Dutch, say he had only fifty. Whatever the number, even the embarrassed Dutchmen have to admit that one night in 1929 Urbina collected a certain number of these Venezuelan refugees, practically captured Curaçao, and helped himself to the arsenal of the imposing yellow fortress that guards the harbor of Willemstad.

To get the full flavor of this incredible exploit you

should know Curaçao—that hive of shopkeepers, foremost commercial port of the Caribbean, with its gaudy streets full of blaring radios and Hindu and rival Dutch shopkeepers fighting it out to sell cheap Japanese goods. See it on a peaceful night as I did, gazing at the romantic scene; the moon playing on the bright aluminum paint of the Shell Oil Company's tanks.

No one had ever thought that the fort would be used. It was just a comforting symbol of Holland's might. Any watchfulness that had been inculcated into its garrison had been to look for danger, mythical as it may have seemed, from the open sea. No one had ever conceived of an attack from where the policeman stands on point duty, directing, from beneath a cement pergola, the stream of American motor-cars that flows all the twenty-four hours across Curaçao's pontoon bridge.

Urbina shot the policeman on point duty, walked his Venezuelans into the yellow fort, imprisoned the Governor, and helped his irregular army to the garrison's arsenal. Then, armed with the latest Dutch rifles, he marched his men across the pontoon bridge to where an American Red "D" boat was discharging cargo. Urbina suggested to the captain that he might swing in his cargo booms and shove off. When the captain demurred, he found himself gazing into an automatic behind which was one of those "killer" faces that the mixture of Indian and Spaniard has given to the Venezuelan countenance. He cast off.

Urbina then took the Red "D" boat across the Caribbean and up into Lake Maracaibo—his revolution failed. Chiefly, it is said, because he did not have enough money to buck Gomez. South American revolutions are strictly business propositions. Urbina made his escape, and was heard of from time to time in Porto Rico and Panama. When Gomez died, he returned to Venezuela, and, so I understand, is now the Governor of a rich province himself.

He was a startling example (to the Dutch, at any rate) of the way politics are run in these twenty-one Latin-American Republics with which the United States is now hopefully trying to form some workable Pan-American *bloc*.

✓ ✓ ✓

Further example of the accepted role of the individualist in South American politics is the case of General Eustacio Gomez. Cousin of the dead Dictator, probably believing that the control of Venezuela was a purely Gomez family affair, Eustacio Gomez resented it when the Minister of War, General Don Elezear Lopez Contreras (now President of Venezuela) took over power immediately upon the Dictator's death. General Eustacio Gomez came to Caracas single-handed to stage a *coup d'état*. He was too brave. He entered the palace single-handed. He had a revolver in his hand. But he never got a chance to use it. He was shot in the back by a palace officer and died on the presidential palace floor, with a brick for his pillow.

✓ ✓ ✓

The day after leaving La Guaira we woke up in the morning to find our ship moored directly opposite the yellow walls of Fort Cabello. In the wan morning sun it looked particularly doleful. Low down, where the walls slide into the sea, there was a row of small slits—about a foot by four inches wide. An American machinery salesman, who had come down from Caracas, said there was still use for the dungeons.

"There's still a lot of 'disappointed people' in Venezuela," he said—"that's what they call them down here —who would like to get back to their good old days of graft under Gomez. Only way they can do it is to get rid of Contreras. Contreras, by the way, looks like a skinny edition of the late King Albert of the Belgians—eyeglasses and all. He's been trying to work this country round to a constitutional Government. But it seems too soon after Gomez—too much change. Funnily enough, it's the students that are making the most trouble; they think he isn't going fast enough to the Left. So he had to jail some of them. Maybe they're in there. Now he's got both sides against him!"

He stared at the sinister little slits of Porto Cabello fort. "Yes, Contreras tried to rule by kindness, but he found it didn't work."

In the meantime, he said, I could take it that Venezuela was about as quiet as an inactive volcano.

Chapter VII

COLOMBIAN CONTACT

As MY Colombian visa was obtained for me while I lay in a nursing-home in London—and I had to give evidence of my moral and financial character, innocence of abortive political affiliations, and imperviousness to alcohol, all of which were very difficult—I had never seen a Colombian before I boarded the Dutch *stoomboot* in Dover harbor.

He was a virile youth. Quite disconcerting after the placid young men one sees about London. He had black hair and pale gray eyes, which showed he was probably a mixture of Indian and Spanish blood. He had been away a whole year in Europe and the United States collecting agencies for the wholesale business he and his brother ran in Bogotá. His luggage was full of German and Czecho-Slovak samples of cheap but sporty men's wearing apparel. On the boat he always walked about in American basket-ball shoes. The kind with the round leather pads over the ankle-bones. And I'm sure, coming to know this thrusting young man as I did in eighteen days' shipboard companionship, those American basketball "sneakers" are now all the rage among the valleys of the Andes.

The hot afternoon we ran before a following wind to where a mile-long wharf sticks out into the Caribbean at Puerto Colombia he stood in the bow with his field-glasses for a first glimpse of his country.

"I feel as nervous as a wild monkey just shut up in a cage," he told me, quoting a familiar Spanish saying in South America. Then he lowered his field-glasses and turned upon me; the indignities of a year in Europe and the United States were welling up within him. In the cafés of Paris, and especially among the complacent English, he had discovered that all South Americans were lumped together under the generic term "dagos." And in a country that should know better, the United States!

"Do you know what a young man in New York said to me? When I asked him if he had ever been to Colombia, he said: 'No, but my brother went there. Class of 1915!'

"That shows you," scowled this young Colombian, "all you Americans know about my country."

I felt like telling him that unfortunately it was about all we cared. When I set out for South America I had to look Colombia up on the map to see where it was. Up to then I had almost forgotten that Colombia even existed. I was sorry, I told him, not to have remembered.

"You ought to be. You stole the Panama Canal from us."

"Well, well, I'd even forgotten that."

"Well, we haven't!"

And neither have they, as you will discover if you broach this topic in the Republic of Colombia. You will also see that some of the political leaders have, as apparently part of their claim to office, the fact that they are known as good "Yanqui-haters."

When I had looked up Colombia on the map I was astonished to see that it had both an Atlantic and a Pacific seaboard. And when I located its capital, Bogotá, it seemed that there was no way to get to it. I discovered that it lay at the eerie perch of 8,500 feet; and that there was no railway to it from either the Caribbean or the Pacific.

"Only way to get there is to fly?"

I could do that, said the young Colombian. I could fly up to Bogotá in six or seven hours from Barranquilla, the new seaport of Colombia. A fast and very well-run German air service using express American planes. But that would be very expensive if I had any luggage. Otherwise I could go up the Magdalena River—eight days in a stern paddle-wheeler—always provided that the ship didn't get stuck and sit for a week on some sandbar. Quite a common occurrence. Even at the end of that there was another day across the mountains to Bogotá by rail and motor-car—again providing the landslides occurring in these regions during the rainy season had not washed the road away, another not infrequent occurrence. The best way to get to Bogotá was to go on to Panama, through the canal, then two days down the Pacific. Then, at Benaventura, take a two days' mixed journey of train and motor-car over the 10,000-foot passes of the Cordilleras to the high *sabana* of Colombia's condor capital. We decided to take that. But first we had to get our boat off a sandbank. After traveling uneventfully 3,600 miles down across the Atlantic, she had, at the last minute, run aground twenty-five feet off the wharf of Puerto Colombia—and there, all of us now as nervous "as a wild monkey in a cage," the Colombian port officials made us spend

the night. No amount of argument would move them—
nor could our reversed, rumbling twin propellers.

Trying to reach Bogotá via the Pacific meant that actually we should be in the Republic for only a short visit,
and then have to leave it again and make a long detour
through the Canal Zone in order to get back to it. It also
meant that, at Barranquilla, I would have my first view
of what Florida and California are doing to South American architecture. Quite awful, I think. And my Colombian friend would have a chance to sell some of his haberdashery. It would also let me see the end of the tragedy
of the Englishwoman on our boat who wanted to destroy
every scarlet poinsettia—a desire I immediately appreciated, for the stucco villas of Barranquilla are simply
smothered with them. These violent, eye-searing poinsettias, and the depressing sight of the split-tailed frigate
birds and vultures planing through the scorching sky over
a blatantly raw and self-satisfied stucco sub-development,
are enough to dismay any heart except a real-estate salesman's.

It is an interesting fact that, probably because of the
way inventive American architects have out-Spaniarded
the Spaniards in the buildings of Miami and Hollywood,
rich South Americans have now abandoned the orthodox
Spanish style and have brought down Americans, chiefly
from California, to build their new model towns and
country clubs. To the tourist looking for the "quaint,"
"picturesque," "Old Spain" sights of South America, this
rather knocks the show on the head. But South Americans
are wildly enthusiastic over the new residential sections
outside Bogotá, Lima, and Valparaiso. Who designed the

new buildings outside Quito I cannot guess—unless it was
some American architect suffering from the altitude and
a bad dose of Barcelona—Catalan city—which has, unless the esthetes have used the excuse of the civil war to
destroy them, the finest collection of architectural mon-
strosities known to man.

One legation outside Quito—I've forgotten which nation cares to own it—had a Reckitt's blue dome of shiny
tiles, with four cement minarets sticking out of it. And:

"It's not finished yet," said a passer-by, as we both
stood appalled before it.

✦ ✦ ✦

Barranquilla's attempt to build a Colombian Miami has
other points of interest to Americans. It is said that practically all its civic improvements have been made with
American "frozen dollars." These are the loans which the
American investors cannot get back from Colombia. They
can't get their money out of Colombia because of the exchange restrictions which that country has put on to protect its currency. On a small section of the American
loans small payments are now being made into Colombian banks, in Colombian scrip. The Americans can put
this money out to work in Colombia if they want to. Hence
Barranquilla's development.

✦ ✦ ✦

When we lay in Curaçao my young Colombian friend
had vanished among the Dutch and Hindu shops with a
long cardboard canister in his hand. This was full of felt
hats. He came back aboard ship in a furious mood because

the Japs had got there ahead of him with imitation Panamas, and felt hats were not the mode at Curaçao. But at Barranquilla he returned to the hotel all smiles.

"Just sold a large order," he said. "Those German ones, green, with the imitation chamois brush. The rich *hacendados* who come down here for the winter season will be crazy about them."

ィ ィ ィ

Sitting in meditative soliloquy in the tiled foyer of Barranquilla's Miami-est hotel can be found at almost any time of the day a tall, distinguished-looking man in a suit of pinkish cotton drill. He is the owner of so many "frozen dollars" that he has stayed on in Colombia to see what is going to happen to them. Might as well, because he can't get enough out to live comfortably elsewhere. They are not frozen loans; they are the dollars he made in twenty years as an engineer in the tropics. Enough to retire on, have a home on Long Island outside New York, and drive in whenever he wanted to see a show. But New York seems just as far away to him as it did in the days when he was a young man down in the jungles of the Choco. To keep his dollars and himself occupied he is building stucco houses, and cashing in on the boom. But he looks bored with the process. I saw him so constantly hanging around the foyer of the Barranquilla hotel that I thought he was its manager.

Several times he looked at me as I walked past, and seemed on the point of speaking to me. Finally he did.

"How's things?" he asked.

"Oh, so-so," I said. I passed on. I wanted to talk with

the man because I liked his looks a lot—that lean, weather-worn, gray-haired type of American who has been seasoned, instead of rotted, by the tropics. I knew that over a few drinks he would have an interesting story or so to tell. But I could also see from his looks that about the first question he would ask me was: What did I think of Barranquilla?

So I did not take up his offer of conversation. He had enough to bear.

Chapter VIII

SPANISH MAIN—BULLFIGHT

SUNDAY. Cartagena was even more depressing than London. The British tourists had gone the rounds of the yellow walls that had been sacked by their compatriots; they were tired of letting the condor out of its cage to fight the palms in the hotel patio; their consciences had rebelled at again getting the monkey drunk; they decided to go to a bullfight.

This was at a village about twenty miles back in the country. Cartagena is a seaport; and it is significant that, after the centuries when Drake and Morgan sacked it, it is still only a seaport, with no roads behind it. The British tourists had not gone ten miles back into the country before they were debating whether it would be wisest to push on or try to get back. The road which had sped out of Cartagena with such asphaltian deceitfulness, the instant it got out into the country, where no one could see it, turned into a causeway of oiled dirt. After a mile or so of such encouragement it suddenly erupted into a succession of shell-holes, craters, pools, and swamps, then became just a path of burnt undergrowth through the jungle.

A young American engineer, brought down from the States to bring order out of this chaos, had been lost somewhere along this road the night before. This had caused a social scandal in Cartagena. The Town Gossip, dropping in for a good-night drink with an American official, came on that American official in the act of trying to comfort the new road-builder's weeping wife. "Sorry," said the Town Gossip, and ran off as fast as he could to spread the glad news—for Cartagena is a spot where the foreign colony welcomes even the merest excuse to dish the dirt. Unless he could produce that new road-builder, dead or alive, the American official's reputation was gone.

There had been labor troubles—and no wonder—along that road. Hence the agitation of the young American engineer's wife. She did not know whether her husband had been split open by a machete or not. As a matter of fact, his car had broken down or been mired three times along the road during the night; and he limped into Cartagena at lunch-time, just as the British tourists were speeding so blithely out.

✼   ✼   ✼

The village bullfight began at four o'clock, and the tourists tottered into the ring just in time to see it start. The ring was made of bamboo, about two hundred feet long by half that wide. And the bamboo stands kept crashing, coming down with a shattering succession of pops throughout the four fights. The sunny side of the stands was white with peons and cowboys in white cotton drill and chin-strapped straw sombreros. These Centaurs of South America had spurs strapped to their bare feet.

In the "shade" was some silk-clad Cartagenan society that had come out by train.

A party of young bloods was drinking rum out of a bottle—neat.

✼   ✼   ✼

The first matador was an old Spaniard who needed no civil war to drive him from the rings of Spain. I felt sorry for him as he stood there, sweating in the sun, flourishing his *capa* so gallantly before the local mayor. I felt particularly anxious for his safety when the first bull was pushed in. It was a Zebu bull, with a large hump on its back (like the sacred cattle of India); and, apart from its ability to shed a sword with that sharp, ridge-like back, a Zebu bull doesn't play the game. A Zebu bull will frequently change direction as it charges. Bullfighters are afraid of them; most will refuse to fight a Zebu bull.

But old matadors can't be choosers.

It made matters more ironic when we were told that the first three bulls were not to be killed. The matadors were merely going to play with them, exhibit their skill. We expressed our opinion that that looked like cheating; when you go to a bullfight you expect to see something killed. One of the bloods with the bottle replied: What did we expect for a peso? That was all we had to pay to get in. What we got was the sight of a matador being gored within twenty feet of us.

✓   ✓   ✓

One of the stock stunts of a bullfight is for the matador to walk up to the bull, flourish his *capa* in its face, stamp his foot, shout "Hi!"—and make the bull back away. This establishes the matador's superiority. Then he turns his back on the bull, contemptuously, and walks across the ring to bow before the local mayor, or some local belle, or very likely the girl he is living with, who is there to

watch her man play with his death in the arena of blood
and sand. It is a brave gesture, and it always brings down
the stands.

✓ ✓ ✓

It did in this case. But it was not the applause that
crashed the bamboos. It was the antics of the crowd trying to warn the bullfighter of his danger—for the Zebu
bull was charging. It was not playing the game. At the
last instant, something in the faces he was walking towards caused the matador to look behind him. The bull
was almost on top of him. The matador tried to run. But
he was too slow to reach the safety of a barrier. The bull
hit him.

Three times the matador and his cerise cape spun round
like a ball of colors in the sun. The third time, as he
came down, the sharp black horn of the Zebu bull went
through the matador's gold-braided jacket and pierced his
lung.

The matador squirmed like a freshly caught fish on
the hot sand. A young man in his shirt-sleeves rushed out
from a corner barrier and dragged him to safety. This
man was Ivarito, the other Spanish bullfighter, who was
dressing at that moment for the next fight. Instead of
putting on his gay jacket, with its gold epaulets (and thick
protection of cotton padding), young Ivarito, with the
blood of his comrade still wet on his soft white shirt,
went out to fight that bull.

✓ ✓ ✓

He was unexpectedly handsome, with a pale, clean-cut
face and fine forehead. He frowned thoughtfully as he

stepped out from behind the barrier, and before he left it I saw him drink about a third of a glass of dark rum. Unlike the vast rings of Seville and San Sebastian, where the bullfighter is usually so far away that he looks no bigger than a doll, we could watch every expression on Ivarito's face. It made the fight very intimate. And it was obvious that Ivarito, taking the matador's revenge, intended to humiliate the bull by driving it into a frenzy of frustration and fear. He exploited every risk for all there was in it. Time and again it was hard to distinguish man, cape, and bull. It seemed folly to take the chances he was taking in such a shabby ring for a mere country crowd. He was due to fight a few weeks later in Bogotá, where he would get a hundred times the purse he would get for this village exhibition. But if he had been fighting in Madrid itself he could not have given the crowd more for its money.

The people and the cowboys seemed well aware of all this. If they had been a British football or American baseball crowd they would have been yelling their heads off. As it was, being Colombians, they behaved with great dignity, and their applause was more unconscious exclamations of delight than any conscious cheering. It was my first chance to witness how unmoved the Colombian can be even in the most exciting situations.

In merely his soft white shirt, Ivarito was taking twice the chance he would have run in his heavily padded gold jacket.

When he had reduced the bull to such a state of jitters that it backed away from him the minute he came near it, Ivarito gave a contemptuous nod and ordered it to be removed from the ring. The next two bulls he treated with similar but more absent-minded disdain. He was now going to have his complete revenge; kill the bull which had gored his comrade.

A personal affair.

✻   ✻   ✻

But when the bamboo door was opened to admit the final bull, all four bulls trotted in. They were accompanied by a cow of sorts. They all stood there, looking around uncertainly, as if wondering what they were expected to do now. The original bull—the one who had gored the first bullfighter—had two *banderillas* dangling from its sharp hump, and its spotted hide was glistening with red blood. Even so, it merely stood there and gazed at Ivarito sullenly. It knew him by now. Yet it no longer seemed to have any feeling about him, one way or the other.

Any sense of danger in the bull-ring simply evaporated from the scene. This was barnyard. Ivarito, casting all professional etiquette aside, picked up a piece of broken bamboo from one of the stands and whacked the bulls over their behinds. They moved about peevishly—and suddenly burst like a rocket, to charge in all directions. Then they began to take an interest in this new game. Two bulls came after Ivarito at the same time.

From then on, Ivarito and his two assistants became as active as Swedish gymnasts. The bamboo stands made natural ladders. With four bulls and a cow charging hysterically round the small enclosure, the bullfighter and his aides were kept climbing up and down the stands like a troupe of acrobats. It wasn't the performance they had contracted to give; but, once it had begun, there was no way to stop it. One after another, the charging bulls demolished the barriers. They were flimsy affairs at the beginning. Now they were nothing but kindling-wood. The original bull gave a diversion and charged into a bamboo grandstand, getting half-way through it. And, as the bamboo supports gave way, the peons on top rose into the air like a flock of white birds. Finally, at the risk of his life, Ivarito managed to put back the bamboo door that the bulls had butted down. And one by one, like the marbles in a puzzle, the three other bulls and the cow were maneuvered out of the half-demolished ring.

I don't think any bullfighter ever had such a busy and versatile afternoon.

✦　✦　✦

Ivarito and the original bull—maddened with the pain of two fresh *banderillas*—faced each other. It was death now. One or the other was going to be killed.

The bull is "killed with the cape"; that is the acme of Spanish technique—to draw the bull past you with the cape as you reach over and drive the sword into him. And Ivarito gave a perfect performance.

He put his heels together, raised himself on his toes, aimed down his curved sword, and drew the bull with the cape. The Zebu bull charged. Without moving, Ivarito drove the sword into him. The bull gave a low, swinging motion, and sank on the sand. A man rushed and jabbed a dagger into the back of its skull. The crowd broke what remained of the bamboo stands in its rush to reach the carcass.

"They will eat it tonight," said a British diplomat who was with the tourists. "How could they?" they exclaimed.

✶   ✶   ✶

Everybody had forgotten about the other bullfighter—except perhaps Ivarito—and the two doctors who were operating on him underneath the stands in an attempt to save his life.

Chapter IX

SPANISH MAIN—SAILORS
DON'T CARE

HE CAME into the Navy Bar at Cartagena and, by a process of levitation, carried on among the dancing couples until he reached the handle of the cash register—which he turned backwards. Then he steered into the *cantina's* toilet and reappeared with an armful of dirty paper, which he distributed. The unsuspecting inmates of the Navy Bar at first thought they must be pamphlets of some sort. Then he reached across and slapped the fat señorita tending the bar on her silk behind. She did not like this—not in public—and shrieked for help.

" 'E's 'armless," exclaimed his pal. " 'E don't mean nothing by that. Everybody knows Bill."

Bill was one of the 278 British sailors and officers who had come out here in 1932, with two brand-new British destroyers, to settle the Peruvian "war." The advent of the two destroyers settled it all right—although the League of Nations, poor thing, takes the credit—and today seventy-eight of those British sailors are still in the Republic of Colombia. So are the destroyers, which, by the time the sun slides down behind the mangrove swamps and coco-nut palms, are hot enough inside to broil a chicken. Hence the nightly appearance of Barnacle Bill and his pal Jock in the Navy Bar.

Cartagena is a quiet town. Most people go to bed about ten o'clock. Ever since the days of Drake it has been quiet. Drake and Morgan—the British! What they have done to this town! They'll never let it alone. The Navy Bar itself is an enterprising jazz roadhouse put up at the harbor edge by a Jamaican Negro. For girls, he has the local Colombian belles, dressed in evening gowns of robin's-egg blue velvet or Japanese silks of mauve and scarlet—colors almost exclusively favored by these coffee-colored Colombian tarts to show off their protuberant charms. The strain of Spanish blood in them makes them always feel a little *gauche* about being handled so familiarly by strange men in such a public place. Their chief attraction, they believe, is an air of cultured propriety; and, whenever they can tear themselves loose from a clutching, frustrated sailor, they gather together around a far table from which their laughter sounds quite girlish again. This technique may be all very well with the Latin men, who always like to bring seduction into their love-affairs, but with the forthright Anglo-Saxon more immediate response is required. When he feels that the sailors need a change, the Jamaican Negro goes up to Colon and brings down a couple of French strip-dancers from the Canal Zone. This is quite an adventure, both for the French girls and for the Colombians.

There were no French girls tonight. And Bill was bored. He was a lean, melancholic creature with a bald spot on the top of his head; and he wore his hat on the bridge of his nose. Except for the gilt letters on its black band, which showed he was in a foreign ship, there was nothing to distinguish his outfit from the regular British naval uniform. Jock was just the opposite from his pal. Short, bow-legged, no teeth, full of talk, he wore his hat on the back of his head—and how it stayed there only a British sailor can tell you. When he asked if Bill and he could sit down at my table he apologized.

" 'E's 'armless—Bill 'ere don't mean no harm to nobody. Everybody knows Bill."

Confirmation of this had been given me by the Jamaican Negro as he clung on frantically to the handle of his till. Whether he thought that Bill, by turning it backwards, was going to reduce the cash receipts, I don't know. But he bore no anger towards the British sailor. He said:

"Don't worry, mister. I've known him for years." Then, when Bill had been pried loose, he said seriously: "Mister, I can't make these sailors out. They comes in here an' they drinks up their pay every night—an' when they goes broke I take their chits—but they don't never have nothing to do with no girls. I can't make that out."

"Maybe," I said, thinking of sailors I'd seen in other parts of the world, "they get drunk before they get that far."

"Yes, mister, I guess that must be it."

✓ ✓ ✓

Although neither Bill nor Jock would have believed it if you had told them, nor would the Jamaican Negro—a human King Kong, by the way—their presence in Cartagena at that time of night, with a calabash orchestra banging away on its dais, was a poignant comment on Colombian morals, militarism, and social life.

To begin at the last count and work backwards; Latin-

American cities—to the great heartbreak of all tourists—
do not have an exotic night life. The balconied streets of
old Cartagena, with their wooden and iron grilles before
every ground window, become empty and quiet after darkness. There is a midnight coffee-stand by the clock tower
where the old Spanish gateway breaks through the li-
chened walls. There is a soft-drink café bearing the ironic
name "The North Pole," where night-hawk Colombians
have a last pineapple sundae or glass of Barranquilla beer
before going home to bed around ten o'clock. Otherwise
Cartagena nearing midnight has all the propriety of the
grave.

The Navy Bar, the Pullman, and the Dancing Bar;
these three clattering *cantinas* that have sprung up down
by the waterfront outside the city itself are set-ups for
the tourists and foreign sailors—and nothing else. The
fact that young Colombian bloods are to be found in them
merely shows you the contaminating influence of European civilization on the more primitive mind.

To take the next count—Colombian militarism. The
fact that Colombian soldiers and sailors are not to be
found in these *cantinas* may arise from one of two things.
First, there *are* hardly any Colombian soldiers and sailors.
The two British destroyers swinging at their mooring-
buoys in the hot harbor *are* the Colombian navy—except
for those impromptu affairs, their stern paddle-wheelers,
that usually go up the Magdalena River, which the Colombians boarded up and put guns on when they thought a
war with Peru was imminent. But these "wet-tailed Janes"
have now returned to carrying passengers up the Magdalena again. And as for the army, Colombia, with a popu-

lation of ten millions, has an army of only 12,000 men.
In Colombia, moreover, a soldier, a sailor, or an officer
has no social status (although they are now trying to give
them one), and, such being the case, they do not appear
to swagger about in midnight dancing-bars. All of which
is something distinctly different from the conventional
idea of South America.

The chaperons for this evening were the Colombian
police, of which, it seemed to me, there was at least
one for every Colombian girl—police prerogative found
throughout this wicked world. After all, what is the use
of being a policeman if you can't get in to see a floor-show
free? And then—and, if I was warned about this once, I
was a hundred times—these quiet, *gauche*, Colombian
prostitutes (in places like this) have a habit of carrying
safety-razor blades in little gadgets made from discarded
rubber motor-tubes. And they have a bad habit of using
them when they think someone is going too far. So the
Colombian police had a reason to be there. And it was they
who tried to quell the riot raised by Barnacle Bill.

✓   ✓   ✓

Bill, after moodily telling me that he intended to remain in Colombia until he was sixty-five, whereupon he
would return to England and apply for the old age pension—"No use me going home when I don't know nobody there"—had reached that stage of cynicism where
he had apparently gone to sleep over the back of his reversed chair. But while Jock was saying that he couldn't
go home "because my wife's a Christian"—a thing which
apparently kept Jock always at sea—Barnacle Bill actu-

ally had his eyes focused on the feet of the dancing couples hopping past. Then, very solemnly, he removed his sailor's hat from the bridge of his nose and took something from it. To me, it looked like a stick of peppermint candy wrapped in tissue paper. Bill looked at the dancers again —and then back at this stick. Then he picked up my lighted cigarette from the ash-tray and pressed it against the stick. Then he threw it among the dancers.

* * *

Volcanic—and that's the only word that comes near it —was the reception of this act. The dancing couples went straight up in the air. They knocked each other down trying to get out of doors and windows. They jumped on tables. . . .

They had a reason to. For a signal rocket was whizzing around like a fiery snake between their legs, belching a tail of sparks. I was appalled at the speed, the endurance, the diabolic fury of the thing. I don't know how many miles it would have gone up into the air; but it zigzagged a couple of kilometers around that dancing-floor. It darted after Colombian couples caught in corners, who tried to leap straight up the wall. It zithered back and sent two petty officers hopping into the open, smacking at the sparks burning pin-pricks on their legs. It hit a fat Colombian beauty where she did not expect to get a rocket—and altogether that rocket simply raised hell.

The calabash orchestra stayed up on its dais. But the Jamaican Negro, trying to save his establishment, squirted two soda-syphons on the floor. The Colombian policemen attacked it with truncheons. Finally it was beaten to death, charred and inanimate on the empty floor.

Bill stared at it indifferently. He had done the thing he had come there to do. Now he turned to the table, folded his arms, and went quietly to sleep.

Chapter X

SPANISH MAIN—SHEDDING ILLUSIONS

CARTAGENA is an old walled town whose yellow stones rise out of the green jungle and heat haze as you come at them across the Caribbean. There is something heraldic about it, for these ramparts have not changed very much since the days of Morgan and Admiral Drake. The little conical turrets still stand on the sharp corners of its bastions, from whose peepholes the apprehensive Spaniards watched Admiral Vernon cast anchor off the sandspits, preparing to fulfill his boast that he could take that city with six guns and one hundred Devon men.

I got off in that hot corner of the Caribbean to await a letter which was coming down to me by Pan American Airways from New York. The letter was to contain instructions of just what I was to do in South America and, I hoped, a check.

On the Dutch *stoomboot* people said: "Cartagena! Oh, that's the very spot to use as a stepping-off place for the tropics or South America. Only over-night, you know, from Colon, up in Panama. Boats call every day. Regular tram service."

But once I had complacently watched my Dutch *stoomboot* nose out through the sandspits on her fifty-seven day trip from Amsterdam to Amsterdam, I discovered that I was not going to get away from Cartagena for eight days

at least, for it would not be until then that another boat
came along bound for Panama.

I got this bad news while I was arguing with the port
captain about my shotgun. That shotgun! The fuss they
made about it might have made you think that I had come
to these South American countries to stage a revolution
single-handed. And I did feel very inclined to, that day.
But if that shotgun caused me trouble, and didn't kill such
a lot of South American fauna, it did provide me with a
beautiful litmus test of the local manners. In Peru, even
though I had left it in bond at Callao, they tried to make
me get an export permit from Lima to take it out of the
country. In Guayaquil, that "pest-hole of the Pacific," I
retrieved it from the customs to find its case an inch deep
with cockroaches. In Colombia it introduced me to the
best-mannered port captain in all South America.

Although I could not take it into Colombia without a
permit from Bogotá, he said he would look after it for
me. He put it on the top of his own roll-top desk and
gave me an American cigarette from a carton he had just
removed from a shore-going sailor. So I left the masts and
funnels and limp flags of the seaport, all bound for the
opposite direction from the one I wanted to go, and entered the hot city.

In there, I was informed by steamship company clerks
that I couldn't be sure of a berth on the next boat, even
after a wait of eight days. A moot, but not a mute, point,
I can tell you. I would not be allowed to go as a deck-
passenger, as it was illegal to carry more than a stated
number of passengers per lifeboat. I couldn't even work
the old dodge by signing on as a member of the crew—

trick by which obliging steamship companies can often evade the regulations. The man in New York had some grand ideas about geography, so that my letter of instructions did not reach me until I had landed in the Canal Zone. All of which led to the point at which I turned to the Hotel Americano, where I met Mr. MacWithers— also trying to get away from Cartagena.

And every day before lunch or dinner, Mr. MacWithers and I created a breeze by rocking ourselves swiftly back and forth in the rocking-chairs of the Hotel Americano's patio, sipping Tom Collinses made for us by a happy, expert, and very busy little mestizo boy.

↗   ↗   ↗

The Hotel Americano had once been a convent. Around the second floor of its patio was a balcony of rich brown wood. The rose tiles of its roof had been placed there by Negro slaves when Colombia was a colony of old Spain. There were green palms in the patio; and, looking up through the square box of its white walls, we saw a light blue sky in which there was never a cloud.

The ex-convent stood in a city of narrow streets, where the sun beat down between houses whose walls formed unbroken blocks of purest white. Overhead, their balconies were painted apple-green, blue, and rose. The walls of the church houses were painted dappled marble, faded now to take their place in the soft pastel of the color-scheme. The Palace of the Inquisition that flanked the main square still retained its original color of rich orange, with its archways and windows faced in white. The main square itself was a pool of cool shadow under its stand of royal palms. A patch of sun in its center shone on Simon Bolivar the Liberator, reared on his bronze horse with an uplifted sword. Heroic, as is all the statuary in South America. The ground-floor windows of every house in Cartagena had an old iron or painted wooden grilles. There was sarcely a pane of glass in this tropic city.

✓   ✓   ✓

Colombia is what is known as mestizo country. This means that the predominant strain of its population is a mixture of Indian and Spanish blood. And a very good mixture it is too: in Colombia it has produced some men of exceptional brilliance. But down in the hot jungle along the Caribbean and Pacific it is the Negro who has survived. The streets of Cartagena were full of dusky Colombian clerks, and slightly paler office managers. All in white cotton drill. Of *café au lait* ladies dressed in every hue of the paint-box. Of duskier, dingier Negroes, some absolutely jungle black, dressed in hardly anything at all. More prosperous among these were mule-drivers, directing huge two-wheeled carts up through the narrow streets from the waiting ships. The foreign element went about in pith helmets and American motor-cars.

✓   ✓   ✓

Mr. MacWithers was a gold-miner. He had arrived in Cartagena after a mysterious mixed journey of mule and aeroplane from the choking jungles of the Choco, over on the Pacific slope, where he had been one of the hydraulic engineers for an American concession. He wore a "seersucker" suit, which, for the benefit of the uninitiated, is a ribbed cloth of vertical blue and white stripes, which is always rumpled and practically shows no stains, so that a "seersucker" suit is probably never washed or pressed from the day you buy it to the day it is thrown away. Mr. MacWithers was not going to throw his away, be-cause, as he explained, he found the summer weather in New York and Chicago much fiercer than in the jungles of the Choco.

"But it wouldn't do to say that," he said. "It would make me unpopular in New York. The boys wouldn't like it. Anyway, this is my last trip out. I've had all I want."

It seemed none too soon. For Mr. MacWithers's blue eyes had been bleached by the tropics until they were now the color of watered milk; his patchy hair (I sup-pose to preserve it) he had cut off at a half-inch height wherever it remained on his melon-shaped head; his sal-low, damp flesh looked as if he had coated his face that morning with a thin layer of candle-grease—and he had a mean sense of humor. Mighty mean.

This was embodied, mostly, in a collection of clippings that he kept in an enormous black wallet in a back pocket, with the result that his right hip looked almost deformed. And, swaying back and forth, Mr. MacWithers produced his clippings to illustrate what he thought of South Amer-ican life. He handed me a local newspaper cutting.

"Shows," he said, "what the Church thinks it can still do to the women of South America."

The Church (this was one of Mr. MacWithers's sore subjects) still tries to dominate the life of the women in the Americas below Panama. It is fighting a very tenacious battle. The women are its last stronghold. The women still obediently put on their black mantillas to go to church. The priest of the village still dictates the mode and manners of their social life. And what he does not do consciously is done for him by centuries of tradition. More than that, in some of the remote parts of South America the priest still tries to dictate the entire life of the community—even its civic enterprise. A Jap I met up in Popoyan, in Colombia, who had been taking a circus through the Andes, told me that until only a few years back he had to placate the priest of the village before he could get permission to have a show. So strong is this dominance of the Church that a Liberal in South American politics usually turns out to be no other reformist than a man who wants to "throw out the Church." And a "Liberal Government" is usually the term for a Government which has dissociated Church and State. But, even under such lay Governments, women are still susceptible to the influence of the priest.

✓   ✓   ✓

Mr. MacWithers had been to a Hallowe'en party in Cartagena the previous November which had led to an excommunication.

A local American oilman had got the thing up. It was held in the Popa Club. The Popa Club is very respectable. A proper institution, very much like the Century Clubs of small towns in the United States. Mrs. Grundy's club. Men and women could always go there for lunch or dinner. But the women did not go there very often. Even though they did not feel it was exactly sinning, they did feel a bit awkward. Yet it is difficult to see why this

Hallowe'en party should have led to the excommunication of the late Governor of the Province.

✓   ✓   ✓

"It was a dud show," explained Mr. MacWithers. The women had all sat in an uncomfortable jumble at one end of the hall. The men sat by themselves at the other end of the tiled floor of the Popa Club. There was a curious little cabaret, where a few girls shrouded in sacks hopped about in what was supposed to be taken for a Witches' Dance. When this was over, a feeble attempt was made by the few couples who knew some steps to have a dance among themselves. That was all.

"One or two of the men did get a bit tight," said Mr. MacWithers. "Don't blame them. But everyone was a perfect little gentleman. No scenes. It was just damned dull, and that's all I can say for it. Much rather have stayed home and gone to bed."

✓   ✓   ✓

Why the Archbishop of Cartagena, the next morning, should have pondered over the idea that he would excommunicate everyone who had been at that party was beyond comprehension. But he did. And it was only after the lengthiest argument that he was persuaded to select one particular participant for a scapegoat.

He selected the most important figure present—a former mayor of Cartagena and one-time Governor of the Province. Him he excommunicated.

The Archbishop then wrote an open letter to the Press

to explain his action—clipping removed from Mr. Mac-
Withers's wallet. The Archbishop said:

*This grave affair regarding the ball at the Club de la
Popa has been resolved favorably . . . the real culprit
of the disorder has now been discovered. . . .*

The Archbishop then let the cat out of the bag as to
what seemed the real reason why he had selected that
particularly distinguished figure, the ex-Governor, for the
victim of his private Church vendetta. The letter continued:

*This sympathizer of the cannibals in Spain, this black
heart who seems to desire that similar crimes should be
committed among us, this depraved gentleman, in addition covered the ladies of Cartagena with ignominy by
saying that the time would come when men and women
would smoke equally, drink cocktails together, and dance
the rumba. . . .*

The Archbishop then concluded:

*This unnatural being without conscience, and who
has always been a repugnant scandal, deserves an outstanding censure. We therefore excommunicate Señor X
for the inhuman sentiments that fill his soul and for his
infamous conduct, shown in the past incident. . . .*

✦   ✦   ✦

"That's going some!" said Mr. MacWithers.

Mr. MacWithers had given me this clipping after we
had been sitting at a cock-fight. I shall never cross the

street to see another cock-fight. In fact, I would cross the
street to get away from one. It's a dirty affair; and I
didn't like the audience. Around the octagonal fence of
boards and stands enclosing the main, sat tiers of sallow-
faced men, mostly old ones, several with diseased eyes,
looking a good deal like vultures gathered for a feast. Indecent old age. They were betting thousands of pesos on
a bird.

One cock had natural spurs. His owner sharpened them
before the bout with a penknife. The owner of the other
cock strapped a pair of dead cock's spurs on to his bird
with adhesive tape. Then they dropped the birds on to
the sand and sat down themselves on little stools inside
the ring.

Each cock had its wings clipped. Its legs and back were
shaved to a point where they looked quite naked. Their
red combs became even more nauseating as they began to
drip blood. And their courage was terrifying.

From time to time, when a cock was groggy—and they
fell back with a gesture that would have been comic in
any other circumstances, on their tails and elbows—its
owner would pick it up and twist a feather down its throat
to clear out the blood. Then he would take a mouthful
of water and spray it over the cock, like an old-fashioned
prize-fighter's second. Or he would take the cock's head
in his mouth.

The gameness of the birds was heartbreaking. No wonder the Romans encouraged cock-fighting to inspire their
centurions. In whirls of feathers they flew up into the air
and struck their spurs together. Then one cock lay on the

sand in the most sickening contortion. It had stuck its own spur through its own eye. . . .

"Jolly little world, isn't it?" said Mr. MacWithers.

✓ ✓ ✓

"Game as a fighting-cock" and "Live like a fighting-cock" were expressions I shan't forget after seeing a fighting-cock's life at the home of a breeder on the outskirts of Cartagena. He was a wizened man, living in a vast house of plaster-red emptiness whose dark rooms, leading off the tiled patio, housed the families of his married sons and daughters, his wife, and their own brood of un-mated progeny that he and his wife (judging from her figure when I came on her in a wrapper at 4 p.m.) were still breeding without any sacrilegious obstacles such as birth-control.

Each cock had his individual cage among the splash of banana palms in the jungle of the back yard. There were a few hens in a harem to provide for their less war-like pleasures. The cocks were fed on a diet calculated to give them the maximum of strength and viciousness; and from time to time, to keep them in condition, they were carefully rubbed with rum. Shaved, their high red hips looked particularly indecent. To keep their tempers peppery, showing us how it was done, the breeder and his son each took a cock in his hands and waved them back and forth, beak to beak, until, infuriated, they tried to strike at each other. Then they locked one bird up in his cage and dropped the other one on the sand. It hopped up on to the stump of a coco-nut palm and screamed with triumphant crows. . . .

"Muy bien, señor!"

This was a bird, I was told, destined to be cock-of-the-walk in Cartagena.

✝   ✝   ✝

Social life being what it is in Cartagena, it is natural that there is not a side-walk café or cabaret in the whole city. I must say that I didn't pine for the cabarets so much —there was always the Navy Bar for myself and the lower sections of the populace—but I did want to see some of the Cartagenan society for a change.

But as "society" in South America recognizes your blue blood by the percentage of your Spanish blood, it clings with a perverse perseverance to the life and customs of old Spain. This means that you may meet the men at the club (if there is such a thing), in the office, or, if you argue with them enough, get them to invite you to lunch at a hotel. But the women of the household are behind the iron grilles of ground-floor windows, peeping down at you with infuriating coy coquetry from trellised balconies high over your head, or else sitting in their dressing-gowns at all hours of the day in the flowered patios of their private houses—enchanted seclusion of which you occasionally catch a glimpse through an inadvertently open door as you pass by in the street. There is not even a restaurant in Cartagena where you could at least sit down near the people you would like to meet and watch them eat.

Therefore, I was lonely. And it was a loneliness in which I was not alone. Mr. MacWithers produced other clippings from his wallet to illustrate just this particular form of South American sadness—this feeling that Americans and British have, everywhere except in Chile and the Argentine, of living in a life in which they are always on the outside. Result of the Church and the customs of old Spain.

"Just look," said Mr. MacWithers, "at this bunch of tourist bait."

✓ ✓ ✓

Mr. MacWithers, in his days of exile in South America, had picked up the habit of reading all the advertisements in the American magazines. There were so few magazines, generally, where he was. When he had finished the stories, there was no other reading-matter, except what he one day discovered was the perfect gold-mine of unconscious humor at the end.

"Don't they beat hell? Now you know why the tourists always go round looking for señoritas and fandangos—and are sore as hell when they don't get 'em!"

The advertisements were pathetic. Created by some romantic ad-writer in New York, who had probably never been any further south than the piers of Hoboken, they were so convincing that they left you with the impression that the ad-writers themselves must have believed South America was like that.

"But don't you wish South America *was* like that?" I said.

Mr. MacWithers winked. "Bet your sweet life I do. I wouldn't be taking next Tuesday's boat for Panama."

✓ ✓ ✓

For Mr. MacWithers and me, the Cartagena days were long and hot and drowsy and uneventful. This was the tropics; people got up round about six o'clock. The Colombian family in the room next to mine on the balcony of the Hotel Americano had both a radio and a parrot. They played both of them all day long. Emerging from a stifled sleep under my mosquito net, I removed my dripping wet pajamas, hung the two separate pieces up on two separate coat-hangers (remembering the Bishop of the Dutch *stoomboot*), and then I stood for a long time under the shower-bath in the corner of my room—shower which, of course, had no need for a hot-water tap. Then, selecting a fresh suit of tropic white, because they would only last clean and unwrinkled for one day—if that—I dressed without haste, for that would make me sweat and ruin my suit, yet as quickly as I could while the cool of the water was still in me. I had a complete outfit of tropic suits, drill, silk, and pongee, that I had bought out in India five years before. I had not thought that I would ever use them again. And many of them I never shall.

The laundry is chancy over most of South America. In the villages they beat your clothes on the rocks of streams. This is not bad, because they bleach them a startling white in the blazing sun. But when they wash them in a "modern" laundry, such as in Guayaquil, they just toss them into a vat with whatever other laundry they have in hand. As violent scarlets, blues, and oranges are colors particularly favored by the Negro and mestizo women of South America, and as these are by far the majority of the population (excepting Indians, whose clothes never go to the wash), something usually happens to your white suits. Dyes, for instance, run. And, while they run in, they don't run out.

The result was that, after Guayaquil, I did not have a suit in which I did not go about looking like a rainbow.

✓   ✓   ✓

Mr. MacWithers always groaned about the coffee in the mornings. "This country, around Medellin, is supposed to grow the finest coffee in the world. Now why in hell can't they make a good cup of coffee? I *like* a good cup of coffee in the mornings; helps you to put up with a lot of things."

In the twenty-odd years he had spent knocking about the tropics, Mr. MacWithers had come to look upon his boat-trips up and down the coast of South America as little visitations from home.

"I always try to make an American boat. There's ice-cream there. No other country in the world knows how to make it, 'cepting the Americans. Waffles and stacks of buckwheat cakes—with maple syrup in the mornings. . . ."

"Shut up," I said, "until we get out of Colombia. What do you think is the matter with this cooking here?"

"No imagination. No sauces. Nothing. Strikes me there's probably a good reason for it, too. Y'know, in the old days, when the Conquistadores came out here, and these countries became Vice-Royalties, Spain wouldn't let 'em grow anything that would compete with the old country. No spices, I suppose. Anyway, all you can say for this fish we're eating now is—it's been treated with heat.

"Ha-ha!" said Mr. MacWithers, telling me the same story he told every meal in Colombia. "Know how they get their cooks down here? Ranch I was on . . . used to make the Indian girls come in and cook *free* for a time whenever they had an illegitimate baby. Hell! They never had a chance to learn anything. Didn't stay long enough. There was always a waiting-list. Ha-ha! Bet that's the way they get their cooks up in the big hotels at Bogotá."

"Bogotá?" I said. "I wonder if I'm ever going to get there?"

"Oh, maybe you will," said Mr. MacWithers. But he didn't sound hopeful.

✦   ✦   ✦

It was impossible at any meal to get away from a large slab of yellow melon called papaya. Usually we ate it to get it out of sight. But there were two fruits whose exterior looked like a commonplace Irish potato after it is baked, but whose insides were highly exciting. One had a creamy pulp, soft as an alligator pear, and a blood-red interior. It tasted rather decadent, but grew on one. The other, split open, revealed a crystalline green substance that both tasted and felt like ginger as you bit through it. Then there were green oranges, exotically succulent, whose skins had been split open so that they lay in four green petals, like the leaves of a flower. Twice a day, in addition to soup, meat, or fish, there was a heavy rice dish—rice being a staple crop in the valleys of the high Cordilleras.

And it was a heavy, hot meal like this that Cartagena ate after it left its offices around 11.30 in the morning. From then on, until around three, the city dozed.

Down in the harbor, the fishermen and the sailors on their local cargo-boats slept in the shade of their furled sails. Fish-vendors and fruit-sellers in the market-place slept on the cobbles beside their stalls. So they did at night, in spite of the smells of decaying unsold produce. Taxi-drivers by the city gate sprawled backwards in their cars. Outside the yellow walls, on the stretch of sand between Cartagena and the tepid sea, the poor Negro colony in tattered huts slept on their beds of bamboo slats and the children curled up to drowse beside the sleeping dogs.

About 2.30 Cartagena begins to yawn and stretch itself. Iron shutters before stores are rolled up with metallic clangs. Banks open; cafés; the ironic North Pole begins to serve the villainous soft drinks that Colombians seem to adore. Loud speakers renew their blaring from radio shops. The two-wheeled, lumbering mule-carts have resumed their clumsy passage up from the cargo-boats, pressing you flat against the walls. Fords and Chevrolets, after they have practically run over you, honk in passing. Clerks in shirt-sleeves, who have just gone into their offices, dash out again for a quick *tinto*—that thimbleful of black coffee so essential to the tropic morale. A small contingent of the army marches past, the men in German tin helmets and bare or sandaled feet. The last man in the column is carrying a dead rabbit by the legs.

At six this movement stops. Night has fallen. Another meal is being eaten.

✦ ✦ ✦

After dinner, on the broad causeway across a channel of the Caribbean, squirming with reflected harbor lights, there is the evening promenade. This causeway is lined with the marble busts of the Colombian martyrs, executed by the Spaniards for their part in trying to cut South America loose from the Motherland. And they are very real and numerous martyrs. There is, therefore, a heroic background of blind eyes watching this evening stroll of the young men and women of this ancient city. And there they walk; up and down, up and down, up and down. . . . From the orange tower of the illuminated clock over the gateway through the city walls, a radio plays operatic airs. At the far end of the causeway two open-air movie houses run to capacity every night.

But when the clock strikes ten the causeway begins to drain. By eleven the movie crowd is already home. By midnight, as I have said, except for the tinkling *cantinas*, the Navy Bar, the Pullman, and the Dancing Bar down by the harbor, or the bungalows of the red light district among their suburban palms (both communities outside the city walls), old Cartagena is sound asleep, slowly revolving under the brilliant tropic stars.

Chapter XI

NIGHT IN THE COOLER

AN EARNEST United States official told me that he had
spent three years trying to see the inside of Colon jail.
Well, I had a good look at it the first night. My only
trouble was how to get out.

It began, as many things do, with a taxi-driver. I had
been dancing in the Moulin Rouge, and I thought I had
had about all I could stand. But I wasn't sure—so, when
I was driven back to the Hotel Washington, I told the
Jamaican taxi-driver that, if he wanted to, he might wait
about. I might come down for more. Again, I might not.
Then I went straight upstairs and went to sleep.

About one o'clock I was awakened by a very polite
American Negro waiter, who said: "Yo taxi, suh, am still
waitin' at de doah."

"My taxi? *My* taxi? . . . What on earth are you talking about?"

"Well, suh, he's waitin'—an' he says you owe him foah
dollars."

"Go on!"

"Yassuh—dat's what *he* says."

✓   ✓   ✓

I got up and dressed. And let's draw a veil over what
happened then. Just see me standing before a local magis-

89

trate in the Panama night court. Then see me, still refusing to pay that taxi-driver, being conducted under police
escort across the street—a short walk but not a gay one—
to where nothing but the bars broke the lights from inside
the jail's office. Here papers, watch, money—and penknife
—were removed from me. . . . Sanitation ceased, and I
was paraded down a corridor stinking of human offal, and
clunk!—horrid sound—the bolt of a cell shut behind me.
I was not alone. . . .

✓   ✓   ✓

And here I want to interject something—some politics. Don't walk away with the idea that the Panamanians
and Colombians love us Americans; they don't. The
Colombians have long memories; as I have said, they
have not yet forgotten or forgiven us for stealing the
Panama Canal (remember Teddy Roosevelt's famous
statement: "I took the Canal!"), even though we did
eventually pay them $25,000,000 "conscience money,"
the last $5,000,000 being paid in 1930. The Panamanians
have an inferiority complex from living under the lee
of that terrific, terribly efficient Canal organization, and
the 17,000 U. S. soldiers, sailors, marines, and fliers who,
with their imposing forts, naval bases, and flying-fields,
dominate this narrow neck of the American continent.

Therefore, when one miserable little Americano stands
before a Panama magistrate . . . not that that little man
did not lean over backwards, to be scrupulously fair. He
was a model of precision—but he saw his chance.

✓   ✓   ✓

I was not alone. . . . This story saddens abruptly. There was nothing amusing about the inside of that pen. Ten Negroes and Panamanians and one Frenchman were inside a cement box. It was like a cage at the zoo; it smelt like one. A cement pit in the corner was the communal toilet. There were two bunks made of steel piles and canvas. But two Negroes had pre-empted these. The rest just lay on the dirty floor.

1   1   1

"Bon soir, m'sieur," nodded the Frenchman, without a smile. I was dressed in spotless tropic white. He had on a pair of the dirtiest under-drawers I have ever seen. He had not shaved for weeks. And no wonder—he had been in there that long. He had spread a piece of straw matting out on the floor to make a bed and was using his coat and trousers as a pillow. I sat down, and, somewhat grumpily, shoved him slightly sideways towards the edge of his mat. Without a word he moved over to give me a little space. Then I lay down beside him. Without thinking about it, I produced a packet of cigarettes and casually offered him one.

"Ah, *merci . . . merci . . . merci . . . !*"

It made me ill to see such gratitude. If I had known the feeling inside that cell I would have brought a carton. The Frenchman's joy brought some of the realities home to me. These men had lost their liberty. And very likely some of them would not soon get it back again. They were in the first stages of a long period of despair.

I then noticed that the Panamanian beside me, rocking back and forth with his hands around his knees, had a badly broken nose, with a piece of bone sticking out of it. Back and forth, back and forth; moan, moan, moan. . . . He was entirely isolated by his misery.

"What's he done?" I asked the Frenchman.

"Caught another man with his wife. Stabbed him."

"And you?"

"Nothing, m'sieur."

I smiled. "Neither have I," I said. Then he smiled.

✶ ✶ ✶

It was not a flattering smile; for it seemed to say: "You are a clever one: you know better than to talk!" His story was that he had come from Costa Rica and, when they were examining him, the Panama police had taken his passport and thrown him in here. He had been here two weeks. He couldn't get a letter either out or in. What was he to do? As he was an obvious crook of the worst sort, and as the jailers had taken all my valuables away from me, I said good night and went to sleep. Back and forth . . . back and forth . . . back and forth . . . the last thing I remembered was that bleeding Panamanian rocking like a Japanese balancing doll beside me.

✶ ✶ ✶

At 3 o'clock I was awakened and saw a jailer leaning over me. He nodded. I followed. "I will fine you three dollars," said the magistrate. I gave it to him. "Now," I said, "may I tell you what I think of this business? And you," I said to the taxi-driver, who was sitting on one of the benches. "I—"

The magistrate jumped up. "You hit that man," he

said, "and I'll fine you the limit. I'll give you ten days in jail. Yes—and when you get out I'll send you back."

"I merely wanted to speak to him," I said, turning towards the taxi-driver. And as I said this his honor made a sign. A policeman grabbed my arm; and I was led back to jail again.

✦ ✦ ✦

Froggie was asleep when I came in this time. When I started shoving him off my part of his mat he woke up. "Good God," he said. "I thought you'd gone." "So did I," I said. I still had about half a packet of cigarettes. I was afraid to give them all away, as I did not know how long I was in for. So I gave Froggie one. We smoked them until the fire burnt our lips. A Negro groaned, got up, and used the toilet. *"Pas de papier!"* said the Frenchman. He shrugged his shoulders. Sleep seemed the best way out of it, so the Frenchman and I lay back, and he was soon breathing heavily.

Two overhead lights blazed in our faces.

✦ ✦ ✦

Just before dawn the jailer came back again. I was led out into the empty street and liberated. My papers and valuables had been given back to me; but the jailers had kept my penknife. Dangerous weapon, I suppose. Incidentally, it was a Toledo blade that I had been given by a Basque in the high Pyrenees.

It was a long way to the Hotel Washington. I looked round for a taxi-driver—and I knew the one I wanted to find.

✦ ✦ ✦

The cabarets along the Balboa Boulevard were just closing. A few of the girls, a bit puffy under the eyes by now, were having a drink by themselves in the Moulin Rouge. They waved to me. I sat down, bought a round of drinks, and found they were seventy-five cents each. More expensive than jail. I told them so.

"Mister," they all said very seriously, "don't be funny with the magistrates. They can fine you whatever they please. Don't give them a chance to do the dirty on you."

*   *   *

Bearing upon the interjection I made in this account on politics—later in the day I met one of the two magistrates. The minute he saw me he crossed the street and hastily invited me to have a drink at the Strangers' Club.

"I'm sorry," he said, "about last night."

"Oh, that's all right," I said. "But tell me; why did that other magistrate throw me back in jail the second time?"

"Because you were impertinent," he said.

Even so, I was glad I had not given them the chance to do the dirty on me.

Chapter XII

ALONG THE CANAL (I)

THE BUTTERFLIES came out to meet our ship as we passed through the yellow concrete blocks of Colon breakwater. They fluttered around our white superstructure. The waters of the Caribbean going into the Canal were a rich cobalt blue. There was a fresh breeze. Inshore, two white yachts were heeled over, their crews up on the weather side as they raced across the harbor. The sun glistened on the white sides of a United Fruit Company boat as she went out past Toro Light on her way up to the States and the snows of New York. Funnels of red, black, and white marked a big German round-the-world liner lying at the long cement docks of Cristobal. The coco-nut palms along the waterfront were vivid green against the powdered blue of the distant mountains of Panama.

"Not bad, is it?" said the ship's doctor. He was an inwardly emotional man, surcharged with repressions, with small, red-rimmed eyes that betrayed him and filled with moisture when he talked about beauty. His hobby was color photography. Of clouds and sunsets. His other hobby, I imagine, was drink. The card he gave me showed that he belonged to a good London club. A rich, sporting lot, however. If he liked you, or felt that he could trust you not to gush about them, he would invite you to his cabin and show you his Lumière plates. He had a little

95

black box, with an electric light bulb, that showed up their colors.

The chief steward usually saw that any "lady" traveling alone, particularly if she were *blasé* and beautiful, was placed at his table. They were the M.O.'s kind of people. The steward knew better than to place a certain type of eager, out-to-see-the-world tourist with the doctor. He liked 'em cynical and snotty, he did.

Most of the morning coming up to Panama I had spent in a bathing-suit, swimming round like a fish in a bowl in the pool that had miraculously been contrived out of the ship's forward hatch. When this was drained I got into cool white and hung over the rail, watching the glistening jungle of Colombia. The Conquistadores, those unbelievable supermen, had crossed the Isthmus; but there were stretches of Indian country in this jungle that had never been seen by a white man. Between long distances there was an occasional native village on the water-edge. You could always pick them out by the lighter green splash of their banana plantations, which stood out against the dark-shadowed depths of the jungle itself. And, although I was then unaware of it, I was to meet a French convict in Colon, escaper from Cayenne, who had achieved the remarkable feat of coming up along this coast by the means of stealing Indian canoes as he progressed from village to village. The sloppy sails of the banana boats lying off these habitations also signaled their presence. But, for the most, that wall of green, shining in the heat haze of the Caribbean, was no man's land.

This coast seemed to fascinate the doctor. And for a long time that afternoon he leaned beside me on the rail, absolutely silent—as if he were contemplating some act. Finally he remarked: "Wonder what it's like to live in there—to *live*, you know?"

Then he said: "I'm afraid No. C206 is in a bad way. She has a temperature."

C206 was a society beauty—erstwhile photographer's model, and a "girl of the twenties." The days of the bottle-parties. All I knew of her then was that she had red hair and Nofretete eyes and nose. Much too fragile, she seemed, for her reputed will-power. The man with her also had red hair—and a red beard. He had blue and very bloodshot eyes; result, said the doctor, of being neither quite tight nor quite sober in the twenty-one days he had been aboard the ship—and yet, in the short dive-and-out he had taken into the bathing-pool that morning, he had displayed a pair of shoulders in which the muscles still stood out like ropes. Once, at any rate, he had been a fine specimen. I was not surprised to hear that he was a British colonial. And I knew the explanation of his red beard without being told it; Paris—the Left Bank.

They were coming out to the tropics *en route* to some South Sea island—to settle their personal equation. This I learned later. All I knew now was that they had had a hell of a row in the smoking-room last night. It had begun with a cocktail party celebrating the end of twenty-one days at sea. She had called him a "bloody amateur" and said: "All you can do is copy people who really know how to paint." And down in their cabin she had thrown his sketch-book out of the porthole. He had hit her.

✦   ✦   ✦

The Canal Zone has three lives—and a hotel which is part of two of them. This is the Washington. It is run by the U. S. Government; has the finest open-air bathing-pool in all the tropics, in which a genius of an instructor teaches the children of the U. S. Zone employees to swim the Australian crawl at the age of six; and the cool, green lawns of the Hotel Washington stretch all the way down to the walk of coco-nut palms that wave along the sea-wall of the Caribbean. The coco-nuts drop into the sea and float past you, joining that careless abandon of the thousands of coco-nuts that have dropped into the sea all the way up from Colombia and Panama. The Hotel Washington has cool, dark rooms; white-tiled bathrooms; a staff of immaculate and most polite American Negroes in white jackets; excellent food—and no contact what-ever with one side of life in Panama.

The two lives it does know—excellent lives—are those of the U. S. Army, Navy, and aviators, and the higher-paid officials among the Zone employees. In the final analysis, the ten-mile-wide strip across the Isthmus of Panama—fifty miles from deep water to deep water—is run by the United States Army. A colonel is always its governor. But the bulk of its employees are civilians, many of whom have been down there since shortly after 1903, when Panama declared its independence from Colombia. They live in park-like settlements along the Canal from Colon to Balboa Heights, mostly in two-family gray wooden bungalows built on stilts and enclosed by wire screens. It is a park-like civilization, with practically no class distinction. In a life where the Governor of the Canal Zone can get no more than $883 a month, and a foreman in a skilled trade may earn anywhere from $3,600 to $4,000 a year—and few houses rent for more than $35 a month—there is a good chance indeed to work out something like liberty, equality, and fraternity among the human species. And the Canal Zone is doing it—has done it, in fact.

Liberty has a gentle curb put on it by the fact that the employees of the Administration are rated as U. S. Civil Service officials. They are living upon Government property, with, of course, the attendant restrictions as to what they may or may not do with the houses they are occupying. And they are both freed and deprived of that financial competition which is supposed to be the backbone of American "rugged individuality," and which at the same time gives us that set, taut look to the lips—so distinctly American that you can pick out an American business man at a glance in the Savoy Hotel, or among the throng that strolls past you on a spring morning in Paris, as you sip your *apéritif* outside the Café de la Paix. From where Toro Point Light throws its revolving beam over the Caribbean to where the green lawns of Fort Amador stretch out into the Pacific, this life of the Canal employees is one of the best working examples of a Government's paternal Socialism in existence.

It is a life that is almost vegetarian in its propriety. With careers easily wrecked by bad personal conduct, these U. S. employees lead scrupulously healthy and upright lives.

A Colon hospital doctor showed me a room.

"We used to use that for the d.t.'s. We don't use it any more. And it's amazing how, when there was a cut in the salaries of the Canal employees during the slump, the drinking stopped. They just pulled in their horns, and decided that would be the first place they would economize. And they have not taken it up much since."

For me, I would find it a bit dull. I can understand an engineer, in love with his profession, simply reveling in the marvelous efficiency and the amazing exploits of the machinery he is directing with so little obvious effort. You turn a knob no bigger than a door-handle to close the 600-ton leaf gates. But the women must find life a little too uneventful at times. I met one who keeps a perfect aquarium of microscopic fish. Minute, jewel-like fish. She can never get enough of them. Her home is walled with glass battery-cases in which these flashing fish flit about as you have tea with her. It takes up most of her day looking after them.

"One must have a hobby," she explained.

⚹   ⚹   ⚹

The officers of the 17,000 soldiers, sailors, marines, and aviators in the Zone live their Service lives in the most immaculate green-lawned forts and naval bases and around the mess at France Field. To many of them the Canal Zone overseas appointment of two years at least is two years "off time." They are far away from the small-town gossip of U. S. navy yards and military posts; they are free, except for occasional visits from busybody U. S. Senators—that curse of the Service. And, like the British officers in every mess in torrid India, they drink as much as they want—when they feel like it.

The Services are clubby. Usually they invite only each other out to dinner. Zone people think they're snobbish.

*   *   *

But these two trim lives keep to themselves. Neither of them seems even aware of the colorful existence lived on Colon's painted balconies; the life of the ten thousand happy Jamaican Negroes in the Canal Zone—all British subjects brought in to do the spade-work. Nor of the life of the enlisted men, Uncle Sam's soldiers and marines in trim tropic khaki and the sailors in their flapping white, making whoopee under the twittering neon lights of the cabarets that line Balboa Boulevard. The life of Panama.

This life has a color, a lustiness, a rich humanity—full blown by the tropics—that makes the other two lives seem gray and sterile. After a few days at the Hotel Washington I gave up my salubrious room one afternoon and went down and took a room in a native hotel whose balcony overhung Balboa Boulevard.

Here I found the red-bearded Australian.

*   *   *

"It's a toss-up," he said, "whether she will die or not."

I had just been thinking that here was *life:* the barefoot nigger boys running by in the street; slim wenches, smiling to open wide mouths full of white teeth; continuous passage of soldiers and sailors past the bar's open doors; Panamanian bar-tender cracking jokes with three dusky customers as they tossed dice for drinks, feet on the brass rail; a real tramp—shooed away by the proprietor; a broken-down white man soaking beer at a side-table, his face the color and texture of a ripe strawberry—none of which could be seen in the golf-club atmosphere of the Hotel Washington. They made me feel alive again.

The Australian was obviously overjoyed to have company. He had been drinking heavily. His face was puffy, and his white coat was wrinkled and full of patches of damp sweat.

"I've been sitting here pretty nearly all day," he told me. "Take a taxi every now and then to the hospital. She has a fever of 105 . . . and a pulse of 140. That's pretty bad, isn't it?"

I nodded. I did not tell him I thought a normal pulse was around 80.

"She's had a blood transfusion," he said miserably.

✓   ✓   ✓

As he was not going back to the hospital until round 9 o'clock, I suggested we walk along to Bilgray's Tropic Bar and have some food. "Might as well eat, I suppose," he said, trying to laugh at himself. "All I've had today is whiskey."

He ordered a club sandwich and I had a big half-lobster, grilled with drawn butter, for which the Tropic Bar is famous. The life inside the bar cheered him up a bit. It is a lively spot, with a Caribbean seascape painted over the bar in robin's-egg blue of coco-nut palms, tropic islands, and a luscious Carib girl. The three winning numbers of the Panama Lottery are always written on the bar's long mirror in whitewash. So, in the seasons, are the U. S. football and baseball scores. Above the bar was a large glass frame over some strips of paper, under which was the caption: A GOOD PLACE FOR BAD CHECKS. There were photographs of semi-naked Indian girls; Antarctic explorers in their fur parkas; one of Admiral Byrd himself, and one of Captain Scott's ship, the *Discovery*. Bilgray is one of the characters of the Canal Zone. Of him a young local editor said to me: "It's an honor to know that man. He's so straight. Old Bilgray never cuts his whiskey."

I was beginning to wish he had cut some of it, for the Australian was taking on a boat load. His club sandwich lay neglected. When a crowd of hilarious tourists came in from an American ship, he said: "Let's get the hell out of here."

His Parisian *patine* had gone completely. "It's been a damn' nightmare!" he exclaimed as we drove to the hospital in an open taxi. "It's hell—you feel so damned impotent, unable to do anything. The doctors must think I'm crazy, the way I keep after them."

I waited downstairs in the hospital while he went up. The smell of chloroform and the hot night and the babies crying; I thanked my stars I didn't have someone I cared about lying there. He came down, looking just as worried as when he went up. "Her temperature's down a bit," he announced. "But that enema . . ."

He turned to the colored Panamanian nurse who was following him downstairs. "Look here, Sister," he said, trying to hold on to himself, "what about that enema? She was to have had it this morning—doctor ordered it—and she hasn't had it yet. What's the matter? Why don't you give it to her? What?"

"Oh, now you go along," tried the nurse. "Doan' you worry yourself—she's coming along all right."

"Don't try to kid me like that. I want to know—why didn't she get that enema?"

"I—I don't know. The Sister that's looking after her is off duty."

"Off duty. . . . Isn't *anyone* looking after her?"

"Yes, I am."

"Are you going to give her that enema?"

"Yes, I'll give her that enema."

"Well, what about *now?*"

"I'm getting along to it."

✶   ✶   ✶

He came up on my balcony. I still had most of a bottle of Johnnie Walker.

"Gamest thing I ever saw," he said, "was her that first morning. Of course we neither of us knew how ill she was. I felt that if I could make her eat something it might buck her up. She said she'd try. So I got her an egg sandwich. She can eat that when she can't eat anything else—she's got good plebeian taste about food—but she couldn't even *bite* it. It just stuck in her mouth. Then I didn't say anything—but the minute I got out of the room I ran like hell for a telephone. I had a hell of a time. It was too early to ring up the Consul and get the name of a good doctor. That fool on the desk kept trying to put me on to one of his Spanish friends. I was lucky to get hold of that young American. I've got confidence in him. He had her over in the hospital inside of twenty minutes. It's the first time I've ever seen a doctor show the wind up—when he came out from that blood count . . ."

The Australian stared at the tin roofs of Colon. They

were clear as day under the bright tropic moon. "I've spent the last two nights over in that hospital. Sitting out on that balcony on the second floor—that's just by her room. My God, how that infernal rasp of those palm fronds got on my nerves. Ever notice it? It's bloody.

"You're going out, aren't you?" he asked.

I told him I was; but it would not be until around midnight. I thought I might as well see the floor show at the Moulin Rouge.

"It's a good idea," he said. "I'll go with you. I want to get good and tired so that I'll get some sleep. This is a hell of a town. . . . Always singing and dancing. There's a happy nigger family down there on that balcony across the street . . . wakes me up five o'clock every morning, when they start their day singing hymns."

In the Moulin Rouge he said suddenly: "Look here, I'm going on the wagon. When I drink I lose my nerve. Just haven't any guts. I'm going to quit. Somebody's got to keep his head in this damned business."

Chapter XIII

THIS ROUGH WORLD

THE *Santa Lucia* lay at Cristobal, in the Canal Zone, with three stowaways under 180 tons of coffee in her forward hatch. They had been down there ever since Guayaquil, in Ecuador; four days. Nobody had known that they were there until they had made their presence known that morning by a frantic banging. It was now nearly midnight. An officer had managed to locate them in the lower hold, get past the coffee, and send them down some soup with a hot-water bottle and an enema tube. But for several hours no sound had been heard and no soup had been sucked from the tube; the betting was, they were dead.

"Serves 'em right," said one of the men peering down into the hatch to where two gangs of Jamaican Negroes were piling the 154-lb. bags of coffee into cargo slings just as fast as their glistening ebony could make it.

The rest of the men looking down at this scene—ship's officers, a couple of privileged local correspondents, and a gorilla dressed in the uniform of a Canal Zone policeman —turned and stared at the fellow.

"Well, it's their own fault, isn't it?" he said, defending himself.

"What the hell's that got to do with it?" demanded the gorilla.

✶ ✶ ✶

That was just the point. And if the harmless civilian who had thus spoken out of turn had had any savvy he would have replied: "Absolutely nothing!" For it hadn't. The whole thing was automatic. Men in trouble; get them out—and *then* attend to them. That was the attitude of the higher command. Otherwise, why should the big *Santa Lucia,* one of the finest ships of the Grace Line, upset her entire unloading routine to save three miserable wretches who had deliberately got themselves into such a fix?

But it was funny that the gorilla should have taken that point of view; for, just before he turned on the civilian, I had been watching him unconsciously clenching and unclenching his two massive hands as he stared down into the hatch—obviously dying to get those hands on those stowaways.

I know what was the chief (perhaps only) emotion that animated everyone else engaged in that scene, including even the sweating black stevedores—just plain curiosity. How many were there? The ship's officer had said he *thought* there were three. Who were they? And what would they look like, alive or dead?"

✦ ✦ ✦

"I'll bet they're squashed flat as frogs!" said one of the local newspaper men.

The youngest of the ship's officers grinned at him. "Didn't think that coffee was on *top* of them, did you? No—they're down in the lower hold."

He explained how heavy planks covered the hatch that went into the hold; the stowaways were under no pressure —but the hold was absolutely black dark, and had no ventilation. There was also practically no head room. King Kong, the Canal Zone policeman, who had been listening to this with the deepest attention, then surmised: "Maybe they're suffocated?"

"You've said it," said the ship's officer.

✓   ✓   ✓

There was not even rancor in the scene, although there was soon to be reason for it.

For a colorful, dramatic stage-set, that scene around the *Santa Lucia's* forward hatch would be hard to beat. The spotless white superstructure was blinding white in the big deck-lamps. It was a pale blue tropic night, with silver-rimmed clouds floating past the stars. Rows and rows of lights shone through the ports of the big German round-the-world liner as she went out past Toro Light. A beautiful sight. They would be dancing on that liner, and the crowd from the *Santa Lucia* were either over in Bilgray's Tropic Bar, or watching the U. S. soldiers and sailors making whoopee over in the cabarets of Colon. And can they make it!

"Looks like a good story," declared a local reporter. "Stowaways aren't much. They're always snatching them out. Stick 'em in Colon jail . . . send 'em back in the brig of a boat of whatever their own country happens to be. But four days under 180 tons of coffee . . . feeding 'em with a hot-water bottle and an enema tube. . . . Boy! this is sure where I hit the first page . . . specially if they're dead."

✓   ✓   ✓

I never saw a ship unloaded so fast in all my life. The level of the 154-lb. bags of coffee sank like the water in Gatun Lock. It really was a race against death. Finally a space was cleared big enough to allow the young ship's officer to crawl along on his stomach and look down into the lower hold.

"There they are!" he yelled back. "See 'em?"

Through where the plank covering had been chipped off we caught a glimpse of something moving, a light reflection in the patch of darkness. The plank was pulled further back, and, like a dog entering a rabbit-hole, the ship's officer slid his head and shoulders into the aperture, finally vanishing from his waist on.

Then his feet began to beat a tattoo on the hatch-covers. He was struggling. But from his stern view it was impossible to tell whether he was trying to pull someone up or whether someone wasn't trying to pull him *down*. Just when another officer wormed his way forward to assist him, he emerged and stood up. He held a long knife in his hand.

"Isn't that gratitude?" he grinned, as he held it up to show us. "Tried to stick me!"

"Grrrrr!" said the gorilla dressed in the uniform of a Canal Zone policeman.

✓   ✓   ✓

They were three Ecuadorians: one nearly dead from suffocation, starvation, and heat—the one with the knife; one only slightly dopy; and one who might have been traveling four days first class as far as any sign of exhaustion was concerned. The Zone policeman looked at them mournfully.

As they had behaved themselves since they had been pulled out into the open air, and as they had all stood obediently against the white bulkheads in a line, as he had ordered them to, he could not touch them. All he could do now was put them in the "pie-wagon" quietly, and let the magistrate attend to them. The Zone police are well-behaved policemen.

*   *   *

This policeman was suffering from a bad case of frustration. But it was soon ended. As he was walking the Ecuadorian stowaways meekly through the dock shed, several taxi-loads of the *Santa Lucia's* tourists came back to the ship: men in white dinner-jackets and tropical drill, women in light chiffon. Among them were a couple of young-men-about-town who came tootling back to the *Santa Lucia* with a large cargo of their own on board. One of them, seeing the huge sign NO SMOKING in the shed, stopped deliberately under it and lighted a cigarette.

King Kong waited until he had got it fully alight. Then he removed it from the young man's lips and stamped on it.

"You—" said the roisterer.

*   *   *

It was beautiful. The thing that poor King Kong had been waiting for all the evening. An excuse for action. As the rest of the *Santa Lucia's* passengers went up the gangway, King Kong quietly picked up the young tourist and lifted him deftly into the "pie-wagon." "Grrrr!" he said, and slammed the door.

"Okay!" he said happily to the driver.

Chapter XIV

ALONG THE CANAL (II)

Why is the Lighthouse Bar famous throughout the tropics? Because our drinks are second to none, and they include the standard mixture of drinks, and the others which are mixed by none other than I. Kresch and his most able assistant, Prof. Max W., which are accepted throughout the Service world. Our Bar is supplied with the best liquors from Vodka to Napoleon Brandy. . . .

SITTING with a bunch of khaki soldiers, shaking his Dempsey-like head as he tried to get his eyes into focus to read this encouraging testimonial, I found Skeeter.

Skeeter was in civilian clothes. That is, he had on a pair of white drill trousers and a soft-collared shirt open down to his navel. That is, they had been white. About two days back. Skeeter was on a blind.

Skeeter had been a radio operator over at Coco Solo, the submarine base. Skeeter had "purchased out"—bought his discharge from the Service. The U. S. Government, not wishing to pile up human driftwood in the tropics, does not ordinarily discharge a Service man in the Canal Zone any more. He is released from the Service back home. But if a man has had a good sheet during his term of service, and can convince the skeptical authorities that he has a good job in the Zone, he may buy his discharge from the Army or Navy before his term of enlistment expires. Skeeter, therefore, was no longer a servant of Uncle Sam.

But he was still a fine physical specimen of the U. S.

regular Service man; generous to the point of being sentimental about it, sentimental about life itself, a bit lonely and anxious that chance acquaintances should like him; but quite willing to give you a black eye if he thought you had it coming to you. Skeeter, incidentally, had been a Navy boxer.

He had a bottle of rot-gut whiskey which he shared with prodigal hospitality. Unwrapping it, he dolloped it into the empty glasses around the table.

"Down the rat-hole," he said.

✓   ✓   ✓

The argument, when they invited me to their table, was over a new tattooing process—the electric needle.

"Don't go deep, like a Jap's does. Not like a real needle. Kinda common. Always looks new."

An old Gob who had hands hardened by salt water until they looked like a turtle's back, stared at them regretfully.

"No," he said, "I shouldn't 'a' done that. That was a mistake. That don't look well in a Tuxedo, does it, pal?"

The hands he held out for me to examine bore, on the right one, a blue and white design of a nautical compass card. On the left was an outstretched bird clasping a handful of arrows and an olive-branch; the American eagle. When I asked him where he had had his done, he said:

"Buddy, that was a Barcelona drunk. A Bar-ce-lo-na drunk! Ever had one?"

My stock went up immediately when I said yes, perhaps I had been tight in Barcelona. Anyway, I'd been there several times.

"Well, maybe you got good likker. Kind I had—all I had to do in the morning was shake my head and be drunk all over again."

↗   ↗   ↗

There was a Professor Schmidt in Colon. He was behind Dutch's place, I think. Pub whose motto has it: NORTH, SOUTH, EAST, WEST—DUTCH'S PLACE YOU'LL FIND THE BEST! Professor Schmidt's office was behind the pool tables; and he would leave his game of pinochle and do you a good tattoo for one dollar. The walls of his office were lined with what looked like all the face cards in the pack. These were the colored designs that Professor Schmidt could do for you. He had a celluloid stencil for every one. Professor Schmidt rubbed tattooing ink into the grooves of the stencil, pressed it against your arm or chest—then he traced out the design with the hot, spluttering electric needle. You were marked for life.

A young Gob bared a forearm to show a tasty frigatebird of Professor Schmidt's, under which were the block letters: COCO SOLO—1936.

Comment was guarded. It did look a bit raw, and only surface deep—like a child's transfer.

"Well, I got the other kind," he said testily, trying to pull up his white sleeve to show his shoulder. "I got it done in San Diego."

"When was *you* in San Diego?"

"Remember Smutty Williams?"

"*Do* I know Smutty Williams!"

↗   ↗   ↗

Outside passed the night-life of Colon. The Zone is the U. S. Service man's idea of heaven. It is a long way from home. And there are probably more cabarets and cafés along Balboa Boulevard than along any other street in the world. About all of the 17,000 U. S. soldiers and sailors in the Zone seem to be trying to get into them every night. They are always full. And yet the street outside is a river of khaki and white, a roar of music, a quivering blaze of red and blue neon lights. I lived over this street for a couple of weeks and it was worse than having to go to a circus every night.

The cabarets and *cantinas* are below the balconies. On the balconies are the 10,000 happy Jamaican Negroes that inhabit the Zone. They are dancing buck-and-wings, playing banjos, mouth-organs, radios, gramophones; and the more exotic among them are wailing African hymns.

The dark street paralleling Balboa Boulevard is called "Bottle Alley." Cheaper, and in some ways a more exclusive section, it is used by men who have been in the Zone for over a year, and therefore rate as old-timers; and this street is full of beer saloons, shooting galleries, and hot-dog stands.

One street further and you have reached the dividing-line between the Republic of Panama and the United States Canal Zone. This is Front Street. Front Street is just one long line of Hindu shops selling Japanese goods. Just about an unbroken mile of plate-glass windows full of flowered silk kimonos, pajamas, shirts, blouses, shimmies, socks, bamboo hats, and ivory elephants. A Panamanian shop sells crocodiles converted into handbags, belts, and boots. Another retails eighteen-foot anacondas cut up into snake-skin cigarette-cases and more handbags, belts, and boots. There is no closing hour along Front Street when a big tourist ship is in port. And the tourists, after a mad orgy of shopping in this duty-free gaudy street, turn up in the cabarets along Balboa Boulevard looking like the chorus from *Chu Chin Chow*.

"God damn their souls!" said the red-bearded Australian. "Doesn't it make you ashamed of the human race?"

⚹ ⚹ ⚹

As a matter of fact, it does have the most extraordinary effect upon you, this city. If you've ever felt that you wanted to go wrong, in night-life, Colon will cure you. It's a lesson in the futility of immorality; or of merely trying to be naughty, to be more exact. This got through to Skeeter, who was on a blind when we met him, and stayed on a blind miraculously for three days. His philosophic faculties were aroused by the Australian's comment on the soda-fountain quality of Colon's sin.

"I guess some of us do come into Colon with the original idea of raising hell, but by the time we finish standing each other drinks, why, we're broke. We never get around to it."

The marvelous vitality of Skeeter and his pals is a tribute to a thoughtful Government. In the Zone an ordinary U. S. private gets $21 a month and a sailor gets $30; and the colored proprietors of Colon's *cantinas* get nearly all of it. The minute they wake up in their forts or ships, however, they must fall in step with a life that keeps them so healthy that it hurts. Hangovers probably cause their possessors a certain amount of keen physical pain. And,

bowing to Socialist progress, I am told, the U. S. higher
command has reluctantly let up a little in its notorious
passion for physical jerks. But with the great husky mass
of German, Slav, and Scandinavian stock to recruit from,
the U. S. Army and Navy still turn out the finest physical
specimens of fighting men in the world; and, mentally,
they are several school classes, very often a university or
so, ahead of their brothers in European conscript services.
To see this mass of unfulfilled desire prowling along under
the neon lights of Balboa Boulevard is one of life's sights.
It is human dynamite.

"But," philosophized Skeeter, as we watched a strip-
tease girl from Texas do her act, "I don't see the use of
sitting here looking at something I know I can't get."

✦   ✦   ✦

These strip-tease girls, and the less exhilarating professional performers brought down from the United
States, are another example of a thoughtful Government.
They are brought into the Isthmus under a three-months'
rigorous contract. The proprietor of the place of enter-
tainment who brings them down must put up a bond of
$500 for each girl, and deposit ticket-money for their
passage home. And at the end of three months, unless
they can get another contract, home they have to go. The
U. S. Government will deport any American girl it catches
trying to go on the loose in Colon.

"For many of these girls, my dear," said Kate, who
runs Kelly's Ritz on the other side of the Isthmus at Balboa Heights, "it is Panama romance. Life in the tropics,
you know. It's to be their one great chance. They're just

as anxious to see life, my dear, as you are, who are looking at them. What *they* expect, I don't know. Anyway, I
usually make 'em go home after their three months are up
—I seldom give them another contract. The Zone is no
place for them, you know."

Kate has been running cabarets down in the Zone for
over twenty years. What she doesn't know about men
could be put on a needle-point. Or women, either. Perhaps that is why she locks her girls up at night. She
doesn't want to lose her $500.

Kate began with four of the fattest and ugliest girls in
the Zone. She opened her cabaret in one room over a balconied shop in Front Street, Colon. She capitalized on
their obesity. The sign over Kate's cabaret read:

"1,000 POUNDS OF FEMALE BEAUTY!"

The stunt failed. The four fat girls left the Zone. But
Kate stayed on. Kate knows ship captains who first came
through the Big Ditch as second mates. She knows majors
and colonels, a bit grisly about the ears now, who first
came down to the Zone as second lieutenants, or even as
enlisted men. She has seen the soldiers and sailors and the
ships of the world pass through the Zone, until today
something like 17,000 U. S. soldiers and sailors rotate in
the Zone every two years—and go their ways; and 7,000
ships passed through the Canal in 1936—and went their
ways.

Kate is an institution. I was taken to see her by a captain who was one of the first men to take a ship through
the Canal. He is just about ready to retire now; and, for
a lark, he introduced me to Kate as his son.

"Well, well!" said Kate. "I thought you told me your boy was in the Navy—flying out at Pearl Harbor?"

"This is another one," lied the captain. "What do you think of him?"

"Well, well!" said Kate, enigmatically. Then: "You know, that's what I've always wanted to do. I've always said that if I ever had any children, and I traveled, I would take them around the world with me. That is the way I'd like to see life. I suppose he favors his mother. I must say he doesn't look like you—except that you've both got blue eyes. How old are you?"

By this time I was trying to change the conversation and I asked Kate about her Christmas dinner. This is also an institution in the Zone; and, in its way, is a real romance of the tropics. There are lots of men in the Zone—old-timers like Kate, who would like to have a family of their own, in particular when Christmas rolls around. And this is where wholehearted Kate throws overboard her professional position as proprietress of Kelly's Ritz. Grandly waving aside the small fortune she might have taken in, Kate closes Kelly's Ritz and gives a private dinner there to all these old-timers on Christmas Day.

"My dear," said Kate to the captain, "we had sixty-eight sit down this year. Bill was the Master of Ceremonies. Bill," she said to me, "is an old bar-tender of mine. Man who has struck it rich, for one, thank the Lord. *And,* Captain Johnson, I kept a vacant chair at the end of the table."

"Sadie?"

"You just bet."

"Sadie," said Kate to me, "is my partner. Seventy-four,

my dear. But she's much sprighter than you are. You should have seen her last year, climbing up the ladders to hang the holly. . . ."

I sat silent.

"She's up in San Francisco now," resumed Kate, after a thoughtful sip of cognac. "Having an operation."

✓   ✓   ✓

It was Christmas, as a matter of fact, that nearly destroyed the Australian—the sight of the sedate American families over in Colon driving past the hospital, bringing home imported pines for Christmas-trees.

"There is something obscene about it," he said. "All this heat . . . and those damn' trees."

His girl was getting better. But nowhere near fast enough to suit her imperious will. "I told the doctors"— he laughed a little sourly—"I said, 'You may think you know something about mules, but . . .' I'm sorry for them. They're afraid to tell her how ill she still is—and she insists on getting up."

Colon, on Christmas Eve, is just about the last place in the world for a man in a desperate frame of mind. The sight of so much feckless gaiety on the part of everybody else is hard to bear. And any chance of sleep was absolutely prohibited by the happy Jamaican Negroes along the balconies, who burst into song and sang hymns all night.

The Australian was still on the wagon. His eyes had taken on an amazing baby blue, like a china doll's. Color emphasized, of course, by his flaming red beard.

"Funny, isn't it," he said, "how the drink gets you?"

He rubbed his hands together, one over the other, as

if he were putting on a pair of invisible gloves. "These little fingers of mine—they have no feeling in them. Doctors tell me it's the alcohol . . . poisoning my nerve centers at the roots. Weird feeling. Sort of half-dead.

"Queer, too, the way, when she'd completely busted my sense of values, she started to *save* me. Blow the masts down, and then try to sail the ship into port. Had a hell of a row once . . . over in Paris, when I said I thought any white girl who slept with a Negro was absolutely unclean. She called me a *prig*. Honest. Liked to say things like that—just to burn me up. Well . . ."

He turned away from his gloomy inspection of the tinsel decorations down in Balboa Boulevard. And it was what he said then that makes me wonder what will be the end of their story. He said:

"I'm not so sure . . . if I do straighten out . . . it won't be the end of *us*."

Chapter XV

PRICE OF FREEDOM

"Je suis libre! Je suis libre!"

He was a French convict who had escaped from Cayenne. After his fifth attempt. That had been eight months ago. And yet all he could say in answer to all my questions was: "I am free! I am free!" As if he couldn't believe his good luck yet.

I had never thought much about what liberty meant until I met this Frenchman. And such a liberty! It takes something like the United Fruit Company to master the jungle. The jungle usually masters the people who try to live in it. Certainly lone-handed white men. And some slight idea of the country this Frenchman was hiding in may be gained from this story.

"I'm not asking you to believe in black magic," said the banana-buyer. "All I can say is that I believe this thing myself. There are two Americans up there, deserters from the U. S. Army, whose Indian girls can make them get down on their knees and go about like dogs."

This was in the Darien Indian country, a large part of which no white man has ever seen. An Englishman who had heard about the strange conduct of the U. S. deserters went up into that country to see for himself.

"He came out *pronto*," said the banana-buyer, "and he

was half scared to death. 'I saw them,' he said. He'd seen them walking round like that, and that was quite good enough for him."

1   1   1

An American "explorer" had penetrated a little further along the edge of the country and come out with a few bleached creatures that he took to New York and put on show as "White Indians." The Indians, whom the Zone people declare must have been albinos, died in New York. An Indian revolution followed in the wake of the explorer; and the Panama Government tried to hold him. The San Blas Indians, when they revolted, killed several white people, including a school-teacher. Panamanians assert the "explorer" was inciting the Indians to declare themselves an independent republic. The U. S. Government sent a warship to take off the "explorer."

But, even so, old-timers in the Zone declare, he did not get into the real Darien Indian country. He only went along the edges. Another party of Americans came down from New York, sensation-bent, with an arsenal of Thompson sub-machine guns, saying they were going to shoot their way through. After a few days in the jungle, they came back. They had not, they admitted, realized the jungle was such a tangled place.

The banana-buyer went up the rivers, buying bananas from the more tame among the Indians. But, when he tried to cross overland, he said that with two men cutting a jungle path with machetes he counted at the best on making only three miles in a day.

"The Indians," he said, "are funny little people. When they think you've gone far enough up into their country, they stop you on the trail, turn your head round, and point back down trail. If you have any sense, you'll go. If you don't—you'll get a fish-arrow shot into you."

✓ ✓ ✓

Stories like this seem improbable when told over a couple of beers in a Colon saloon. Yet an instant's reflection allows you to realize that, except for a road going up to the Pacific to a seaside resort, once you step off the ten-mile-wide strip of the U. S. Canal Zone the jungle swallows you. The banana-buyer had had fifteen years' contact with the more remote Indians, running his independent banana business.

"I flirted for weeks with an old chief, trying to get him in a good humor so that I could go on up the river into his country. We seemed to be getting on quite well. I don't know what I can have said one night; something, I guess, that must have alarmed him.

"In the morning when I woke up I found all my gear down on the beach beside my canoe. My two men were down there, scared stiff. The Indians were standing around them, most of the men holding their bows and fish-arrows. The old chief took me down to the bank and pointed back down the river.

"I went. No fish-arrows for me, thank you. And that's where this Frenchman is."

✓ ✓ ✓

If it had not been for the personality of the banana-buyer and the young local newspaper editor who had appointed themselves protectors of this French escaper from Cayenne, I don't think I would have believed his story. It was too much of a feat.

To begin with, after his fourth attempt at escape, they had him down in those underground cells on Devil's Island where the bars are overhead, and a sentry paces up and down over the cages where the convicts are kept like wild beasts. This Frenchman had escaped from that. Next, he was the only survivor of the seven convicts who made the original attempt. Yet, when I did see him, there seemed still no more life in him than in a small mummy. But that, of course, was convincing evidence of the horror he had gone through. As were these three stark words he had in answer to everything: "I am free!"

✓   ✓   ✓

The Frenchman wanted to put his story into a book. Which was one of the reasons why he took a chance on his liberty in coming to the Canal Zone to see me. I met the three o'clock train across the Isthmus from Balboa; and the newspaper editor and the banana-buyer got off, followed by what looked like a very mangy and minute replica of the thin partner of the team of Laurel and Hardy. Movie stars fit well into the description of this trio; for the taciturn banana-buyer was a perfect double for Ronald Colman, pencil-mustache and all, in the desert costume he wore in *The White Sister*. He was a handsome specimen of the white man who has been trimmed down and made by the tropics. So was the young newspaper editor. Both the results of rigid self-discipline. The newspaper man, who wrote very good stuff, had, so the story runs, begun life in the Canal Zone as a pug. He is one of the most upright men I have ever met. And I hope he will forgive me if I say that too many hours "on the desk," after the stimulating activity of the prize-ring, might result in his getting a comfortable look one day, somewhat like Charles Laughton.

The Frenchman was just a walking mummy. Almost as inarticulate, in a pair of overworn dungarees and an open blue shirt.

1　　1　　1

"*Je suis libre!*" was not particularly descriptive of his miraculous escape, although those three words did hold the horror of it. Details were furnished by the banana-buyer and the newspaper man.

Seven convicts made an escape from the island of death in a small boat. They reached the shores of Dutch Guiana. In coming along the mud coast of that bit of South America, one of them died from exhaustion. Six kept on. In British Guiana, the sporting English at Georgetown outfitted them with another boat. If you look at a map you will see what an experience lay ahead of the convicts: to go up past the mangrove mouth of the Orinoco, past Trinidad, and then along the coast of Venezuela. It was off the Dutch island of Aruba, I think, that they capsized and two of them were drowned.

It becomes like the story of the Ten Little Nigger Boys. Four Frenchmen went on.

They were very nearly dead from lack of food and the sheer strength that had been sapped out of them by the way they had to keep off all traveled paths. Which meant, of course, that either they were pulling their way through jungle undergrowth—a most exhausting process—or they were dragging themselves through the mud of the mangrove swamps.

Nevertheless, they had reached the Republic of Colombia and were facing the almost impossible task of coming up along that coast to Panama, when the ultimate tragedy happened.

Two of the party dropped behind. One was so exhausted that he had begged his comrades to leave him alone—not to force him to go on any longer. It was too much agony. He wanted to die. The other convict, a burly man with a peg leg, offered to stay behind and help him catch up with the other two.

Peg-leg rejoined the other two. Alone.

"Oh, he's dying," he said, answering the others' questions. "Leave the poor devil alone. He wants to die in peace."

He protested so much that the other two became suspicious and went back to find the other man. They found his body. He had been murdered.

Then these two men stalked the man with the wooden leg. They felt too weak to face him openly. They ambushed him. They killed him. And so, the surviving Frenchman said, they made a fire of his wooden leg. It is not at all beyond suspicion that they ate part of him.

The horror of the whole struggle affected the other Frenchman. At the very last lap he turned back. He refused to go on another step. And there this Frenchman that I talked with left his comrade. Asked what he thought could have happened to him, he shrugged his shoulders. *"Je suis libre!"* he said.

That was all that mattered.

✓ ✓ ✓

He was your superb realist, this Frenchman. *Chacun pour soi* was a weak way of describing his attitude. His crime, as a matter of fact, had been so paltry that one can well understand the complete selfishness he felt towards all the rest of mankind for having been sent to Devil's Island—condemned to a living death—simply because one day, out of work in Paris, unable to find a meal, much less a job, he had broken into a house in the suburbs and stolen a necklace. The necklace happened to be so valuable that the pawnshop was afraid to handle it. Instead the police were informed; and, when the Frenchman came back to get his money, he began that long career of torture—which included a transatlantic passage in a cell surrounded by pipes of live steam which would be turned on him if he became rebellious.

Then the years in the penal settlement.

✓ ✓ ✓

The only time he smiled during our whole conversation was when the banana-buyer, the newspaper man, and I, in our various forms of French, made him talk about how he did the impossible—came up the coast of Panama.

There are no trails through that jungle, except a few that the Indians know. To follow those, of course, meant certain death. So the Frenchman stuck to the shore, making from village to village. He hid outside the villages, and at night sneaked in and stole a canoe. Paddling all night, he shoved the canoe off at daybreak and let it float out into the Caribbean, where, he supposed, it would be found by his pursuers and the chase would be given up. This worked beautifully. The Indians, as we were left to imagine, chased a lot of canoes up and down the Caribbean. And the Frenchman, one day, in the last canoe, paddled into Colon harbor.

What that sight must have been to him—a city, for instance, something which he had never thought to see again —was expressed in a past tense:

"*Jétais libre!*"

ꜰ   ꜰ   ꜰ

It was very dramatic.

"But, of course," said the banana-buyer, "he's really not free. He's more or less got to stay up there, where he is, in the Indian country. He's doing a small trading business with them. He's down today, buying some small trinkets that he's going to take back with him. We are helping him a little. Grub-staking him."

He smiled at the Frenchman, whose sallow face with its deep, sad eyes and long lines beside the mouth broke into a radiant horror of receptive wrinkles. It was one of the saddest sights I have ever seen—that pain-ravaged face trying to put on a happy look. It was terrible.

"Well, the little devil's got guts!" said the banana-buyer. "I'm all for him. He thinks he's doing a grand job up there, starting a new business—a new life, you know. And as long as he thinks so, why, that's all that's needed. Isn't it?"

ꜰ   ꜰ   ꜰ

The little Frenchman was nervous, looking round him all the time. He wanted to get back to the safety of the jungle. We shook hands and I wished him luck. He went out to do his shopping. And also, I dare say, to enjoy the thrill of walking with the crowd along the side-walks of Colon—the nearest he will ever get to the streets of his beloved Paris.

Chapter XVI

SEEING LIFE

I ASKED the little blonde what she thought of the Panama Canal. She said:

"Oh, I think it's *cute!*"

This was when we were coming out of Gatun Locks. They are a mile and a fifth long. A man standing half a mile away in a control tower turns the knob to close the 600-ton leaf gates behind you. As soon as the gates close you start to rise, and you rise eighty-five feet.

A British sea captain, first time he took a ship through the Canal, was heard to mutter: "Not a word . . . not a sound . . . nobody shouting at you through a megaphone, ordering you to stop your bloody engines when they've already stopped; it must all have been a dream!"

When the process was reversed and we were being lowered into Pedro Miguel Lock, the red stacks of a Royal Mail boat appeared in the twin lock beside us, coming up. Said my blonde:

"The power of the water must be awfully strong to lift that audacious big thing!"

*   *   *

You simply could not invent that girl. No place but a virile country like America could have produced her. "Beautiful but dumb"; but was she so stupid? She was the most puzzling mixture of innocence and experience.

130

"I can't make her out," said the ship's captain—a sea-dog who had sailed before the mast in the old square-rigger *Shenandoah*, now master of one of the finest ships on the New York-Canal-West Coast of South America run. "Her father said to me in New York: 'Keep an eye on her, will you?' Well, I'm afraid I'm going to lose an eye."

She came from the Middle West. She looked like Jean Harlow. She asked me, in fact, if I didn't think so. She was getting off at Callao, in Peru, for Lima. And she had a shiny black Packard sports model in the hold.

"What are you going to do with that Packard in Peru?" I asked her.

"Now don't you be goofy," she said.

✓   ✓   ✓

Unanswerable. So was the captain's continual question to me: "Now what do you think that girl's up to? I don't know." "Neither do I," I told him. Although we both spent a lot of valuable time trying to find out. Anent the Packard, she said she was going to drive from Callao to Lima.

"By yourself?"

"Uh-huh."

I went to my cabin and looked at the map. Then I came back and challenged her.

"I suppose you know," I said, "it's only eight miles from Callao to Lima?"

"Sure I did."

✓   ✓   ✓

The captain used bucko-mate tactics, to which she reacted like a lamb. The night we lay over at Balboa she said she wanted to go ashore. She turned up in the captain's cabin in a cream white suit, scarlet hat, and black gauntlets.

"I wouldn't wear the gloves," I suggested. "Too hot."

"Oh, it wouldn't be genteel," she said, "to go in a restaurant without gloves and hat."

"No?"

"Course not," she said.

The latest racket in the Canal Zone is the huge open-air beer-gardens being built all over the outskirts of Balboa by the rival brewery companies. Poor Colon has nothing as classy as their cement dance-floors, on which the U. S. Army and Navy officers make the scene look like a White House ball every night. We took "Sweetie"—the name the captain and I had automatically agreed upon— to the Rancho. Sweetie and the captain ate T-bone steaks almost two inches thick—"I want mine rare!" said Sweetie —and then she ate several plates of preserved-strawberry ice-cream.

"Isn't there anything to see in this dump?" complained Sweetie, after a few ineffective dances with the captain and me.

"Plenty," said the captain. "But you're not going to see 'em."

"Oh, why?"

"Because you're not."

"Well, I am."

"You're not."

"I am."

"Oh, all right."

✓   ✓   ✓

From the sanitary interior of the motor-car we let
Sweetie take a look, as our open-air taxi drove through
the notorious Coco-nut Grove. About as innocent a name
for a red light district as the tropics could furnish. It was
a stifling night. Most of the houses in the Coco-nut Grove
had not only their windows but their doors open.

"Well . . . !" said Sweetie. "I never! Look at those
people *there!*"

The captain looked, then punched the driver.

"Make it snappy," he said. "Go on—I'm in a hurry."

"Now why . . . ?" began Sweetie.

"Now you be quiet," said the captain. "You've seen all
that's good for you."

I waited. Surely, I thought, this blonde is now going
to uncork some remark, suddenly disclose a worldly
knowledge that will take the poor old captain off his feet.
But not that girl.

"Mean old thing!"

She cuddled up to the captain, and put her arm through
his.

✓   ✓   ✓

When we got back on board the ship after midnight I
did not know what to think. Neither did the captain.
When Sweetie excused herself for a moment, after drinking whiskey and soda that was a good half whiskey, the
captain and I were left face to face.

"I . . . er . . . what do you think of that girl?"

"You mean—her air of sweet innocence in the Coco-nut Grove?"

"Sure! What did y'think I meant?"

"Just so."

"Well, what?"

"I don't know," I said. "She beats me."

" 'Keep an eye on her,' said her father. Huh!"

He bit the end off his cigar. "Look here, Sweetie," he said as she returned, "you're going to bed."

*   *   *

"No, I'm not," she said. "I'm going to Sloppy Joe's."

"Sloppy Joe's? Now how did you come to know of that place?"

"Saw it. Saw its sign right beside Kelly's Ritz—when you were trying to get a taxi."

Sweetie turned to an embarrassed figure that had been standing in the doorway. It was the youngest of the ship's line officers.

"Mr. Walker," said the captain, "what do you want?"

"I . . . er . . ."

"Mr. Walker's taking me to Sloppy Joe's, aren't you, Mr. Walker?"

"He's not."

Mr. Walker, that craven-hearted *caballero*, started to back off along the boat-deck. In another second he would have made a clean escape. But not with Sweetie. She shouted:

"Mr. Walker, you come back here. Don't you run off

and leave me like that. You tell him to let you take me to Sloppy Joe's. We'll just have one dance and then we'll come home.

"Honest," she said, turning to the captain. And then: "Look here, Captain Johnson, I'll have you know I'm twenty-one. I'm of age. I'm not going to be ordered around like that."

꜒   ꜒   ꜒

I have always marveled how these big-liner captains, men who began their careers as ordinary sailors before the mast, can make such perfect hosts.

"Come in, Mr. Walker," said the captain. "Have a drink. Let the young lady mix one for you. She's my bar-tender on this trip."

"Thank you, sir." Mr. Walker sat down relievedly and grinned at Sweetie.

"Just a weak one," he said.

The captain turned his swivel chair and pretended to be going through some cargo telegrams. He swung round.

"Did I ever tell you," he said, "about the time I put the camphor on top of the coffee? Now, camphor . . ."

"You look here," said Sweetie.

". . . course, coffee's queer, you know . . . just sucks up the odor of anything that's put next to it. Got to be very careful with coffee. Course when this stuff got to New York . . . and those people got the bags of coffee . . . full of camphor . . . and started to sell it . . ."

"Listen, Captain Johnson, I . . ."

". . . why, I was put in the dog-house for a month!"

"Yes, sir—I heard about that, sir. Well, sir, if you will excuse me, sir, I think I'll say good night."

"Good night, Mr. Walker."

✓   ✓   ✓

The captain snapped out the light over his desk.

"What's dog-house, captain?" asked Sweetie. "Why did they put you in that?"

"Oh, that's just an expression—means putting you on shore for a time. Punishment. We're getting off at six in the morning, so I guess I'll turn in."

"It's been a lovely night!" she said.

Chapter XVII

A SINGLE MAN'S POST

If South America begins at the waterfront, it gained a lot of ground this morning—and they can keep it. When the tide went out at Benaventura, it bared the most morbid miles of mud-flats I have been forced to look at. Squirming between them was a remnant of yellow river wriggling out to the distant Pacific. Framing the dismal picture was a miasmic black fringe of stinking mangrove swamp. The scape was blurred, God be praised, by a smear of slanting rain. It rains at Benaventura some time, sometimes all the time, every day in the year. Four hundred inches per year is that town's record. It also holds a world's record for the finest collection of rusted tin roofs.

The excuse for the town (and all Colombians will agree with me when I damn the place) is that it is the shipping port for gold, platinum, and the mild Medellin coffee, perhaps the finest in the world; and it is one end of the Pacific Railway that goes half-way up to Bogotá. Otherwise there is no excuse.

There are four Americans there; the Consul, his assistant, the Tropical Oil Tank Farm man, and the radio operator of the Pan American Grace Airways. When I asked one of them how they stuck it, he declared:

"Work. Our work is our pleasure. So much to do. If we didn't have that so much to do, we'd go nuts. Absolutely!"

Benaventura is the only place where I have had a man tell me that he remained at the office just as long as he could, even sometimes went back to work after dinner, just to see if he couldn't find something to do. Chief reason being that old Spanish custom, still rigidly adhered to in Colombia, which absolutely forbids the young girls going about with the young men, "Yanqui" or otherwise, after the sun goes down. A custom, incidentally, about which young and old Americans complained to me all the way up and down the west coast of South America, until Chile, where it eases off a bit.

I even had one U. S. Consul grouse about it. He said: "It just makes life hell. Damn it, all I want to do is talk to the girl."

Which brings up another point about Benaventura and South American life. Benaventura, awful as it is, is a marriage mart. If the young girls of the big cities, Cali, Medellin, and Bogotá, are not allowed to see anything of the young men after dark—and can't see much in the daytime, except sitting in the park—they could see a lot of them lolling on the beach at some bathing resort. Seabathing is doing a lot to emancipate the women of South America. But it is not so easy to reach the sea from the cities that lie in the valleys of the 12,000 foot Cordilleras of the Andes. You may fly from Bogotá to Colombia's Miami, Barranquilla on the Caribbean—if you have enough money. Or you may take ten days getting down there in a Magdalena paddle-wheel steamer—if you don't spend your vacation on a sandbank. Benaventura, with a bit of luck and a motor drive over a 10,000 foot pass in the Cordilleras, can be reached in two days from Bogotá.

Voilà! Horrible, muddy as it is, Benaventura, smeared with rain, is Colombia's Pacific sea resort.

Every year, for the short season of a few weeks, a few comparatively wealthy mothers take their daughters (or the daughters drag their mothers) to Benaventura to see if they can't marry a foreign Consul.

They aren't hunting for the poor American or English or German clerks who have to accept the Benaventura post to begin a career; they want someone with "position." And the Consuls of the various South American countries, with their equally poorly paid European *confrères* attached to Colombia, *faute de mieux* have hit upon Benaventura for their short vacations.

The result was that, while I sat in the bar talking with the port officials, and a couple of young Americans and Englishmen who were damning Benaventura as a girl-less post, I could look through the partitions to where a peacock parade was taking place in the lobby. With rain spattering the mud and bowing the scarlet poinsettias, I watched this promenade inside the hotel of well-dressed young girls and men in smart white—quite consciously stalking each other. It was like the beginning of a cock-fight.

One of these young Consuls, a South American, was notorious for philandering.

"Someone ought to tip that girl off," growled an American. "He kisses and runs away and tells and *lies!*"

Then, just as a string of flamingoes will alight at a water edge, rise, and fly over the mountains, the girls and the Consuls are gone.

The recent port captain of Benaventura fell in love with

the sister of the Peruvian Consul, married her—and now he is gone. He forgot that feeling still runs strong in Bogotá against the Peruvians for the "Leticia War," and a port captain of Colombia's only Pacific port cannot be married to the enemy.

"It's just us," grinned the American, laughing at himself and the *distrait* English clerks. "We will be the Foreign Colony!"

The port officials were not taking an active interest in this conversation. They were having a hard job to keep awake. There had been a fiesta the night before. All the drinks in the hotel had been drunk; the conservatory was full of empty bottles. This accounted for practically the entire port staff being down to meet our boat. It was my first experience of this charging mass of white-clad South American officialdom up the ship's ladder—and into the bar. It made the rest of us on board ship feel like the proprietors of a pub at opening time—a feeling which helped us to bear the delay in getting our landing cards.

It is said in Benaventura that the railway company owns the hotel, and when they see a boat coming the train pulls out. That means you have to spend the night at the hotel. But they need not have bothered to go to that extreme with this boatload. One of the new symptoms of the Republic of Colombia's self-consciousness is the law in the customs: COLOMBIANS FIRST. As one Colombian commercial traveler who had been away a year in Europe, had twenty-seven trunks of samples to be passed, valued, and have the intricate duty paid, the rest of our ship went over and engaged rooms for the night.

It was a dismal prospect, with that conservatory full of

empty bottles. In the drinkless bar the port officials tried to entertain each other; talking about anything except the weather. Doing his share, one official announced that he had not spent the night where he should have spent it. "And I did not want to be seen coming from that end of the town this morning when someone woke me up to tell me your boat was coming in. Why did you come so early? Six o'clock!" His only hope of reaching the ship in time had been to make a quick dash through the mangrove swamps—much to the bad luck of his theoretically white uniform.

An American electrical engineer went upstairs to his room and rejoined us in a pair of dirty khaki trousers and open-necked khaki shirt. "Got a job to do in Benaventura?" I asked quite naturally. "Hell, no! I'm just saving my States clothes."

Cartagena has some of the most pungent limes in South America to make a Tom Collins. Benaventura couldn't even produce a lemon to make lemonade. We drank lemon pop out of bottles. Finally a mule was paraded with two casks of beer slung on his flanks like panniers.

I hung on to a vision I had caught through the swamp mist that morning of the blue Andes rising into the clouds. Some day, somehow, I would get to them. Finally the stationmaster came into the hotel and announced that there were so many of us (he did not say how irritable we had been) that it had been decided to run a special train that would take us part of the way. It would take us the sixty-odd miles through the jungle. After that we could see if we could get private motor-cars to take us over the 10,000 foot Quindío Pass in the first wall of the Cordilleras to drop down into Cali—about half-way to Bogotá. Cali had plenty of hotels, he said, where we could spend the night.

I hope the railway company enjoyed our reaction. We all gave up our recently engaged rooms in a body—a very angry body which refused to listen to arguments about payment. A night in the jungle would be preferable to an evening in Benaventura with nothing but beer to kill it.

✦   ✦   ✦

When it wasn't raining in Benaventura there were two men who used to play tennis on the soggy red court of the hotel by the mud flats. One of these was the Ruritanian Consul. He was a good player—but haughty. One day when he took a terrific swipe at the ball and missed it, a spectator yelled: "Ho, Tilden!" The Consul tucked his racket under his arm and strode off the court.

Since then there has been no tennis at Benaventura. The other man can find no one to play with.

Chapter XVIII

LOST SOULS

"Yes, we're back all right!"

Among the many things left on the dock at Benaventura by the big Grace liner before she continued her long voyage down the west coast of South America was the pretty young Colombian girl and her Austrian husband.

They stood there, among a pile of bags and trunks that bore the labels of nearly every Ritz Hotel in Europe, facing a silent but very real revolution in South American life. Just as the slump emptied Paris of a large part of its colony of American ex-patriates, so it did with South Americans. But it is even worse down here, for the exchange restrictions that some of these countries, such as Colombia, Chile, and Ecuador have put on to protect their currency, mean that even people who have the means to live abroad can no longer do so. In Colombia, for instance, apart from strictly commercial purposes, a tax of 23 per cent must be paid to the Government on all funds transmitted abroad—and even then only a limited amount is granted under special permit. The result is that hundreds of fairly well-to-do Colombians—and how they do love Paris!—have been forced to return and settle down in their own country. If this process continues long enough, it will change the complexion of South American life. For the present, it appals Colombian women who have looked

143

forward to a comfortable, sophisticated life abroad, and the foreigners who married them.

✓ ✓ ✓

There was a story causing considerable laughter at Barranquilla of a French dandy who had just passed through there with his Colombian heiress. She had wooed and won him in Paris some years before there was any thought of such hideous thing as finance-control. She was hideous herself, fat, but unbelievably wealthy. In Paris or Nice that had not mattered so much to the philandering Frenchman. There are always ways of arranging things. And she had suffered patiently. But when the exchange-control cut off the flow of her money, just like turning off a tap, she recognized the opportunity that had presented itself.

Her vast income came from ranches and sugar plantations high up in Cauca valley, between the Cordilleras of the Andes. And she passed through Barranquilla bound for the valley—with the Frenchman in tow. The scenery is beautiful . . . but . . . well, the Frenchman might wheedle some money from her and go to Bogotá and play baccarat in the Jockey Club. He might go back to Barranquilla and take a swim in the Caribbean. Otherwise he is exactly like one of those animals in Whipsnade, the London country zoo; he can wander freely wherever he wants within the confines of Colombia—but he can't get out.

✓ ✓ ✓

This case was different, because the young girl and the Austrian were obviously very much in love with each other. They faced the problem of a return to Spanish life.

She knew what it meant. The handsome young Austrian aristocrat didn't know what was coming to him yet. He stood there in the customs shed waiting for their mountain of luggage to be passed—those many-colored bags and trunks with their Ritzy labels—and the best way I can describe his expression is to say that he looked like a man who had eaten some strange new dish and is not sure yet whether he is going to be sick.

The girl's mother, a distinguished old lady, had crossed a 10,000-foot pass in the Andes to be down there to welcome her—a welcome that savored of the relentless. The girl tried to escape it. She knew that with that fond embrace the shackles of the old Spanish family life, so rigidly adhered to in Colombia, were closing round her.

"I know exactly what it will be like," she told me, as our train squirmed up through the jungle toward the distant Andes. "Nothing! I shall do absolutely nothing! On the *hacienda* I shall sit around all day—after a short time in a dressing-gown. Kurt, who likes horses, will ride himself to death for a time. But he'll soon get over that. There'll be week-end parties, when we will ride over to other *haciendas;* but this is all we will have to say to each other: 'I wonder what it is like in Paris today? Don't you love London in May? Remember . . .' Things like that.

"Then we'll go up to Bogotá. In Bogotá I shall play bridge all day. What else? Kurt will go to the Jockey Club—he'll play baccarat. We won't entertain much in the evenings, because people don't do that in Bogotá. And all the nice frocks I've worn in Paris will be no good to me up there—it's too cold, 8,500 feet, you know—and there aren't sufficient fires in the houses. . . . They think they're unhealthy.

"We'll go to the movies, of course. Now that I've married I can do that at any time. If I were a young girl my young man could take me without escort to the six o'clock movie; for the nine o'clock performance he would have to take my father or brother along with us.

"And what will we talk about in Bogotá? We shall say: 'I wonder what it's like in Paris today? Don't you remember London in May?'

"You see," she said decisively, "we can't change the life here—it's too strong for us. Therefore, this system of sending us abroad to be educated, to Paris or London, is all wrong. When we are forced to come back we both talk and feel like expatriated Europeans!"

By this time Kurt looked as if he were sure he had eaten something that hadn't agreed with him.

Chapter XIX

CAPITAL IN THE CLOUDS

THE EARLY Spaniards, I believe, selected Bogotá for a capital because they wanted to place themselves beyond the reach of the English pirates. Those superhuman, illiterate men—the great Pizarro himself could neither read nor write—could fight battles at 14,000 feet in steel armor; march thirty-five miles in one day along the Andes; cross the burning, trackless deserts of Peru and Chile. For "gold and God" one of them crossed the Andes, hit on some headwaters of the Amazon, and went all the way down it to the Atlantic Ocean. Yet the mere mention of Drake or Morgan gave their immediate successors insomnia.

They selected, therefore, this high *sábana*, 8,500 feet up in the Andes, killed off a sufficient number of the Chibcha Indians to give themselves breathing-space, and in this rare altitude has blossomed an intellectual capital spoken of (by itself) as "The Athens of South America." Nearly every literate person in Bogotá writes poetry; they compose it under the cypress-trees of its salubrious plazas; modern bookshops display their collected efforts beside imported British and American best-sellers.

And Bogotá is still the most inaccessible capital in the world. Lhassa? Yes, Lhassa does rather explode my sweeping statement; but the capital of the Dalai Lama himself could not be more unreal in its atmosphere.

✦   ✦   ✦

The unreality of Bogotá really lies in suddenly finding yourself in a city of purring limousines, with shops not much inferior to Piccadilly or the Boulevard des Capucines, after the emotional and geographical gamut you have had to run to get there.

Immediately your train has pulled out from the rusted tin roofs of Benaventura beside its yellow river in the mangrove swamps of the Pacific, it begins a sixty-mile squirm through jungle so dense, dark, and sickening that human beings rot in it. The word rot is in no sense an exaggeration, for the Negroes living in their wretched huts of bamboo slats, among this stifling vegetation, are often covered with sores, distorted, with black feet swollen to clown-like dimensions, and ulcers that eat into their calf muscles and jerk their heels up permanently. It is such human catastrophes that assemble in the clearings where there is a railway station and try to sell you whole roasted chickens, extraordinarily good bread, and bunches of bananas: bread and chicken which you are fearful to eat because of contamination; bananas, therefore, which everybody buys, peels off their protective skins—and then finds himself going round with a bunch, trying to offer a banana to everyone else on the train—who has also bought a bunch of bananas.

No wonder they call the jungle "green hell." Every man, woman, and child walks about with the everlasting machete in hand—for without that there is no way of passing through this misanthropic undergrowth which shuts off for ever any possible glimpse of the hot, overhead sky. Steam. Vegetation that is obviously gasping and straining for air. Every tree with some creeper crawling around it and trying to choke it. Lianas stretching in loops from tree to tree, like nets, catching everything that falls from above, to form another life where parasites and purple orchids grow a hundred feet above the slash of palms. Cactus that occasionally has the effrontery to push out brilliant flowers of scarlet and yellow in this reek of rot and steaming shadows.

The conversation of Kurt, the aristocratic husband of the beautiful Colombian girl, had a brilliant, fragile quality during this part of our road to Bogotá that was too much like the forced gaiety a brave woman feels she must put on the night before a serious operation. A Dutchman in the train, who was being sent out to Colombia by an English Church organization to find a spot where he could settle a colony of fifty German Hitler-refugee families, looked at this jungle and remarked:

"I tink I better go back to Yava!"

◢ ◢ ◢

This egg-headed Dutchman was also unreality on the road to Bogotá. Together with our mass of baggage we shared a vast but asthmatic American motor-car to cross the Quindío Pass, a notch 10,000 feet high in the first Cordillera. This wall of the Andes was drenched in mist —a good thing, perhaps, as it prevented us from seeing how far we had to drop when our frolicsome Colombian driver missed a turn. And at 10,000 feet, where a high wind blew the mist away, showing us that even at that altitude we were in green forests, with purple flowers growing two hundred feet up in the trees, the Dutch-man informed me:

"I shoot a elephant in Yava. He was a mad elephant."

When, after another bus and train ride, we did totter into Cali, we found a *thé dansant* going on in our hotel. Said my Dutchman:

"But these girls are white! Dey vos niggers on the coast. What *is* a Colombian?"

His last remark before reaching Bogotá, after another day and night in the country town of Giradot, where the local orchestra (three pieces) played three tunes at the same time for the dance outside our bedroom door, was to say:

"I tell you what is the matter with the Colombians—the young men do not do enough at nights. Look at them in this train—the young girls are always hugging them and holding their heads in their arms! And yet the night is long—it begins at six o'clock!"

What his poor settlement of Hitler-refugees must think of life as they found it in the Republic of Colombia is a thought I leave alone. The last time I saw him was up in the Cauca valley, nearly a month later, at Popayan. He had not yet found land for his colony. He was leaving with two horses and an interpreter for a valley twenty miles up in the Andes. How the German settlers were going to make a living up there, with nothing but mute, unfriendly Indians about, I can't imagine. Perhaps the land was never found for them. The day the Dutch-man was to set out on horseback from Popayan, to found this Semitic Valhalla, his interpreter was arrested in the act of climbing aboard his horse.

"Orders from Bogotá," said the Dutchman. "They say he do something. He say he don't do anything."

✔   ✔   ✔

The three 14,000-foot walls of the Cordilleras divide the Republic of Colombia into practically four separate countries. Bogotá lies behind the second wall. These sky-scraping ranges are so high and precipitous that their western flanks are nearly always cloaked in blue shadow. From a distance they have a jagged silhouette of broken blue—scene that is almost a hallmark of Colombia. The sun itself takes almost till midday to climb over them. When it does, it shines down into valleys of strange, unreal beauty. Silver rivers curve through the feathery green of bamboo forests and red cachimba-trees. The cattle lie in white clumps on the green plains. Pink squares on velvet-green lesser mountain-tops are the faded roofs of old *haciendas* that have been perched up there since the Spaniards' day. Strange birds, found nowhere else in the world, hover over the fields of rice and sugar-cane. White ibis rise from the dead trees of stagnant marshes. Minute speck in the sky is a condor, taking in all of Colombia in his glance.

Then your train—for you do this last lap by rail—slides into a modern city; and a hotel concierge with brass buttons and the regulation cross-keys on the blue lapels of his uniform, obsequious, omniscient, condescending, makes you feel you have come back to Europe again.

As someone has said, the worst thing about travel is

to arrive. Not so with Kurt. No Mohammedan, waking
in Paradise to find the face of a houri on the pillow beside him, could have been more overjoyed than Kurt as
he booked room-with-bath from the Swiss clerk in morn-
ing-suit at the Hotel del Prado.

✦ ✦ ✦

Warp of the woof of Bogotá motor traffic was the spectacle of the wry Indians. They pattered along in bare
feet, past shops they never went into. They dodged extermination as they trotted with pack-loads, taking the
place of motor-lorries, in and out among the limousines.
They rested for a moment on the stone benches beside
the poets composing odes to the Golden Age under the
shade of cypress plazas. They clattered in with pack-mules
and milk-cans in the early morning, for the coffee they
could not afford to drink. Bandy dwarfs, with a resentful
look.

Those that still lived high up against the sun in their
Andean villages were a dark brown. But the waitresses
in the Hotel del Prado, in green uniforms to tone with
that alligator-pear-colored dining-room, were as pale as
better-bred Japanese women, and looked Japanese. Dis-
senting anthropologists may argue all they want about
South American Indians not being of Asiatic-Mongol
origin. I know it is so. The waitresses in the Hotel del
Prado are the evidence of my own eyes.

They, too, were unreal.

The food had the cardinal quality of all reality; it was
commonplace. The foreign colony of Bogotá prefers to
dine at a curious little restaurant run by an Austrian. Two

odd things about this little eating-place are that space is so much in demand that you cannot get a table unless you are with an old customer—it is as exclusive as a club in that respect—and the fish which is served three times a week has been flown up from the Caribbean in an aeroplane. In this, Bogotá joins with Buenos Aires, which has its lobsters sailed five hundred miles across the Pacific from the Chilean island of Juan Fernandez, and then flown at 14,000 feet over the snows of the Andes and across the Argentine—still alive.

"Which I call being taken for a ride!" as one Chicagoan put it.

✓ ✓ ✓

The foreign colonies in the South American capitals are always full of picturesque figures—but they are becoming fewer and less picturesque every day. Outstanding reason, of course, is the growing self-consciousness among South Americans that they can run their countries themselves. The grand old days of the Anglo-Saxon freebooter who used to exploit, practically make off with the natural resources of the country—with the acquiescence of local statesmen he had in his pocket—are just about over. The World War, the Geneva disarmament and Abyssinian fiasco, and the Wall Street slump, have freed South Americans from their previous willingness to accept dictation from Europe and the United States. They have, they think, seen through our bluff. It is true that the British and Americans still exploit the fabulously rich oil-fields of Venezuela, Colombia, and Peru; the gold of Colombia and Ecuador, together with practically all of the last country's public utilities, and that they mine all the copper coming out of Peru and Chile. In other words, the Americans and British have their hands on the national incomes of these countries. But it is no longer the rough fist of the financial freebooter which is holding on to these concessions—a more "diplomatic" hand is required to pull the strings with these uppish South American Republics.

I put that "diplomatic" in quotes because during the six months I was away from England I met several interesting English and American business men in South America, whom New York brokers would have described as the "cocktail partners" of their firms. They held official titles ranging from the innocuous vice-president to manager; but they seemed to have no connection with the work "in the field"; they lived in the capitals; they were seen most frequently at Government functions or shooting or fishing-parties of the Corps Diplomatique—of which one or two of them had once been members themselves. Libel prevents me from being more specific. But in its order of importance their work seems to be: (*a*) trying to prevent the concessions of their American and British principals from being further taxed or driven out of existence by the mass of new liberal and nationalistic legislation in these countries; (*b*) trying to secure new concessions in the face of such inauspicious conditions; (*c*)— quite hopeless in most cases—trying to collect sour loans from these Republics. From financial freebooting, Anglo-Saxon enterprise in South America has turned to flirtation.

How to Win Friends and Influence People is probably their bedside book.   ✓   ✓   ✓

The type of "men in the field" is less complex and more exhilarating. They usually have adventurous jobs and are picked men in their professions. In Bogotá, this colony (for the British and Americans form a unit) has some exciting individuals. Reason for this is that about half of Colombia, all that jungled part east of the Maracaibo-Bogotá line, is practically unknown, to say nothing of being undeveloped. On the Barco oil concession they have had several men shot by the arrows of the Motolone Indians within the last few years. I have photographs of two men shot in 1935, one still clutching the six-foot arrow sticking into his stomach. He died. The other lying on his back with the broken shaft of an arrow sticking out of his chest. He was dead. He was the night-watchman at the well, shot within a few feet of the protective wire screen (to keep off Indian arrows) erected round the well. All the boats going up to the Barco concession have wire screens round the decks to prevent the passengers from being shot by the Motolone Indians.

"And yet," an American told me in Bogotá, who was working on that concession, "I've been there years and never seen an Indian! Queer. They're all around us in the bush."

To be bow-and-arrowed in this year of our Lord 1937 did not seem at all bizarre to him. It was much too likely to happen.

Scenes like this occur. At Puerto Berrio, on the Magdalena River, a friend of mine saw two men taking turns walking round the hotel all day with a mechanical contrivance strapped on their backs. It was a German oil-divining machine. An amazing invention—but so delicate that the slightest jar might disarrange it and require it being sent back to Germany for adjustment. As it was going to be taken over mountain trails and through path-less jungle, the British oil prospectors were walking around with it on their backs in *order to acclimatize it*.

✓   ✓   ✓

The doyen of the Anglo-Saxon colony is an American "sewing-machine" man who has spent something like twenty-seven years in all parts of Colombia. He is as much at home in a peon's thatched hut as he is in his own comfortable flat in Bogotá. He prefers that "life in the field," in fact. That is why, even in the Negro hovels of the unhealthy Pacific jungle, you will see his sewing-machine. Not to be outdone by the two eighteen-foot ana-conda skins that form the murals for his exciting dining-room, his cocktail shaker is two feet high.

I would like to be more personal about these Bogotá Anglo-Saxons. But that is one of the troubles with travel in South America. You had better leave the friends you found down there strictly out of the account. Reason being, that if you happen later on to say something unflattering about the country they are living in, the politicians of that country blame them.

"You're a nice one!" they say to the local American or Britisher trying to conduct his business with the mini-mum of Government interference. "Why did you tell us that So-and-So was a nice fellow? It was on your recommendation that we talked so frankly with him—and now look at the things he has gone home and written about us!"

↗   ↗   ↗

That is why, when you arrive at a South American capital, the first censorship you have to pass is the silent appraisal of your own countrymen. It's not a bad test, either. They have already passed it.

Chapter XX

HOW THE STRINGS ARE PULLED

Dr. Alfonso Lopez, the President of Colombia, is a banker; the son of a banker; and when the Banco Lopez failed in 1923—a three-day national holiday was declared, so that the Banco Lopez might not go into bankruptcy.

The man who engineered this coup was the Minister of Public Works, Dr. Laureano Gomez—a boyhood friend of Alfonso Lopez. He saved his comrade. Given a few days' breathing-space, the Banco Lopez liquidated in a way that earned the eternal gratitude of all its creditors. Nothing but praise is heard in this Republic in the valleys of the Andes for the way the House of Lopez met its obligations.

Today Dr. Alfonso Lopez is head of the Liberal Government of Colombia. Dr. Laureano Gomez is head of the Conservative opposition. They are both bitter personal and political enemies.

✶ ✶ ✶

Behind the enmity of two old friends is a political drama that shows the way the strings are pulled below the Rio Grande. It is played on a large stage, with surprisingly few actors on it. Rome and Wall Street play leading parts, as they do in every South American tragedy.

The stage is large because the jungles and lofty valleys of Colombia between their 14,000-foot Cordilleras cover an area that is over twice the size of France. The characters are few, because, of the Indians, Negroes, Spaniards, and exciting blend of all three who live in this Andean world, not much over one-third can even sign their own names. Rome and Wall Street are formidable characters on such an empty stage. They have to deal only with a handful of people centered in Bogotá.

✓ ✓ ✓

The play opens with the thundering collapse of the Conservative Government, which had held an unbroken rule over Colombia for forty-four years. Conservatives, strong supporters of the rich landowners and Church of Rome. The unthinkable has happened; the Church, whose Archbishop at Bogotá and black-hatted priests in all the Andean villages had been electioneering for the Conservatives for all they were worth, sees another stronghold lost. A Liberal Government will rule Colombia. And the first thing a Liberal Government does in South America is to separate Church from State. The political power of the priest is broken; the education of the youth is taken out of his hands. Which was exactly what happened. Colombia, which, before the 1930 Liberal election, was more under the influence of the Church than any other country in South America, began making a new Concordat with the Vatican.

✓ ✓ ✓

And here enters the most spectacular figure in all this South American drama. A man who is loved by friend and foe alike. A man who dies on the stage while the play goes on. On the eve of the 1930 elections he is at Washington, where, for eight years, he has been known as "the popular Colombian Minister." Big, hearty, fair-haired man, perhaps few people indeed at the cocktail parties of the Diplomatic set knew that Dr. Olaya Herrera was a full-blooded Andean Indian—known in Colombia as the "White Indian from Guateque."

Colombians knew that the "White Indian" was the one man in all Colombian politics who could break the uninterrupted grip on office which the Conservatives had held for nearly half a century. So several of the leading Colombian Liberals (among whom was Dr. Alfonso Lopez) sent him a round robin telegram. Put briefly, the career of the "White Indian" was then this: he flew back to Colombia, and, after an all-night session with Dr. Alfonso Lopez, agreed to run as the Liberals' candidate for Presidency— and was elected.

This was immediately on the eve of the world slump. For four years the "White Indian" steered Colombia safely through the economic blizzard. Because of friendships made in his eight years at Washington, he was able —even under these panic conditions—to get another twenty-million-dollar loan from Wall Street: then he stopped payment altogether on all foreign loans. Following England, he took the peso off gold. Foreseeing Roosevelt, he re-financed Colombian farm debts and mortgages, slapped on a high agricultural tariff, thus saving the small Colombian farmer from losing his land. And he even fought a more or less successful "war" with Peru over the Leticia affair. During the perilous years of the

world slump, Dr. Olaya Herrera was the Horatio on the
Colombian bridge.

During this time he sent Dr. Alfonso Lopez as Minister to the Court of St. James's. To General Vasquez
Cobo, the Colombian hero defeated as the recent Conservative candidate for President, he awarded the Legation at Paris. The fiery, brilliant Conservative, Dr. Laureano Gomez, he removed from the Colombian political
stage by making him Minister in Berlin.

✦ ✦ ✦

The "White Indian" then had to resign the post of
President after his term of four years in office. There is
a law in Colombia, similar to that in several of the South
American countries, which stipulates that no President may
remain in office for more than one consecutive term. This
is meant to prevent Dictatorships—which it never does—
but, in Colombia, where political morals are probably the
highest in South America, this law is rigidly obeyed. In
1934, Dr. Alfonso Lopez was elected President. And,
soon after, Olaya Herrera went as Ambassador to the
Holy See.

Now, here is the real drama. The "White Indian,"
whose election had been opposed so bitterly by the Church
in 1930, was now sent to make the new Concordat with
the Vatican—to prise the Church loose from the strongest grip it had on any South American country. And in
Rome the "White Indian" died.

It was off the coast of Peru that I picked up my ship's
newspaper and read:

Rome: *Pope Pius the Eleventh prayed Thursday night for the repose of the soul of Enrique Olaya Herrera, former President of Colombia and friend of the Pontiff, who died suddenly in the day in a Rome clinic of a brain blood clot.*

ᛞ ᛞ ᛞ

Instantly I knew that the reams I had written about the "White Indian of Guateque" for the American newspapers would be worthless. He would not become, as was a dead certainty, the next President of Colombia. Instead of quiet Colombian elections in 1938, the fat was in the fire again. Dr. Alfonso Lopez could not run again for President—not before another four years; the Liberals must find a new man. Would he be Echandia, Minister of Education when I was in Bogotá; a pronounced, radical Leftist? If so, what was going to happen to Colombia? And Dr. Laureano Gomez, that fiery potential Fascist, he would have had no chance against the overwhelmingly popular "White Indian." But now—now I saw brigades of Blackshirts in Colombian politics.

Confirmation was a letter which followed me all the way down the west coast of South America, finally catching up with me at Buenos Aires. It was from a highly intelligent Colombian journalist; it said:

Olaya's death has upset everything. You should have been here. Fireworks! Speeches in Parliament. Political duels. . . . Dr. Eduardo Santos is certain to be elected; he controls 90 per cent of the Liberal vote. . . . You should write and congratulate him on his forthcoming presidency. . . . He always asks about you. . . .

With it was coupled the hope that I would be invited as "guest of honor" to the All-American Congress of Journalists to be held in Bogotá in 1938. And so I had passed; I had had my days in Bogotá and gone on. And the calm, dignified editor of *El Tiempo*, the *Manchester Guardian* of South America, with whose pretty, fair-haired wife I had lunched in their book-filled home outside Bogotá, would now occupy the palace where I had spent the best part of a Saturday afternoon with President Alfonso Lopez.

As my boat went out of the muddy River Plate I knew that I would never come to the shores of South America again. But I shall read every bit of news from Bogotá during the summer of 1938. I will hope for Dr. Eduardo Santos, for he is one of the most enlightened men I have ever met—it will be all for the good of South America if a genuine, sophisticated Liberal like Santos becomes next President of Colombia—but I will also watch for the name of Dr. Laureano Gomez, backed by (and strong backer of) the Church and the rich Colombian land-owners; the Leon Daudet of South America.

✓ ✓ ✓

You are probably wondering what is the part that Wall Street has played in this South American drama? It is this; and I will quote the wisdom of Sir Arthur Salter, in his book *Recovery*, as a partial explanation. He wrote:

When a large loan is dangled before a weak Government by the representative of a powerful financial institution, perhaps competitively by several of them, all sorts of political consequences, all unfortunate, are likely to result. . . .

The one thing that Sir Arthur omitted to say was the unfortunate consequences that are likely to result when the loans are dangled before a *strong* Government. Which is precisely what the Conservatives imagined themselves before their unthinkable fall from office in 1930. They were too confident—so sure of themselves that they split their ticket and ran two separate Conservative candidates against Olaya Herrera, chief reason why the "White Indian" got in. And this false confidence was engendered, it is claimed, by the easy, enormous loans they obtained from Wall Street. This, and the twenty-five-million-dollar "conscience money" paid Bogotá by Washington for the rape of the Panama strip, last payment being made in 1930. This overturned horn of plenty, if it didn't happen to corrupt Conservative statesmen's morals, at any rate destroyed their morale.

And these Wall Street loans were the very first thing about which Dr. Alfonso Lopez flamed into action when I saw him in the Presidential Palace.

✓   ✓   ✓

"There they are!" he said excitedly, slapping a long list of the loans New York bankers had made Colombia during the dizzy boom years. "Just look at them. Look here"—he put his finger on the years 1927 and 1928—"just look at them there, pouring in at the rate of ten millions a month. Absolutely unjustified! Absolutely criminal! All they were trying to do then was to get someone to 'accept' a loan—and then they would take it back and sell it in America."

Around eight months in the 1927-28 period something like eighty million dollars' worth of Colombian bonds were retailed by these bond-salesmen of the New York banks to private American investors. The loans were made at terrific rates of interest to the South Americans, and then retailed in the States at boom prices by the banks.

"Many of them," said Dr. Lopez, "were made to municipalities, with no form of investigation whatever as to the municipalities' capacity of repayment. It was a scandal!"

Lopez's anger against these loans can well be understood. Repayment in foreign currency has been stopped since Olaya Herrera got in. Exchange control has been put on to protect the level of the Colombian peso. If and when repayment on these loans is resumed, it will probably crash the Colombian currency. If repayment of the Wall Street loans made to Peru, for example, were today resumed at the rate of interest and capital repayment agreed upon, it would take just half the present Peruvian national budget.

"Whatever you say about this loan racket, you can't say enough," an American business man, who had spent over twenty years in the South American Republics, said to me. "The English *invested*; the Americans simply threw money at them. I've been on boats going down the west coast with American carpet-bagging loan-salesmen on board—simply racing to see which of them could be the first to reach the President and make him 'accept' a loan. These loans have brought down Governments. In

Cuba they took a perfectly good patriot, Machado, and made a crook out of him. It was the hundred million dollars that old Leguia of Peru got out of Wall Street that ended with his dying in jail. If the banks got it in the neck I wouldn't care. But they passed the buck. It's the poor private American citizen who's holding the bag in this case. The more you can give that loan swindle the air, the more all of us will bless you down here."

✔   ✔   ✔

It may seem a bit out of date, after the hammering that Roosevelt gave Wall Street and the New York banks—with their bond annexes—to keep on harping on the same old string. But these loans are a very live issue down here. At least, the numerous creditors' committees for South American loans all over the United States hope they are. Colombia and Chile are very jealous of their international financial integrity; Chile, for one, has never yet defaulted on a foreign debt. But in many quarters the psychology regarding these loans which were showered on South America is beginning to approximate the debonair attitude Europe now has toward the war debts.

It was rather startling to have the Presidents of two countries speak so frankly, and violently, about these Wall Street loans. You have seen what Lopez of Colombia has said. President Alessandri, of Chile, said to me:

"When I was in exile in Paris I wired Mr. X of the New York XYZ Bank and begged him not to make those loans to Ibañez. I told him then Chile would never be able to repay them. And yet they were made!"

I have not given the name of the famous bank he men-

tioned for the simple reason the bank would never have
made the loans if it had genuinely believed that they were
not repayable. What one exiled South American President
said about another President in office could not be taken
as conclusive financial authority. New York loaned plenty
of money to Europe that it will never see again—post-
war. It is just a case where everybody seems to have been
slightly mad.

✔   ✔   ✔

This madness—the realization of it—has had peculiar
repercussions throughout South America. It has discounted
the prestige of the New York bankers. It has discouraged
South American Governments from looking for more help
from Wall Street—except on the most hard-boiled business basis. It has, therefore, for the time being anyway,
broken the money-power of the United States and England in South American politics. An immediate result of
this new-found freedom that these Governments feel
obliged to enjoy is increased taxation of foreign concessionaires. This was the next explanation that President
Lopez was kind enough to make.

I say "explanation," because I had not come into the
Presidential Palace to ask about either of these questions.
I had hardly entered the Cabinet room before Lopez
literally threw the debt question in my lap. He had the
list of loans already lying on the table. And now, without
any question from me, he turned and picked up another
list.

"Here they are!" he said again. "You ask them. Ask
them if they think my new taxation is excessive. I'm only

asking for one-sixth of their year's profits. Is that out of line?"

The list was the year's balance-sheet of some twenty of the biggest foreign concessionaires in Colombia; British and American oil-wells, gold-mines, railways, banks, cable companies—with a couple of German commercial enterprises edging their way in. One of them, a big American oil concession, with its long pipe-line, was paying under the new taxes about one-quarter of the entire twenty million extra pesos that Dr. Lopez was raising to balance that year's budget (8.75 pesos equal £1). It was nearly a double jump in taxation.

"But is it as high as the United States?" asked Lopez. "Is it anywhere near as high as the British income-tax?"

✶ ✶ ✶

No European head of State, with the exception perhaps of Hitler in one of his rages, would have allowed himself to be so human as Dr. Lopez. He is an emotional man, and he kept me on the run, following his slim figure round the Cabinet room as he slapped balance-sheets, charts, and graphs showing his country's progress. There is no reason to disregard evidence of Anglo-Saxons in Bogotá, particularly the very concessionaires who are being hit by his increased taxation. They said:

"Oh, he will talk all right—you'll have a hard job to stop him! A bit too emotional and theoretical, perhaps. But he's honest. Lopez is straight. The hardest job he has at the moment is to keep the Left-Wingers of his own party in check. There's not a man in his Cabinet over thirty-eight."

✶ ✶ ✶

The extreme youth of his Cabinet is one of the stock charges the Colombian Conservatives always bring up against Lopez—similar to the one hurled against Franklin Roosevelt's brain trust. And, like President Roosevelt when I saw him in 1934 in the White House, Lopez seemed the man least concerned in the country about what he and his young aides were going to do—or what the others were going to do about it.

His Foreign Minister, just resigned when I talked with Lopez, was a journalist from *El Tiempo*—aged twenty-nine. And the day I did see the President, I was kept sitting one hour on a red plush Empire seat in the Presidential Palace while he accepted the official resignation of another Cabinet Minister, the Minister for Posts and Telegraphs, a thirty-five-year-old lawyer who felt that he had been officially snubbed at an air review. This didn't worry Lopez, as he is always changing them.

"There are nine chairs round that Cabinet table," an irate Conservative told me, "and they are never full. Those that are are occupied by young, inexperienced, theoretical men, with no previous experience whatever in government. How do you expect to run a country with men like that?"

How indeed! I told him that everything he said bore out my previous information that, in Dr. Alfonso Lopez, I would find a "Roosevelt of the Andes."

It is the Conservatives themselves who are to blame for the youth and inexperience of Lopez's Cabinet. First, as the Conservatives held a monopoly of government for forty-four years, the Liberal Party never had a chance to train its members in the arts of government. Finally, at the 1934 elections, the Conservatives did not have one candidate. On the advice of the fiery Laureano Gomez, a party which had held unbroken rule for nearly half a century did not even go to the polls. The result was that Lopez was elected with a 100 per cent Liberal Parliament —and nothing but Liberals, mostly of the Left-Wing variety, to select for Cabinet members. He rode the whirlwind into office—and if he cannot altogether hold it in check, the Conservatives have nothing but themselves to blame for at least not "weighting" the Parliament.

Youth is the keynote of Colombian politics today. Colombia has always been an oasis of Liberalism in the South American desert of military dictatorships and their thinly disguised counterparts. But the youth of the Lopez Cabinet has a freshness of idealism that frightens many Colombians.

The Archbishop of Bogotá, after a visit to Rome, is alleged to have stated: "There are only two Communist countries in America today—Mexico and Colombia."

✦ ✦ ✦

The day previous to my interview I had walked along with my Dutch friend (the man who was trying to plant fifty German Hitler-refugee families somewhere in Colombia) to see the changing of the Palace guard. The Palace was less imposing than its name. Quite a let-down, in fact, after the grandiose things its statuary had led me to expect of South America. It was just a plain, three-storied building, with lace curtains behind its French windows, whose orange wall formed only part of the continuous wall in a block of one of Bogotá's main business streets.

A sentry-box stood by an archway through the orange wall. In it stood a mestizo guard in a dark-blue uniform with red facings, wearing a black leather *Pickelhaube*, obviously made in Germany. Trams waited for a moment or so to let the new guard, headed by a band, march up the street. The band halted, played a few national airs while the soldiers were changed. Then the army marched away, unobtrusively, as was befitting its meek social, numerical, and political position in Colombian life. And the trams clanged past again.

While we were standing there, a slender man in a brown business suit, with grayish hair sleeked back, and a pair of Harold Lloyd spectacles, came out of the archway and hopped into a waiting limousine. Almost before the guard had time to salute. That was Lopez.

"Why," exclaimed my Dutch friend, "he looks yust like a college professor!"

What we had expected him to look like I cannot say. As it was, for both of us, our first sight of a South American President, I suppose we expected to see a heroic figure with twirling mustache and gold epaulettes, clutching a sword. He was as much a disillusion as the Palace.

↗ ↗ ↗

The walls of the empty Cabinet chamber, hung with maps, did look like a schoolroom that Saturday afternoon. And Lopez, at close range, was the earnest professor of geography as he played with them.

"See that?" he said, tracing with a long finger a ring around half Colombia. "All that is uninhabited. Only Indians."

I had a hard job not to cheer. I have few convictions that I would care to be dogmatic about, but one of them certainly is the right of the Indian or colored man to live untroubled on his own land. I was delighted to see Lopez trace out an area bigger than all France that was still "only Indians."

It was on the tip of my tongue to say: "And I hope it stays that way." I might have if I had had the time. But President Lopez was already off on another excited explanation, this time about how he was going to develop that half of his country.

"All that vast area east of a line drawn from Lake Maracaibo through Bogotá," he said, "all the way down to the headwaters of the Amazon—there's nothing in it. It was the Peruvian war that brought that home to us—the almost impossibility of getting our troops down to the Putumayo River. Now we know that we haven't even the vestige of a political organization in there, and only the flimsiest of police control along the very edges."

A large part of the territory he was describing lies across the hazy Colombian-Venezuelan border-line. The Motolone Indians in there have a habit, as I have described, of shooting the workers on the Barco oil concession with bows and arrows. The Indians are doing their best to prevent the white man from penetrating their country. A Swedish explorer now in the employ of a big American oil combine is going in, as I write, from the Venezuelan side to try to make friends with the Indians. He has been successful with hostile Indians in other parts of the South American jungle. I don't wish him any personal harm; but I hope he will fail in this case.

However, such hopes are useless. There is oil there. That means the Indians are sure to lose their land—probably by means of their extermination. And as there is oil there is also every possibility of another South American boundary war—between Colombia and Venezuela this time. Somewhat like the fight between Bolivia and Paraguay over the Gran Chaco. Oil was at the base of all that. So, say people down here, was the hand of British and American oil interests.

That part of President Lopez's earnest outline of his country's future did not enthuse me. His next subject was agreeable to me but not to quite a number of wealthy Colombians.

✶ ✶ ✶

"One of our worst jobs," said Lopez—he was educated at Brighton in England—"is to make our landlords develop the land they already own."

He sketched a brief picture of the absentee South American landowner, living in Paris on the proceeds of thousands of acres in his own country, which in many cases he has not even seen. The new Colombian exchange control, making it almost impossible to transmit large sums of money outside the country, has brought many back. But, even so, they are lethargic about working their *haciendas*.

"So we have a new law. Let's suppose that a man has nine thousand acres. Very well, we say to him: 'For every acre that you put to work, you may keep one additional acre of your own land. If you cultivate three thousand acres, then at the end of the ten-year period you will have six thousand acres, all told. The other three thousand you will forfeit to the State—without recompense.' That ought to put the acres to work," said Lopez, with a meaning smile.

So it should. And if other South American countries adopt similar land-laws, the colorful South American colony in Paris looks as if it will pass out of the European picture. This is already a topic of conversation which it is just as well to avoid at the Jockey Club in Bogotá.

✁ ✁ ✁

One of the results of sending South American youth to Europe to be "finished" is that the young men return with suits from Savile Row, an Oxford accent, and a disinclination to become farmers. This much one can easily pick up round the long green billiard-table of the Jockey Club, or in the adjacent room, where, at the high altitude of 8,500 feet, the rich young Colombians are playing an all day and night game of baccarat for stakes that take away what is left of your breath. This coming generation of South Americans has learned several things in Europe—some of which can be put to use in South America. Fascism is one of them.

"These new land-laws of Lopez and the Liberals," said one wealthy young landowner whose estates are on the *sábana* of Bogotá, "have just cost me six hundred of my best hectares. I mean that damn'-fool law legalizing Indian squatter sovereignty."

It is the custom in most countries in South America to allow the Indian farm laborers and their families to have a small piece of land, possibly an acre or so, to till for themselves—this in return for so many days a week on which the peon will work on the land of his master. The condition of servitude varies from the new freedom of the squatter-sovereign in Colombia to countries like Ecuador, Peru, and Bolivia, where the Indians are very often nothing less than slaves, and are sold like cattle with the land when a farm changes hands.

"I've always had the idea I could shift those Indians if I wanted to," said the young landowner. "But now I find that I can't. They tell me that they own the land. That's the new rule, they say. Some of them won't even let me go near it. What can I do? Call in the troops to dispossess them? Not likely. This present Lopez Government wouldn't back me up. They don't want to lose votes.

"Well," he said philosophically, "there's lot of land in Colombia. When I ride over my land now, I give those Indians a wide berth. But one day, perhaps, things will be different."

This man was a "Derechista"—a young Colombian Fascist.

✶ ✶ ✶

President Lopez himself is fond of a good game of cards. He likes the good things of life: congenial companionship and the company of pretty women. He is rather off-hand about food. When I was in Bogotá a new Ambassador was about to be given his official lunch with the President. Said another Ambassador: "You will probably get an egg sandwich." But Lopez is not a teetotaler.

He is fanatic in his desire to travel. On one of his famous trips through trackless Colombia, a supporter, intrigued by his schedule, asked:

"I wonder what the President will use—motor-car or aeroplane?"

"No," said a critic. "President Lopez will take another White Horse."

Chapter XXI

ENOUGH OF POLITICS!

THE COLOMBIANS have just held a national holiday to celebrate Twenty-five Years without a revolution. The last one they had, "The War of a Thousand Days," cost them a hundred thousand dead—and the loss of Panama. They don't want any more revolutions.

Communism? Fascism? What of these two movements —those European tabs which our political intellectuals insist on pinning on the South American political parties?

Communism isn't even incipient in the Republic of Colombia. At the last two elections, in 1930 and 1934, the alleged Communists did run a candidate. He was an Indian who could not even speak Spanish. He got three thousand votes out of a total of over a million.

This million vote is interesting, because the entire electoral poll of Colombia is only four hundred thousand. This double quantity comes from the emotional way the peasants and small villages take elections. As a consequence, President Lopez had to invalidate about half his own votes. The village of Corinto, at the 1934 election, turned in a vote of six thousand for Lopez for President. It was a hard job to persuade the Mayor of Corinto that he had overdone his fealty. The entire population of Corinto is only two thousand.

About two-thirds of the population of Colombia can neither read nor write. And Colombia is one of the most literate countries in South America. It is hard for propagandists, Communist or Fascist, to spread the gospel among an unleavened mass like that. It has to be done by word of mouth. Even so, it is practically impossible to enthuse the peasantry over foreign ideals. Just plain revolt they understand. But just plain revolt requires a good reason—a sufficient grievance.

In several countries in South America this grievance is so appalling that it makes the passer-by want to lead a revolt himself. But it is lacking—that is, a lower-class revolt—in the Republic of Colombia.

Because of the high agricultural protective tariffs put on by the "White Indian," Colombia is one of the few countries in the world today where mere farming, as such, pays its way without subsidies. The farm workers see a new freedom and land of their own under the new Liberal laws.

The squatter-sovereignty law of the Liberals brings up an interesting point. Title to almost any land in Colombia is somewhat vague. Any landlord will become nervous if you question the deeds to his land. One slick lawyer in Cali waited until two fellow business men developed a sugar estate of some 5,000 acres and then produced a deed showing he was the legal owner of 2,000 acres right in the middle of it. The deed was quite valid—but it was signed by Carlos V of Spain.

In labor, the factories are running full shifts to meet a prosperity boom such as Colombia did not know even before the world slump. Local expansion, the sharp rise of

the coffee export in value, more money being left in Colombia from foreign concessions, are the basis of this.
There is no proletarian unemployment.

Labor has its eight-hour day; the beginnings of accident
and unemployment insurance. A new law obliges an em-
ployer to pay a workman, if discharged without sufficient
reason, a month's pay at the last rate of wage for every
year he was in his employ. And it is a Government official,
sensitive to its vote-effect, who decides whether the worker
was unjustly discharged or not.

Colombia's growing self-consciousness, the new feeling
in many of these countries that the time has arrived when
they should run their own countries for themselves, has
resulted in a new and very nationalistic law. That is the
Lopez law that 80 per cent of the "white collar" workers
in any foreign concession, and 90 per cent of all the rough
laborers, must be Colombians.

This does not mean that Colombia is a workers' paradise, nor that these laws are always obeyed. It does mean
that the workers are living under conditions not sufficiently
bad to provide good ground for Communistic propaganda.

✼ ✼ ✼

A revolt of the upper and middle class, the wealthy
landowners, is much more on the cards.

As the army plays no part whatever in Colombian politics—and is much too small to be able to take a part if it
wanted to—this revolt must come from another direction.
If it can't be done by straight voting at the polls, then
Fascism seems the only alternative.

Here is where the Derechistas come in. The Derechistas

are the extreme Right Wing of the Conservative Party. They call themselves Fascists. Up to the present they have been just about as effective as Oswald Mosley's British Blackshirts. And just as comic.

Recently the Derechistas of Bogotá gave themselves a dinner to celebrate the first anniversary of the *Derechas*, their newspaper. About sixty-nine were present. The dinner ended in a riot because three of the more militant of the Derechistas took the floor and wouldn't allow anyone else to speak. Present at the dinner was Julio Zulaoga Arango, wealthy young Colombian blood (such as you will mistake for a well-dressed Englishman any day in the Jockey Club), who was the chief financial supporter of the *Derechas*. As he was one of the men who were not allowed to speak, he withdrew his financial support from the paper, which thereupon died.

"*Fan-tas-tique!*" was the way he described that evening to me.

This was over a few whiskey-and-sodas in the American Bar of the Hotel del Prado. With us were two of the militant Derechistas from that dinner. They were now all boys together again. The two militants told me that the Derechistas numbered thirty thousand members in Colombia. They wrote out for me a list of *Derechas* papers and the names of some of the most prominent Derechistas.

I went to see one, in Cali. His name was Don Jorge Garces B. He is reputedly one of the most able and wealthy men in all Colombia. He owns a vast chain of drug-stores, chemical laboratories, and in addition he has factories, farms, and large real-estate holdings. A charming but nevertheless solid man, who has a reason to be interested in Colombian politics.

"Yes," he told me, "I am a Derechista. What? I should say not! If the Derechistas ever adopt the unconstitutional tactics of Mussolini or Hitler I would leave the party at once. Colombia must be kept a constitutional country."

Whether Fascism can function in a constitutional country is a point for argument. Don Jorge Garces B., however, was not inspiring as a Derechista. Neither was another dinner which the Derechistas of Cali recently gave themselves.

There were thirty-eight present at this dinner, shown, by a photograph, to be mostly in black shirts. Also shown was a huge picture of Mussolini over the table. The crowd in the street outside the hotel where it was held jeered at first. Then they threw iodine over the Derechistas.

Iodine which had probably been bought at the drugstore of Don Jorge Garces B.

✓   ✓   ✓

Just one thing remains that might make the Derechistas a force in Colombia—the figure of Dr. Laureano Gomez—the man, you will remember, who, as Minister of Public Works, way back in 1923, engineered the three-day national holiday which saved the Banco Lopez from going into bankruptcy. Unlike the Republicans in the United States at the last elections, who could find neither a man nor a program capable of answering Roosevelt's moral challenge, the Colombian Conservatives have at least a man.

Backed by the Church and the wealthy landowners, there is no telling what this fiery part-Indian can do. Apart from heading the Conservative Party, he is also editor of *El Siglio*, Opposition paper, to whose political polemics he gives the sting of a very intelligent rattlesnake. When I saw him in his dark office he was so voluble in his attack on Lopez, his old boyhood friend, and the Liberal Government (all in hasty French that mine could not follow), that I asked him to put it in writing in a letter from which I was at liberty to quote. The reply is quite South American. It begins with why Dr. Laureano Gomez persuaded the Conservative Party to boycott the last presidential election—proof in itself of his power in politics. Here is the gist of his letter:

The Conservative Party, which unquestionably is a majority in the nation, could not accept to concur at elections that were neither free nor genuine, but only a simple farce in which the results had been pre-established, and where the bullets from the rifles of the official gendarmerie *had more influence than the votes of the citizens. . . . At present there is no policy in operation because there is no policy whatever. . . . The renowned inefficiency of the public officials is audaciously disguised, and the visible and growing unpopularity of the Head of the Government is hidden by the noise of rudimentary demagogy. . . . Communism has no real force in this country and its activities would have no echoes, but from the backing which it receives from the demagogy to which the Head of the Government resorts to cover his lack of authentic popularity. . . .*

This from the old boyhood friend of President Alfonso Lopez! Gomez then goes on to charge:

The methods of bloody violence, the reward and impunity of known assassins employed to frustrate the rights of the Conservatives, are what have originated—as a reaction—the Derechista movement. . . .

✓   ✓   ✓

Laureano Gomez has been holding the Derechistas back up to date. If he decides to turn Derechista himself to try to put the Conservatives back into power you will see fireworks during the summer of 1938 from that part of South America known as the Republic of Colombia.

I was glad when I took an aeroplane up to 14,000 feet over the Andes, to get away from the politics of Bogotá.

Chapter XXII

TWO HACIENDAS

My friend's *hacienda* lay up in the valley of the Cauca, between two blue walls of the Andes. Driving out to it across the green *sábana*, we crossed streams in the upper Cauca that were as swift and clear as some of those that sluice down from the mountains of Austria. But they ran through plumed forests of bamboo, through the darkness of green trunks, matted jungle, scarlet and yellow flowers, and the green splashes of banana leaves. Cattle grazed on the broad plain, but for shade they lay under crimson cachimba-trees—trees larger than giant oaks with the tips of every branch glowing with fiery candelabra. Birds that should have been sparrows had ribbons for tails about a foot long. Colombia has some of the rarest and most beautiful birds in the world. Only the iridescent doves on the red road struck a familiar note.

The barefoot men we passed, mostly Negroes or Indians, carried the inevitable machete in their hands—they would have looked undressed without these long knives—and the cowboys rode barefoot in brass stirrups that were as cumbersome as the toes of diving-boots. Silver spurs with rowels as big as saucers were strapped on to their naked heels.

In a field of sugar-cane we came on my friend's son. He sat like part of his horse. It was strange to hear this young American, graduate of a very select American school and university, talk English with his Spanish accent. But his mother was a Colombian; so had been his grandmother —his American grandfather came there from the United States in 1850—and he himself had married a beautiful Colombian girl, his cousin. His wife's people were jealous of their blood. The women of this family were straight Spanish stock, lineal descendants of the Spanish Conquistadores, who had passed over these same *hacienda* grounds on their road to Ecuador, and of the Spanish families that came in their wake. The low buff ranch-house of my friend has oil-paintings in its long dining-room of the Archbishop of Quito in 1726, and of other stern-faced prelates. There was the painting of the young Colombian patriot whose statue now stands in the main square of Cali, shot by the Spaniards in 1810 when he tried to lead the revolution against them. There was a map on the drawing-room wall that this hero of revolution had drawn as a boy of the *hacienda*. Some of the documents my friend's wife was packing up (before a trip to Paris) were records of the plantation in the 1600's—accounts of crops and slaves.

My friend, sixty-three, had a flat in Paris, to which he thought he had retired before the world slump. Unexpectedly finding himself almost ruined, he had returned to Colombia to try and recoup his resources. Thousands of his spotted cattle now grazed in the fields around us at the foot of the blue Andes; the valley was full of his rice and sugar-cane. His wife had made a paradise of their garden. With a prodigal grandeur its hedges were magnolia-bushes—in full blossom. Billows of mauve bougainvillaea rolled up against the adobe ranch-house walls. A mountain stream had been trained to run like a footpath through the rose-bushes under the shade of the mango-trees on the lawn. You could hear it running everywhere. A patch of strawberries and pineapple lay at the foot of the lawn. The stream ended with a grand whoosh into a deep cement bathing-pool under an arbored vine. When we sat out on the tiled veranda for our tea, time just stopped.

My friend's wife was plagued with domestic troubles. Unless you sat there and watched them, the gardeners did not work. They sat and smoked under the trees. The Indians—you could not trust them any more. When she had first married, her maids had been slaves; anyway, they knew how to behave. Now the cook—the cook had just left without notice. Communism was ruining Colombia.

A *hacendado* who had ridden over for tea pointed to where the blue peaks of the Andes reared above their thunder of clouds. "They live up there," he said, "the Indians. But they are in another world—mentally. We just have no contact with them. When I was young I tried to get an old chief to teach me their language. 'Why should I?' he asked. 'Then you will know our secrets.' What are they?"

✓ ✓ ✓

We drove to the estate of General Alfredo Vasquez Cobo. General Cobo was the Colombian hero who ran unsuccessfully as Conservative candidate for President against the "White Indian" in 1930. "Hello! Hello!" he waved, in his cosmopolitan manner, from his little white ranch-house. He was a large man—very large—with an air of ease, foreign travel, and good cigars. Sitting beside him were two direct descendants of Louis XIV of France; the two nephews of Don Carlos, the Spanish Pretender. They all had that simplicity, that instinctive friendliness, which is only to be found in peasants or the best pedigree stock. The two young Spaniards were fatigued—they had been riding across the *hacienda;* but they jumped to obey the faintest flutter of General Vasquez Cobo's humorous, somewhat bulbous eyes—eyes that closed completely into his face when he described how he fought the Peruvians.

This was when he was Minister in Paris, 1932. When the General heard how that Peruvian fellow, Señor Vigil, failing to force the Colombians into buying his ranch, had ridden into the town of Leticia, down in the jungled rubber country, with his cowboys, and imprisoned the Governor and all the town officials, General Alfredo Vasquez Cobo returned his portfolio to the Quai d'Orsay and donned the sword. All Colombian generals are survivors of the Revolution of 1903. The General bought two steamships—one Scotch, the *Highland King,* which he took over at Glasgow; the other a German boat. The French Government allowed him to purchase a battery of its pet 75's. With these on the decks the General sailed his Armada—manned by whatever Colombians he could pick up in Paris, London, or wherever he could find Colombians—across the Atlantic to Para, up the Amazon, up the Putumayo River, and let drive with the 75's.

His French 75's outranged the Peruvian artillery. But the Peruvians produced an aeroplane. It must have been an excruciating affair. The General described how the Peruvian 'plane flew low over his ship—placing his hand about a foot above the ranch-house floor. The General closed his eyes. At that moment, he confessed, he prayed to heaven.

"*Et voilà!*" The General popped open his eyes. "Boom-boom-boom!" The three Peruvian bombs fell harmlessly in the river.

Some people say that the Peruvians were outranged because they had left that particular part of the country the day before. Nevertheless, the General did buy the two steamships; he did sail them eighteen days across the Atlantic and up the Amazon; he did fire off the 75's— and he does like to tell this tale. So does everybody who hears him.

After telling it, he put on his flapping straw hat and led us into his sugar plantation. There, in a thatched shed among the shooting stalks, was a furnace with about twenty Indians and Negroes at work around it. They were grinding the cane with a water-wheel, and boiling it to make a sweet called *penula*, special delight of the Colombian peon and aristocracy. It looks like a cake of maple sugar, and tastes like toffee. The General called an Indian to give us a cake. We should, he said, acquire the habit. It would increase his profits.

The two young Bourbons opened the bamboo gates of the *hacienda* to let our limousine take the dusty road. The trio waved good-by; two descendants of Le Roi Soleil and the General, who began his astonishing career as attaché at the Court of St. James's, when Queen Victoria was on the throne.

Chapter XXIII

MAN OF LETTERS

WITH two yawning German dachshunds and a fellow countryman of theirs smoking a long cigar directly under the NO SMOKING notice, our 'plane bucked about for two hours at 14,000 feet over the Andes. Most air travel is the height of monotony. But it can be instructive.

Over England, you are continually rewarded by the sight of palatial country homes and their parks. England, still the country of great landlords, in spite of the taxation which that mad young Lloyd George started in 1912. In France the earth's carpet is cut up into small parallel strips. France, essentially the country of small peasant owners. In England the roads run obligingly round the big estates, not interfering with their privileged privacy— roads which themselves show the British genius for compromise. In France, a logical country, the poplar-lined roads run in a straight line between towns, that being the shortest distance between two points.

Over the Andes the scene is different. On the slopes where the coffee is grown you see hundreds of small farms, marked by their houses. But, once you start to skim over the high valleys, it is hours, it seems, before you come on one of those pink rectangles which mark the faded tiles around the patio of a great *hacienda*. Roads are mere trails between them. And you realize that these landlords are almost small kings in this part of the world.

Also, you begin to notice that the presence of any Andean village is always signaled by the sight of the great
bulk of its churches. Grandiose structures, lording it over
the hovels around. And the powerful part that this his-
toric pair of partners—Church and big landowner—plays
in South America impresses you, even from 14,000 feet.

Otherwise (had I not wanted to do in a couple of hours
what would have taken me two days by rail and motor-
car) I could have learned a great deal more about life
between Bogotá and Cali if I had traveled on land.

But I was to learn a lot of things, poignantly, about
South American life in the next days, because I was going
to get off at Cali and try to cross five hundred miles of
the Andes over into Ecuador—during the rainy season—
by road.

✓ ✓ ✓

The Anglo-Saxon colony told me at Cali that I need
not say good-by—I would soon be coming back. There
were landslides in the Andes. A man coming down from
Popayan had just said so. Quite impossible, he said, to
cross the Andes; two bridges had been washed away; it
was quite out of the question to get beyond Pasto. I hunted
him up.

"I wouldn't try it, old chap," he said. "You know what
these landslides are."

"No, I don't."

"Oh, never been in the Andes before? Well, they're
made of clay, y'know. Soft. When it rains—and it can rain
like hell up here—the Andes slip. Slide all over the place.
Last year . . . side of the Andes simply folded over—
buried a whole village of three hundred people. They're

still there—nobody's taken the trouble to dig down to them."

"My God! What were the Andes like to begin with?" I asked. "They must have been ten miles high."

This prophet was not amused. "It's all very well," he said, "to be funny about it. But you wait till you get a landslide. Shoulder your baggage and slide down the mountain to try and get round it. You won't find Indians everywhere, you know, to carry your stuff for you."

Then he added: "Sometimes you can't get round. And if you have two landslides—one in front and one behind—why, you just stay where you are."

"Until hell freezes, I suppose?"

He did put the wind up me, and I waited over several days in Cali to get up my nerve. Then, on the day that I had decided to go, I found I couldn't. The train for Popayan had already left that morning at 6 A.M. One day it leaves at 6 A.M., the other at 1 P.M. So I had another day to listen to travelers' tales, but I did not take this man's forebodings too seriously, as he was the type of Englishman whose conversation is of the type: "The British yokel always knows a gentleman when he sees one."

✶   ✶   ✶

During these days I drew nearer to the Colombians. There is a grand composure about the Colombian that is entirely unexpected from the Latin temperament. How it comes to be there I don't know; it just is. Take the case of a newspaper editor in one small provincial town who was kind enough to call upon me. We spent about an hour chatting in the hotel bar, during which time his mind seemed strangely preoccupied. He kept looking, all the time, out of the door. I mentioned this to another Colombian.

"Oh, he just shot a man," he said.

It was a young doctor who had recently come to town. He at once began an affair with the editor's wife. The editor, as is usually the case, was the last person in town to find that out. When he did, he went to the doctor and suggested that the affair should stop. The young doctor, entirely misinterpreting the editor's quiet manner, didn't stop. In fact he became quite open about it all. Then one day—

"He was sitting just about where you are now," said the Colombian, speaking of the editor. "Looking out of that door. The doctor's office was right across the street. Then one day when the doctor came out of his office the editor pulled a revolver out of his pocket and shot him.

"People who were with the editor said they didn't believe he had come there with the slightest intention of doing it. Nearly everyone in Colombia carries a revolver, you know—especially editors. Just acted on the spur of the moment. His friends testified to that in court and the editor was acquitted."

"I suppose he was thinking about that this morning?"

"Quite possible. His wife's still alive, you know."

*   *   *

The mere fact that the Colombians had dared to build this five hundred miles of flaunting road over the Andes into Ecuador was taunt enough to make me want to travel

it. And when I talked with the Colombians themselves
they laughed at landslides.

"What of it?" they said. "We always shovel them
away. What if you are hung up a couple of days?"

So I went up to Popayan.

✓ ✓ ✓

Popayan is an ancient town, and I had something I
very much wanted to do there. I wanted to see William
Valencia, the great Colombian poet. The Colombians are
very proud of literary figures, and in the Andes they will
direct you to one with all the anxiety of a botanist leading
you direct to some rare plant in his garden, for fear you
might miss it. It was the night clerk of the Cali hotel who
directed me to Valencia. "He is still alive, señor!"

Valencia, apart from being the great South American
poet and one of the two defeated candidates the Conservatives ran for President in 1930, is a vanishing type of
South American—much to my regret.

He looked enough like Shakespeare to make no difference. The Colombians talk as if there were no difference. The poet was ill when he sent word in to Popayan
that I might drive out to his *hacienda* to see him. There
was a young engineer at Popayan, son of a general, who
had been educated at an obscure American university, who
was trying to pay attention to one of Valencia's pretty
daughters; and he took this opportunity to go out with
me. I did not know until we returned to Popayan that
this was the first time he had been allowed to set foot on
the great Valencia *hacienda*.

That might have accounted for the poet's air of almost

painful dignity as he came out on the veranda of his ranch-house to greet us. He was wrapped in a camel's-hair bath-robe. Before discussing anything at all poetic or political, he purposely conducted me into his study, where I noted in succession a signed photograph of d'Annunzio, a letter from Hindenburg, framed with a silver medal he had given Valencia, and the last letter of Simon Bolivar, writ-ten from his death-bed—this was under its own private light, like a painting in an art gallery—a case full of the glittering decorations and ribbons conferred on Valencia by foreign Governments; and a glass statuette of Gandhi, sitting impishly on his ink-well.

He then led me through a darkened long hall, whose floor was old polished parquet, and whose chairs round the wall were of ancient tooled leather bearing the Valen-cia coat of arms, brought over from Cordova by the Counts of Valencia to this same *hacienda*. The muffled grandeur of this room was unexpected from the rambling old ranch-house in its grove of eucalyptus-trees. Valencia then took me to the veranda, where we sat on a couch covered with black panther skins, and he proceeded to bastinado the Lopez Liberal Government. He had a rod in pickle.

"They have let the tiger loose," he said weakly, pluck-ing petulantly at his little gray goatee. "And they have put it into the hands of children."

I had a dim idea that his vast estates stretched away from us to where a jagged blue silhouette of the Andes lay far down on the horizon. In fact I had been watching some horsemen, his cowboys, coming into view across them. I could see them from far off across that green *sábana*. And it was only towards the end of my talk with Valencia that they finally rode into the courtyard and dropped from their horses, which they tied to the long row of other horses along the rail before the kitchen quarters. Then they went in to eat.

I did not realize until after he had been complaining for some time how deeply personal was Valencia's bitterness against changing conditions in Colombia; his feeling of impotence against the new Lopez land-laws, squatter sovereignty for Indian peons, the obligation that he must cultivate his great estates or lose them. The figure of Gandhi did not belong on his ink-well.

The old poet saw the red hand of Moscow behind everything. No British diehard could have been more apprehensive. "I know of three men here in Popayan," he said, with watery-eyed seriousness, "who are receiving money from Russia to make revolution."

There was not the least doubt that he believed it. He was the perfect type of old Spaniard of the Andes, pure-blooded, still living in a world that ended with that last letter of Simon Bolivar's on his study wall. And Popayan was a perfect setting.

Popayan is a Church stronghold in Colombia. It has been that ever since the days of the Conquistadores. Until the five hundred miles of new road were built over the Andes into Ecuador, Popayan lay at the end of a *cul-de-sac* in Colombian life. A railway had zigzagged up along the bed of a mad river to Popayan, but nothing but mules or horses could go further.

A pink church, perched on its green hill, was framed in my window every morning like a Russian ikon. Popayan was very reminiscent of the church. The great archways in the walls of every city block led into cavernous interiors, with gold shining above flickering altar lights. At six every morning I was awakened by the students of the ecclesiastical colleges marching forth by drum-beat to their day's study, which began with about an hour of prayer. And over all of this hung that air of brooding peace that it seems only the Catholic Church can give to a community.

I said to Valencia that Popayan seemed barren ground for Communist propagandists. But he shook his head. I did not know the dark forces at work.

You could understand this. His ranch-house itself had turned its back upon the world. The cowboys might be somewhere below, eating, or in their bunkhouses. But the faded brick veranda, with its couches of panther and cougar skins, faced a little patch of secluded green lawn that went down to a stream which flowed silently through the eucalyptus woods. The mementos of his study were mostly the souvenirs of immediate post-war Europe, during which time the Shakespearean head of William Valencia had represented Colombia at various conferences. But the Europe his mind dwelt in was the Vienna of Franz Josef, the Germany of Nietzsche.

In fact, to get in to talk with the great philosopher William Valencia had once disguised himself as a servant. Nietzsche was old, Valencia was young; they formed a friendship, the poet told me, which had a great influence on his life. But the superman had not materialized. Valencia looked around him now, after talking about Nietzsche, with the hopeless air of wondering why it was, why no man could be found in Colombia to put a stop to this madness which the Liberal Government called progress.

He asked his next querulous question of the world at large.

"What if I do obey the Government's edict," he said, "and cover all my land with cattle? Who will eat all that meat? Who can drink all that milk? What good will it do? We have not enough people in Colombia to eat all we can be made to produce."

*   *   *

Actually, apart from his tremors about Moscow, I agreed with everything he said. His fears of the red hand might or might not have been genuine: in South America these days people of consequence always see a Communist in every woodpile. Mythical monsters, the Communists are used to frighten electorates, encourage police abuses, and camouflage the inherent rottenness of the usual corrupt situation from visiting journalists. Big, bad wolf!

Valencia's question was the answer of all the big *hacendados* of Colombia to Bogotá, and to other capitals. It should be made clear here that few Governments in South America—quite contrary to popular conception—are from the upper classes.

The army, which rules Ecuador and, more remotely, Chile, is a distinctly middle-class affair. Its officers have final political power, but they have no social *cachet* such as they have in Europe. This means a very interesting situation, because the army has no sentimental reasons for maintaining these big landlords on their estates. As long as the army gets its pay and promotion quickly enough

that is about all it cares about. The army is quixotically
heroic and patriotic in fighting for its country over frontier
disputes, chronic cause of war in modern South America;
but in domestic politics it is just a plain gunman's racket.
And the army is not always on the side of the big landlords.

In Colombia, where the army plays no part whatever
in politics, government comes from political intellectuals.
And what terrified the old landowning poet was just these
intellectuals. They also were not necessarily on the side
of the big landowners. On the contrary, with their modern madness for "progress," they were only too likely to
make a drive against the big estates and break up the
feudalism that Valencia and his kind have enjoyed since
the days of the Conquistadores. "Divide the land among
the peasants!" Valencia had heard that often enough when
attending conferences in post-war Europe. It was *à la
mode*.

In South America, these big estates lying so remote
from the supervision of the capitals are actually a form of
feudalism that still exists in the twentieth century. Some
of the Andean farms are so cut off from communication,
so remote from any police control, that the big *hacendados*
make their own laws governing the life of their peons.
And they do not stop much short of the right of life or
death. And these megalomaniac ranch-owners are so con-
vinced of their own power that they will even take international law into their own hands, as is witnessed by
Señor Vigil's marching his army of peons into Leticia and
starting a war which cost the Colombians twenty million
dollars before it was settled.

Old Valencia had no such obscurity as was enjoyed by the rancher Vigil. The railway runs to Popayan. His only chance to save his estate was by proving to Bogotá the illogic of its "progress." Economically his answer was sound. After the nightmare of fueling railway-trains with surplus coffee in Brazil—and the Argentine, where, during the slump, the price of meat fell off so that the steers were not even worth their hides (they were killed, skinned, and left to rot on the pampas while their leather was sold in Buenos Aires)—Valencia had a good case against being commanded to cultivate every foot of his great estates.

Intrinsically his answer masked a greater truth. It was one thing to sit, as I did, in the Presidential Palace at Bogotá and listen to a "progressive" President tell you how he was determined to make every acre in his country pay its way. It was quite another, and an experience that demanded some realism, to sit on the black panther-skin beside old Valencia and realize how the new land-laws would shatter the harmony of this feudal existence.

Valencia and his kind in South America look upon ranching as a mode of life rather than a mere vulgar means of making a living. They can afford to. It may be selfish. Nevertheless, with decent ranchers like Valencia, you can't help feeling sorry for them and wishing that their ranches could remain untouched.

"The days of the big *haciendas* are over!" announced Valencia, in a tone intended to sound like a death-knell.

✓   ✓   ✓

While I was talking with the poet, the young Colombian engineer who had accompanied me sat with Valencia's three pretty daughters at the far end of the long veranda. In that public atmosphere he had no chance to say any of the things he wanted to say to the one he particularly wanted to impress. In fact, in that bright bird-like patter about inconsequential things (which is about all their secluded upbringing ever allows these South American girls to talk about) he couldn't even guess what she was thinking. Or if she did think. Certainly he could find no way of discovering what she thought about him. Which was what he had come there to find out.

When we drove home along the old cobbled road of the ranch to the high road, he groaned and looked back resentfully at the little pink *hacienda* lying so snugly among its secretive grove of eucalyptus-trees. He knew it would be a long time before he could find another good excuse, such as showing me the way, to put his foot on the Valencia estates again.

"I think these old Spanish customs are the limit!" he said.

Chapter XXIV

OVER THE ANDES

AT POPAYAN there was a bare-legged Indian madman who slept on a stone bench outside one of the churches. This was opposite my window. At all hours of the day and night I was aware of his rather unnerving presence. He slept on that particular stone bench because there was a fountain there. He had a fixation. This was a collection of copper cups. If he could fill all these cups with water before a boy ran along and knocked one over, then he had achieved something of great importance. But, until darkness came, he never had the chance to work this out. Someone always dashed in and knocked over a cup. The result was that I usually saw him in pursuit of fleeing boys who were yelling with laughter as he tried to throw water over them. He clanked as he ran because he wore all of his worldly goods tied around his waist.

But it was his hat that was the most interesting thing about him. This was a perfect replica of the "pork-pie" hats worn by the British Yeomen of the Guard—or that worn in Court dress by the early Spaniards. The Conquistadores—one bold group of them—had passed up these Andean valleys on their way from the Caribbean over into Ecuador. And Blasco Nuñez built furnaces at Popayan to manufacture pikes and arquebuses before he marched south over the Andes to fight Gonzalo Pizarro on the plain about a mile outside Quito. My only explanation of its strange shape is that the Indians of those days must have tried to copy the fashions of the Spaniards—in straw. The madman's hat was made of the fine palm fibers from which the Panama hats, that today cover the world, are now made in these regions. From Popayan up to Pasto on the Ecuadorian frontier, all the Indians wear Panamas. But whereas their modern styles are bleached snow-white, the madman's was dyed a rich, dark red.

Somewhere, in one of the side-valleys of the Andes above Popayan, there is a tribe of Indians where all the men and women wear these "pork-pie" hats. Frequently, during the days I lingered at Popayan, I would come on a couple of these strange stunted Indians, tying bales of goods on to pack-mules with ropes made of twisted rawhide; and then I would watch them trot out of the plaza and take the trail that led up a deep forested valley. They wore hard-woven black-and-white blankets—*ponchos*—through a hole in whose center they stuck their heads. Their bare legs were grotesquely short, with great round knobs of calves; and their feet, which had never even known a sandal, had toes the thickness of bananas. They were a distinct mountain people of themselves, and kept to themselves when down in Popayan. Not like some of the other Andean Indians, whose bare toes used to wiggle with ecstasy as they sat licking their spoons after a dish of the local ice-cream. No more incongruous sight could be imagined. Made me think of one day in inner Turkey, when I saw a body of Anatolians leave their camels and march into a shop, drawing daggers from their silver sheaths. They had not come to kill the proprietor. They bought a large chunk of candied *halva,* which they hacked into equal shares and ate with all the gusto of schoolboys.

"Yes, but you wait till these Indians go on a drunk!" said a sallow, erudite Bolivian half-heartedly holding down the job of hotel night-clerk (he had made a fortune, he told me, in San Francisco, and lost it in a Colombian gold-mine). "When they start drinking *chicha* they can stay on a blind for three days."

Investigating *chicha,* an Indian maize beer greatly appreciated by the Conquistadores, I found it inexpensive. But it was, without doubt, the most wishy-washy drink I have ever tasted. The only alternative strong drink, however, was a sticky, dark rum, much productive of melancholia. The young Colombian civil engineers (who had been educated in the United States), the Dutchman trying to found the German colony, and his mysterious German interpreter, and I drank beer made by a German concession down at Barranquilla, on the Caribbean.

The German interpreter, who had lived for years in remote parts of the Andes, firmly believed in a central Indian consciousness. He believed that they had a secret organization, and that its center was on an island in a lake in Ecuador—and that, on that island, there was a place that could only be reached by a secret subterranean passage known only to a few Inca canoemen.

I don't know whether this German was a little "touched" or not. Life in these rare altitudes of the Andes does seem to have a most peculiar effect upon European mentality. They are the most unreal mountains I have ever been in.

✓   ✓   ✓

The five-hundred-mile road which has recently been completed over the Andes from Popayan to Quito is, except for the periodic landslides, just as easy to get across as any mountain highway in the United States or Canada. And the tales I had been forced to listen to down in Cali of the two bridges being swept away were sheer nonsense—because there never had been any bridges. On the first day we crossed the Rio San Jorge in thirty-foot Indian dugouts. This was a strange sight.

At an altitude of around 9,000 or 10,000 feet, the river was already quite broad, pouring down at great speed from the eternal snows of the upper Andes. This glacial-gray flood, at this height, was enough in itself to give some idea of the peaks above us. We were right up against them here, but the river swept around a broad bend of gray boulders beyond which rose a hazy blue silhouette of another range of the Andes. And standing on the edge of this barbaric river, waiting for the Indian dugouts to be poled across for us, were three nuns in their uniform that has probably not changed much since the days of the first Spaniards. In fact, if a couple of adventurous Colombian merchants could have been removed from that picture it was a scene such as this same place on the river had seen for several hundred years.

The nuns were taking a weeping young novice up to a convent near Pasto. Sitting on the formidable pile of our baggage, that in some remarkable manner was to be taken across that swift river in the narrow dugouts, she was a tragic figure. But her tears were not over renouncing this world—in fact, from what I saw of Andean nuns, she was going to take a very active and useful part in it;

her grief came from two heart-wrenching partings she
had undergone that morning. The first of these was when
our bus stopped several miles outside of Popayan at a
convent to pick her up. The bus, as is its tranquil custom
in this part of the world, waited until she was ready to
depart. This was not until an old Mother Superior had
fussed about to see that all her meager baggage was safely
stowed on top of the American bus, and that the three
nuns and she had their lunches, and that she would not
forget to deliver certain messages to the Sisters up at
Pasto. It was like a young girl's first departure for board-
ing-school. The old Mother Superior wept herself as she
reached into the bus to give a last farewell pat to the
novice; and the bus driver nodded his head seriously
when he was cautioned by the Mother Superior to see
that all these things were carried out. He did not tell
the old nun that at the Rio San Jorge his bus would
stop and come back—that it could not swim a river. The
other parting occurred when, irritating as it seemed to
the rest of us, the novice made the driver stop in an apparently uninhabited mountain pass. We sat there, and
then an old Indian came down out of the mountain, shook
hands with the three nuns, gave them some money which
he had to press upon them, and then clung to the young
novice in a last good-by kiss. It was all very touching,
watching this young Indian girl saying good-by to her
father. Even the driver was moved by the scene, and
tried to start his bus in top gear. At another village we
stopped for a long time outside a house while the señora
got dressed. "Ma-ma" would be ready in just a second,
her little daughters kept telling us as half an hour dragged

by. I wonder that we ever arrived at that river in the
Andes at all.

A gigantic Negro, with a silver crucifix strapped over
his biceps, helped the nuns and myself into the waiting
dugout. Breasting the stiff current, he and another Negro
poled the hollowed log across the gray river; and we
landed on the other side to get into a bus with a steamship painted on its side and the large title AMAZONES.
At some 9,000 feet in the Andes its name seemed particularly inappropriate.

The next day we were slung across the gorge of the
Rio Juanamu on steel cables. A little aerial platform was
all that dangled from two pulleys. By twos and threes,
hanging on to our most precious pieces of baggage, we
were hauled across to the other side. The crazy river
roared through its gorge beneath us. The nuns seemed
to like this adventure, and the novice no longer wept.
Life in earnest had begun for her.

✶   ✶   ✶

One of the nuns turned out to have come from Germany. She was much intrigued by my cases of trout-rods
and asked me where I intended to use them. I replied,
"Wherever there are trout"—a logical answer that made
her laugh out loud. In the two days it took us to get
up to Pasto (where I had to get a private motor-car of my
own to get over into Ecuador) this bus-load became quite
friendly. There were no changes in our personnel. And
we did get our landslide.

At the little church town of La Union the driver was
told that a side of the Andes had slid down, obliterating

the road some miles ahead of us. And in La Union we spent the night while gangs of Indians shoveled the slip of the Andes away. The nuns—visitors joyfully received by the Sisters of a local convent—very likely spent a comfortable night.

I ate my dinner in a small hotel, almost deafened by the yells of local guitar players; and, when I closed the door of my room—which had no windows—found that I could not get out, as the key and lock were both on the outside of the door. I added my yells to the local chorus. In Popayan my room had a similar inconvenience. It had only one key. If I closed the door and forgot the key behind me, someone had to climb along the face of the hotel and get into my room to open the door again. There was no master key. And I often wondered what the Indian madman must have thought to see people always climbing across the face of that hotel about midnight.

✦   ✦   ✦

At Popayan a young man began this journey with us whose whole excess baggage, apart from the ordinary business suit he wore, was a huge black-and-white checked muffler, a portfolio, and a tin case such as cinema companies use for shipping reels. As I never saw him open this case, either to put anything in or take anything out, he must have carried his shaving-kit in his pockets—for he did shave, at least once, in the next five days to Quito. Only his brown button eyes appeared that first morning above the checked muffler as we waited an hour, from 6 A.M. on, for our casual bus to turn up. He was a solemn young man. It was only on the third morning, at Pasto on the Ecuadorian border, that he silently produced a letter of introduction and handed it to me. Why he waited two whole days before presenting it I don't know; the unflattering thought could not be ignored that he had waited that long until he finally made up his mind whether he wanted to know me or not. From the letter I read that he was a well-known Colombian journalist, whom I shall call Jesu Christi X, and that the paper he represented was one of the most rabid Derechista die-hards.

At Pasto, Jesu Christi announced that his original intention was only to come as far as there. But now he would see more of the world. He would share a motor-car to Quito with me.

I am sorry to think that he had cause to regret it.

✓ ✓ ✓

Trouble, if it could be called that, came on the Colombian side, from the shattering way Nature rang the changes on climate and altitude. There is plenty of cactus, at 5,700 feet, at Popayan. But the green hills and valleys of the Andes around this ancient town have almost as pleasant a climate as a northern county in England. I wore an overcoat coming out of Popayan that first morning. Two hours later our wretched bus-load was sweating in a tropic jungle that is one of the worst on the Equator. We had simply dropped down so many thousand feet into a chok-ing valley that the Equator had caught us. After about an hour of this stifling heat we were climbing steadily into cold thin air, so rare that Jesu Christi wrapped him-self to the eyes again. Here, my blood thinned already from the tropics, I shivered even in my thick British over-coat.

For long stretches the bus swung along the sides of the Andes at elevations of over 10,000 feet. I did not know which to admire most; these battered American motor-buses which hardly ever got out of second gear, either going up or coming down, or the nonchalant Colombians who took every bend as if there was no one on the road except themselves. Theoretically, this was supposed to be the case—most of this Andean road is barricaded by chains whose police-guards are put there to see that no two vehicles may meet on that section of road. It is a good precaution; but it doesn't take into consideration the trains of Indian pack-mules that come down from the slopes of the Andes, or vaqueros driving long strings of cattle, or the bullock trains which carry all the freight up into this part of the world. A bullock, plodding along with a machinery-case tied on either side of him, has a road-tread wider than a motor-bus.

And the mestizos who spend their romantic lives taking these slow-moving pack-trains up into the heights of the Andes were no way near as mild-mannered as our drivers when they suddenly saw coming around a turn a bus that threatened to push them off over a precipice—and at the same time announced an arrival that would eventually put them out of business.

There were some weird sights along that road. One was the rather startling sight of Indians wearing anywhere from two to a dozen Panama hats. They were taking them in to the town markets to sell them. And, as they leave the ends of the palm fibers still sticking out of them, they all looked as if they had gigantic brushes on their heads. There was one village of pure Negroes in this Indian world. For some reason, very likely affected by the rarefied air of the Andes, they had shot up grotesquely tall. But most of them were diseased, with piebald patches of white and swollen sores disfiguring them. I found them in a market-place where the chief things for sale were the yellow, blood-dripping entrails of some cattle that had just been killed. I learned afterwards that leprosy was common in that part of the Andes.

The constant feeling of unreality you experience in crossing the Andes comes from their everlasting greenness. At altitudes of around 10,000 feet you expect to see rock-masses. But flowers and forests grow in the Andes to above those heights. When you look down into the valley in which you see the two towns of Pasto and Tulcan, one in Colombia and the other in Ecuador, both lying at 9,000 feet, the valley below you is a bright green, and the tall trees in the mist-drenched pass you are in have wild, spiky pineapples growing like fungus in their branches, other queer spines with reddish flowers, and clusters of a purple flower like wild azaleas growing a hundred feet up along their limbs.

Up here, between Pasto and Ipales, on the Ecuadorian border, you pass along six extinct volcanoes, their cones usually lost in the clouds. And it was up here that I learned that volcanoes are safety-valves. If there is a subterranean convulsion, from which they do not "let off steam," an earthquake is usually the answer. There had been a heavy earthquake here at the end of 1936. Ipales was still in ruins, with a galvanized iron church arising out of the debris of the old stone structure; a one-roomed hotel, called "Merry," in its cypress square; and the walls of most of the houses left standing being propped up with long props made of trees. About half that fairly large town was still living in board shacks put up in the main square. The police headquarters was one.

It was outside Ipales where I saw the landslide that had buried an entire village. I thought its white gash in the green Andes was a vast quarry at first. Then I saw that it was too big for that. Then I realized that this was where a side of the mountain had folded over and buried alive an entire village of three hundred people. The whole village—men, women, children, chickens, dogs—lies entombed for ever in the side of the Andes. As my friend at Cali had stated, no one has made any attempt to dig down to them. And why not leave things as they are? Jesu Christi and I agreed that any man-made monument would be puny compared to the landslide that marked their grave.

And that was about the last pleasant exchange of words that Jesu Christi and I had with each other.

Chapter XXV

A BUREAUCRAT'S HEAVEN

THE WORST feature of an entrenched bureaucracy is that it always feels it must find some work to do in order to justify its existence. Otherwise it gets nervous. That accounts for all the documents you have to fill out in triplicate in South America, where it seems that with port, police, and customs officials about half the population is in uniform—riding on the taxpayer's back.

That was why I welcomed it when Jesu Christi suddenly said he would accompany me on my crazy expedition of trying to get over the Andes into Ecuador during the rainy season. Jesu Christi, as I have said, was a Colombian journalist—of the Right. He was good with the driver of the private car I had engaged at Pasto to take me over the Andes to Quito. The driver took the money I gave him in advance for petrol and then made a night of it. He turned up two hours late the next morning. Jesu Christi had been very good in damning the driver. I thought he would be a stand-by in an hour of need. But:

"He's a Rightist," I heard him telling the Colombian officials on the frontier.

"Shut up," I said. "I'm not a Rightist. I'm not anything. I'm not taking sides with any faction down here."

He looked at me mournfully. Wasn't I the stupidest man! Didn't I have enough savvy to understand that this was an indirect but very convincing way of assuring them that I was not a Communist?

"But why the hell should they think I'm a Communist?"

"Ah . . ." Jesu Christi shook his head. Did they think I was a low smuggler? No! Why did I think they took all precautions at the frontier? At the Grecian temple to bureaucracy that marks the Ecuadorian frontier on this pass over the Andes, Jesu Christi plucked a book from my bag and handed it to the customs official, who was writing down what I looked like and my whole family history back to William Tell. The book was *The Autopsy of the Monroe Doctrine,* which had pleased Jesu Christi very much when he saw it on my table at Pasto. It is all on the South American side. And now I heard him telling the customs officials that I was a good *amigo,* a warm friend of South America.

That, of course, aroused their suspicions more than anything else could. I had a lot of luggage, as I was out on a long trip away from London. The Colombians had made me open every bag as I left that country, and now these officials made me open every bag again. They lay in a circle round me, like a plate full of oysters on the half-shell. Jesu Christi—I now appreciated why—traveled with nothing but that portfolio, tin case, and checked muffler. He did not mind opening all his baggage; but it took me a quarter of an hour every time to fit my bags into the car again.

A few miles after we left the frontier we came to the first town in Ecuador—Tulcan. I invited Jesu Christi to have a glass of beer. When we came out into the street

I saw the back of the car open and all my bags going off up the street on the backs of Indians. I lit out after them, and came on a group of Indians watching the police going through my bags on the second floor of the local station. Our own driver was helping them! Diving into the scrum, I slammed shut my bags, orated a bit about the impudence of opening my bags when I was not even there, and altogether made such an unpleasant row that the police let me go rather than have to endure any more.

Half-way through the row I saw Jesu Christi make for the door. He was not going to be embroiled.

We drove on until, just as the sun started to sink beyond a snow-capped volcano, we came to a town where I suggested we get some dinner. When we came out, I found our driver again helping a policeman open my bags, which were once more lying like oysters on the half-shell all over the dusty road. Driven quite insane by such official nonsense, I clutched the policeman and pulled him loose from a bag full of white tropic suits. It was a mêlée that was to cost me three dollars in laundry bills in Quito afterwards.

My driver, the instant I began the all-in wrestling contest with the policeman, simply disappeared. I found him afterwards having dinner with Jesu Christi, who was drinking beer. As I came in, they stopped talking. The driver, who was an Indian, simply set his face into one of those completely blank masks that the Indians wear in the Andes. Jesu Christi arose and wrapped his checkered muffler round his face so that nothing showed but his brown, button eyes below his beret. Obviously I had ceased to be a friend of South America.

We drove on through the sandy roads and eucalyptus forest of upper Ecuador, continually nearly running down squat Indians, always trotting, carrying some massive pack-load that was held by a head-strap on their backs.

Feeling guilty that I had added another cause to the Latin-American's many reasons for not loving the "Yanqui," I stared at the backs of their two impassive heads. They did not speak to me. Neither did they speak to each other. And in that way we climbed and slid down mountains until the moon rose over the table-like peak of Chimborazo, and we dropped down into a deep gorge that was still holding the heat generated by the midday sun. Here, I knew, was the last customs—*the third inside Ecuador!*—before we got to Quito. And here I was quite prepared to give in; they could do anything they wanted to me here. I was beaten.

It was a wretched village of thatched mud hovels. From the door of one stepped two huge Negro policemen. My heart warmed when I saw those familiar African faces shining in the light of their lanterns. While I set myself to go through that ordeal of opening all the bags, I asked if by any conceivable chance I could get a bottle of beer.

"*Sí, señor,*" said the biggest Negro, disappearing among the mud huts. There was the sound of an excited female voice and the deep growl of a man, obviously complaining about being kicked up at this hour of the morning. The Negro came back holding a bottle and a glass, which he first washed carefully in the stream before handing it to me. As he did, the lantern light fell on both our faces; and when I saw that broad grin of his I laughed. So did he. As if he could read my thoughts, he nodded; he and

I could understand each other. When the Indian driver, with his idol-like countenance, voluntarily got out of the car to take out my bags, the big Negro waved him to shut up the car and drive on. We left him standing there in the lantern-light; he was something human and warm. The mere sight of him gave me the feeling of having, for a few moments, been in contact with my old life again. The two heads in the front seat before me never spoke—or moved.

✔ ✔ ✔

When we reached Quito the next morning Jesu Christi jumped out of the car the first time it stopped, and I never saw him again. The Indian, after he had parked his car somewhere, came back to the hotel for his money. I paid him the sum we had agreed upon over in Colombia, and was debating, after the way he had acted, whether I would give him a tip.

"No, no, señor!" he said, putting the money back on the table. I must pay him for the time we had lost going through the customs. Because of the customs we had not reached Quito the previous night, as we would have done had there been no customs. Therefore I owed him for another day.

At this incredible suggestion—remembering how he himself had helped, yes, practically invited the customs officials to open every one of my bags on every occasion—I collected my few words of Spanish and prepared to unburden my soul. But the load was too heavy. I merely sat there in the Metropolitan Bar and stared at the Indian. He stared at me. Then I gave a desperate laugh. At that harsh sound the Indian seized the money and dashed away.

Chapter XXVI

MILITARY DICTATORSHIP

In Ecuador you come face to face with a question that is always presenting itself in South American politics: Is a military dictator ever justifiable? Paez, of Ecuador, will make no attempt to deny that he is that; in fact, one of the first things that he tells you is that he was put in by the Army. He is kept in, his friends as well as his enemies will tell you, by a couple of crack regiments and the loyalty, at the moment, of the general staff. Federico Paez rules without any form of Constitution whatever. He has a Council which might be called his Cabinet, but he has no Parliament. At first hand this looks like dictatorship in its most rabid form. But is it? In this part of the world, people who know what they are talking about declare that Paez of Ecuador is a Liberal to the point of being a dangerous Socialist. Also, in the South American scene, it is quite possible for a Radical to be a dictator.

First, to get some understanding of this apparently impossible paradox, consider the Army. The Army in Ecuador, as it is in many of these South American Republics, is a distinctly middle-class affair. Its officers are not the young sons of the wealthy landowners. It is a thoroughly professional body, which until the end of 1936 did not even have conscription. It was a career for the middle class, as far as its officers were concerned. And for the poorer Ecuadorians of Spanish, or mixed Spanish and

Indian, descent—mestizos—it provided a good future as common soldiers. Even now, since conscription has been started—chiefly in order to break up this formation of professional janissaries—Indians are not conscripted for the Ecuadorian Army. Now, what was the Army's chief concern? Good pay and quick promotion. What did the Army fear? Instability at the top—incessant change of Presidents. Why? Because the general staff and the higher officers could never feel sure of their jobs; a new President might appoint his favorites in the Army over their heads.

The thing that makes the Army-revolution so personal and so old-fashioned in South America is that it dresses itself in no creed. It is purely a case of self-protection. But behind the Army *junta* is usually a patriotic intention as well.

It is putting it on its lowest basis to give the Ecuadorian Army credit for nothing but the materialistic intention of protecting its jobs. Look at the following facts.

In the last six years there have been nine presidents in Ecuador. Two lasted for less than three months. Two others lasted only a month each. And when the President immediately preceding Paez assumed dictatorial powers, he was arrested by the Army.

Dr. José M. Velasco Ibarra was legitimately elected President. He forced the Army to depose him because of his own political recklessness. Ibarra was President of Ecuador from September 1st, 1934, to August 10th, 1935. The reason why he finished his career that August was this: every year on August 10th, Parliament meets in Quito to sit for ninety days. Ibarra's Parliament—as have been all Parliaments in Ecuador within recent years—was overwhelmingly Liberal. For a Conservative to be made President of Ecuador was just as unthinkable as to have a Catholic for President of the United States. Ibarra was a Liberal—but during his term of office he had given several posts to the Conservatives to weaken their opposition and strengthen his own position. On the eve of this Parliament meeting in Quito on August 10th, Ibarra got the wind up—he was afraid of a Liberal Parliamentary revolt because of those posts he had given away. Accordingly he dissolved Parliament, annulled the 1929 Constitution, and declared himself dictator.

After that he lasted just six hours.

When the news got about Quito that Ibarra was ordering a certain number of arrests to consolidate his position and the dissolution of Parliament, the Army promptly arrested him by ordering him to remain inside his own house. The Army told Congress to convene and go about its duties. Congress immediately accepted the "resignation" of President Ibarra and appointed Dr. Antonio Pons, his Minister of State, as Acting President. The new President thereupon immediately set the date for new presidential elections to be held on September 11th to 14th.

Now, here is something in Ecuador which explains both the action of the Army and the reason why Paez is now calling himself dictator. It might also explain why, when Parliament is asked to re-assemble in August this year, Paez might still retain his position in office as a confessed military dictator.

That reason is the lamentable confusion within the ranks of the Ecuadorian political parties. When the elections were called for, the Liberal-Radical party in Ecuador was in such chaos that it ran three candidates for President. Any one, if he had been running alone, was certain of election. With three of them running against each other it made it certain that a Conservative would be President of Ecuador. As I have said, a Conservative President for Ecuador was an unthinkable thing. At any rate, the Liberal Dr. Pons thought so. He at once called for the resignation of all his cabinet—and then resigned himself.

Then the Army spoke. It had not taken any part in this political madhouse up to date. Now it took over all power. It dissolved Parliament for the second time within two months. Then it looked about for a suitable man to whom it could transfer its power. Dr. Federico Paez, Minister of Public Works in the Ibarra Government, an engineer who had worked in nearly all parts of Ecuador and knew the country, seemed the best man. The Army summoned him to take office and placed the power in his hands.

That was how Paez got in; it was no military *coup d'état.*

Now, once the Army was satisfied that its pay, rapid promotion, and security in office were guaranteed, it stepped into the background of the picture. Remember, Ecuador has a population of only two millions—two-thirds that of the city of Chicago—and nearly all of its public services, such as railways, electric light and power, street-car companies, and most of its biggest factories are owned and operated by foreigners, chiefly English and Americans. The Army has very little graft to lay hold of. It has no political program for Ecuador by which a general staff could fill its pockets. Its paramount concern is its professional future. Therefore, the Army lost nothing by giving Federico Paez a free hand to run the country.

So far so good. Political intellectuals in New York might say: "Oh, that's all very well, but he's not telling the truth when he says the Army gives him a free hand." Best neutral judgment on the spot declares that he has got a free hand. And I think my exposition above explains why.

But here is the real danger of a military dictator. The Army puts a "President" in office: the Army will keep him in office; but what about dissension within the Army itself? That is exactly what happened on November 28th, 1936, when the Calderon Regiment mutinied, and 60 people were killed and 101 wounded in the streets of Quito in the six hours before the revolt was suppressed.

Ecuadorian official Government spokesmen, not wishing the real reason for this near-revolution to be known, have given it out as the result of Communist agitation. In reality, the Calderon mutiny was fomented from the outside by some officers of the Army who had either resigned or lost their commissions, and the idea of the revolution appealed to a certain section of the common soldiery because they had been told that under the new conscription law their careers would not be permanent—the Government was getting ready to supersede them. One of these army officers on the outside had recently held a very high position in the Government.

The final criticism of a military dictatorship, such as the present one in Ecuador, is not that the Army is used as an instrument of oppression of the people, but the political dissension it causes within the ranks of the Army itself. It places peace in Ecuador at the mercy of stability within the Army. But even that could not be as chaotic as the instability of the Ecuadorian parties themselves. That is why neutral observers on the spot say that a military dictatorship may, in some cases, be justifiable, even desirable.

Chapter XXVII

THE MILITARY DICTATOR

With a six-foot Army bandmaster twirling his staff as he led a crack regiment down Quito's main street, bugle-calls, the clatter of horses' hooves, and the tramp of marching soldiery, André Roosevelt, fresh from flying over the snow-capped volcano, Chimborazo, flung open the door of my hotel room and yelled:

"Hop into your clothes—the President awaits you!"

It was eight o'clock in the morning, and I heartily wished that Federico Paez, the Dictator of Ecuador, did not keep such outrageous hours. The Presidential Palace flanks the main square wherein, among the royal palm-trees, is a female on a plinth holding an arc-light in her hand, whose kindly light had helped me to find my way home only a few hours back. Inside the Palace, a white Parthenon affair, were other women, the beauty chorus of official secretaries and stenographers. At this early hour —for I had got over to the Palace in less than ten min-utes—they were chattering with some smart, spurred young staff officers, while they took the covers off their typewriters preparatory to getting about Ecuador's busi-ness. In a small room at the end of all this sat a man with gaunt Indian cheek-bones, gray eyes, and the ability to laugh at impertinent questions.

"Were you put in by the Army?"

"I was."

"Why?"

"Because I was unlucky—they couldn't find anyone else. Someone had to be the Chief of Government."

"Do you run the Army—or does the Army dictate to you?"

"I," laughed Paez, "am the Chief of Government."

"I know that, but you are a military dictator, nevertheless?"

"Of course I am."

That stopped me.

"That's what every foreign newspaper says about me," continued Paez. "Military dictator! But I told the Army, when it transferred its power to me, that if it did not give me a free hand I would go home."

I have explained how this paradox of a military dictator given a free hand by the Army can, and does, exist in Ecuador. Today I was interested in trying to see what were the dictator's problems. One I already knew: the difficulty of getting any more foreign loans. There are any amount of sour Wall Street loans in South America. They smell to heaven. And Ecuador's credit has been hurt by these, as well as its own instability of government. A new President always lays open the danger of new legislation, possible repudiation of former loans, and fresh taxation on foreign concessionaires which would impair the repayment of new loans. A stable Government is now one of the prime requisites for the New York bankers with their burnt fingers. And Ecuador hasn't got that yet.

"Stupidity," answered Paez, when I asked him his chief problem. "There are too many people in Ecuador who can neither read nor write."

What was behind that statement was this: 90 per cent of the population of Ecuador are Indians, very few of whom are literate. Nearly all are exploited, often sold with the estates by their landlords, and, with this mass of uneducated, unhappy people in the country, Ecuador is always wide open for trouble. Whether they believe it or not, the people at the helm of Ecuador make much of the Communist bogey.

Automatically, after he had mentioned Communists, Paez reached in his desk and drew out some papers. They were alleged Communist propaganda, captured recently in some raids against alleged Communist agitators. One, found at Riobamba, always the center of Indian discontent, was very interesting. It was a letter written in longhand; and, as if to save paper, its author, when he had finished writing horizontally across the sheet, had continued his message by writing all around the edges of the paper in concentric circles. Paez held it up to the light for me to look at. The letter itself, when translated, was merely a domestic letter to a relative about family affairs. Against the light—now that it had been treated with a chemical solution—a typewritten message stood out. It was directions to the Indians at Riobamba about how to stage a revolt. It came from Nijni-Novgorod.

Another was a letter in Spanish, also to the Indians at Riobamba, predicting the mutiny of the Calderon Regiment. This one looked more authentic and practical than the letter supposed to have come from Nijni-Novgorod. This letter said: "Our brothers in the Calderon Regiment in Quito will help you to behead our oppressors." And it gave directions for a local uprising to support the Calderon mutiny.

The police caught what they declare are eighteen genuine Communist agitators in these raids. They are exiled now, over on Galapagos Islands, among the turtles, together with some thirty members of the mutinous Calderon Regiment. But the raids unearthed dozens of suspects whom Paez has now deported from Ecuador.

When Uruguay some time ago broke off relations with Soviet Russia and told its Minister to go back to Moscow, the Communists who had been flourishing under his wing were deported. They spread all over South America, some to Ecuador. And some of them came in with good passports.

"Everything seemed in order," laughed Paez, "so we let them in. Now I have taken a leaf from Uruguay's book. When they deported those Communists, Uruguay gave them a certificate of good character [a thing required by some South American countries in addition to your passport visa—if you are, or happen to look like, a poor man]. So," smiled Paez, "I am also giving them certificates of good character as I pass them on to other countries."

Chapter XXVIII

MUTINY IN ECUADOR

AT 11 A.M. on November 28th, 1936, a battery of the Calderon Regiment was lined up outside its Quito barracks. It was ordered to proceed to a farm called Lalorena, some distance outside the city. While the lieutenants were inspecting men and equipment, two sergeants walked out into the sandy barrack square and shouted to the battery: "Don't march!" At the same time, other officers of the regiment, lolling in their quarters on the balconies, saw their doors suddenly jerked shut and heard keys turned in the locks. They were prisoners in their own rooms.

This is extraordinary. The reason why that battery was being marched out of Quito was that it was to be disbanded—disaffection had been found inside the regiment. The officers knew it; they thought the men did not. And here they were, at this critical moment, without their arms!

The two lieutenants confronting the battery repeated the order for it to march. The battery refused to move. For a few seconds the scene was static; nobody moved. During this period Commandant Pinto, who had been working in his office, strolled out into the barrack yard. He took in the situation, drew his revolver, and walked towards the sergeants. As he did so a machine gun fired a short burst from over his head, and Commandant Pinto fell dead. The two lieutenants were also squirming about in the bloodstained sand.

A revolution had started in Ecuador.

"That was how it started," said a friend of mine who was forced to be a witness of most of this affair. "It started at 11.30 and it was all over at 5 o'clock—and I don't think that during that time anyone in it had any idea of what was going on. It was a circus, with side-shows going on all over the town. One of the main rings was around the Calderon barracks, where they'd set up field pieces at all four street corners and were firing shrapnel point-blank down the main streets of Quito. The other was the post office, where one of the sergeants had led a gang of mutineers to cut off communications with the rest of Ecuador. Why they didn't make straight for the Government Palace and take the President, God alone knows. He was sitting there within a few blocks of them all the time."

As an example of the ludicrous side of South American revolts, it might be said that during the whole of that morning, and well into the afternoon, President Paez, the Dictator of Ecuador, sat with his Cabinet in the Government palace and debated just how they ought to handle this revolt. And at 2.30 the Minister of State left this extraordinary Cabinet meeting to go home. But the license number of his car was No. 1. Some mutineers, seeing it pass them outside the public library, stopped the car, forced it to drive to the Calderon barracks, and locked up the Minister of State with the already imprisoned Calderon officers.

With one of the mutinous sergeants and his gang

already inside the post office, the Chief of Police of Quito was actually upstairs, trying to get into touch with the rest of Ecuador. Coming down, he saw the sergeant threatening the girls at the telephone exchange—the Calderon didn't want all communications cut off, as it wanted to telephone to other regiments to get them to come out and join the mutiny. The Chief of Police opened fire from the stairs and shot the sergeant. Fifty shots were fired around the heads of those girls at the telephone exchange, and they kept plugging in on the switchboard all the time—which I think is one of the most amazing exhibitions of nerve I have ever heard of.

The sergeant had brought with him to the post office five men and a motor-car set up with a machine gun. While the Chief of Police was shooting from the stairs, an Inspector of Police upstairs was telephoning police headquarters for reinforcements. Comic side of this minor engagement must have been that the gallant telephone girls were actually plugging in calls for the other sergeant at the mutinous Calderon barracks, for he was telephoning to the Iquito Regiment asking the men there to come out with the Calderon. Outside the Calderon barracks, soldiers were distributing arms to the populace, shouting: "Down with dictatorship!" And some sixty civilians were taking them.

My friend saw some raw conscripts of the Calderon trying to load a gun. They didn't know how to do it, and a passer-by, obviously an ex-artillery man, showed them how. They loaded it; then did not know how to fire it. "You do it like this," said the obliging stranger. "And at that moment," said my friend, "he was standing right in front of the gun!" One shell hit a trolley-wire, exploded, and killed seven people on the Esmeraldes. At four in the afternoon there seemed to be shooting all over the city.

The sudden increase of shooting around four o'clock was the Iquito, and the crack Yaguachi cavalry regiments firing on the mutineers. The Yaguachi was commanded by Colonel Enriquez, now Minister of War. He is an Indian who began life as a peasant boy. He is now only forty-two years old, and a redoubtable fighter. When the appalled mutineers of the Calderon saw the crack Yaguachi closing in on them they began to draw back from the streets into their barracks. As they did so, the Yaguachi, some of the best horsemen in South America—that continent of centaurs—charged through the archway of the barracks. In a few minutes a bugle-call from inside that fort told the citizens of Quito that the revolution was over.

✶   ✶   ✶

Sixty people had been killed in the heart of Quito. Forty of these were mutineers. Fifty now lie in prison awaiting trial—and a sure sentence of sixteen years. About twenty-eight are prisoners among the turtles out on Galapagos Islands. What started it? It is the fashion now, in South America, to use the Communists for every alibi. The Government's officials have stated this was the cause for the mutiny of the Calderon. Communism!

But when I asked Colonel Enriquez himself whom he blamed for it, he instantly named a former Minister of War—former general in the Army. "Perhaps not directly," he said, "but he knew what was going on—and he encouraged it." The reason being that dissatisfied officers now outside the Army would like to incite revolt to get back into power again.

*   *   *

An American friend of mine saw seven people killed in her street. A shell burst there. Two women going to the market were among them. One was cut in half; the other lay, her basket still on her arm, with no head. While my friend was looking down at this horror from her balcony, the municipal garbage-truck came along and put the bodies in it. A few minutes later the garbage-truck came back. This time it had a Red Cross freshly painted on it. It had collected some more human remains.

Chapter XXIX

COCKTAILS IN QUITO

COCKTAIL conversation in Quito consists chiefly of: "How do you get your breath?" At 9,500 feet no one knows a good answer. It was a Cossack who first asked me. He was a large, gloomy Cossack, wearing one of those fanciful uniforms which the exiles of the 1917 Revolution still cling to, many of them using that sad regalia to make a living in this cold world. It was very cold that morning in Quito when I came on him outside my hotel. He was walking a dog. The dog was a little fox-terrier, shivering in the thin air, with a very dissolute, morning-after appearance, coming from the fact, I suppose, that its toenails had been rouged a bright carmine. "Manicure," explained the Cossack.

Walking slowly with the dog, the Cossack told me that he had been evacuated with Baron Wrangel when the White Russian Army abandoned the Crimea in 1919. Since then he had been singing his way around the world. The cabarets of Constantinople during the Allied Occupation; then Paris, full of White Russians, nearly every one of whom was finding it impossible to fit into the Western world; then for eleven years he and a band of brother Cossacks had been on a world tour. They had been practically everywhere—except Russia. Quito, he said, had been the worst yet.

The reason why he had asked me how I was able to

231

get my breath—which I couldn't—was because in Quito the troupe of Don Cossack singers had literally been winded. He was already making arrangements to take the singers to some other South American city, and he tried to get me to give him some good American dollars for the Ecuadorian sucres they had been paid. He found me stony-hearted; I was also having difficulties trying to cash some perfectly good travelers' checks, so that I might get on to Peru.

"Somewhere low," he said vaguely, when I asked him where he would go from Quito. "People will not believe us—but the reason why we could not sing up here was because we just could not get enough breath."

*1 *1 *1

It was a bitter comment on Quito, "city of eternal spring," as the guide-books will have it.

The dog belonged to the White Russian girl who ran the Hermitage across the street. The Hermitage is listed as a restaurant and supper cabaret, but is much more than that. It is a life-saver. If you want to find one of the foreign colony of Quito, you will probably find him having either his lunch or his dinner at the Hermitage café. It is not necessarily its food which has brought him there. The pretty White Russian who runs it is much too young to have known much about old Russian dishes. And Quito itself has some most original and appetizing ideas about food. The hotel bars, for instance, which begin to fill up about 11 A.M., serve a pastry with the cocktails—and a little squirter full of lime-juice. You jab this into the crisp pastry and produce one of the most seductive,

destructive snacks in the drinking world. You eat dozens
of them. Then, twice a week, when the railway train
gets up into the Andes from Guayaquil, there are iced
prawns from the Pacific. This is a gala day, and about
9 o'clock the bar-tender shows up and begins to prepare
the prawns in goblets with a rich tomato cocktail sauce.
Or there are strips of fresh, uncooked fish lying on little
platters of fresh red peppers and rings of onion. And at
lunch the Ecuadorians make a marvelous fresh salad of
alligator pear with beetroot on beds of crisp lettuce. As
Colonel Blimp would put it: "Gad, sir, only a cad could
complain about Quito food!"

Nevertheless, you will find Colonel Blimp in the Hermitage. The foreign colony of Quito, more than in any
other capital in South America, seems to like its own
company. And what a company they are!

At one table in the Hermitage one night I sat with
André Roosevelt who, as I have said, had just come
down from flying over the snow-tipped volcano Chimborazo. Chimborazo, just outside of Quito, is 21,220 feet
high. As it is on the Equator, fattest part of the earth,
the top of Chimborazo is further from the earth's center
than the tip of Mount Everest. Previously he had been
exploring a jungle lagoon, walking on its bottom, with a
diver's helmet on his head, taking moving pictures of fish
and submarine bugs.

Walking with him along the bottom of that tropic
lagoon was an English captain, D.S.O., who tripped and
knocked out two of his own teeth against his diver's
helmet. The English captain was with us that night, in

fact, for practically every other luncheon and night. I found him an engaging companion.

He had just returned from an expedition fantastic enough to satisfy Rider Haggard. He had been eighteen months over in the Oriente, the unmapped jungle country around the headwaters of the Amazon, trying to catch up with the "Phantom Indians." No white man has ever seen them. Neither did this English captain. But he did find rivers which were either unknown, or which the Ecuadorians had mapped running in the wrong direction; he found Peruvian military outposts way up inside country which Ecuadorians claim is their territory. Interesting point this; claims by Ecuador, Peru, Colombia, and Brazil conflict in the unsurveyed drainage basin of the Upper Amazon. The accepted estimate of the area of Ecuador given in world geographies and almanacs is 118,500 square miles. The extreme official Ecuadorian claim is 275,936 square miles. And the English captain, following up a known river where he came on several *haciendas* whose population had recently been murdered by head-hunting Indians, found that that river could be navigated by a good-sized launch—so that the Peruvians, if they wanted to, could bring troops by water almost up to Quito's back door. His official thanks for making this known to the Ecuadorian War Department was the retort of some jealous Quito map-makers that he must be a Peruvian spy.

All did not go well with this Englishman. Yet, because of a combination of treachery and accident, he did stumble upon what may or may not be the lost treasure of the Incas. At any rate, he found gold; and four gold fish-hooks among the nuggets showed that he had come upon gold that had been *worked*. This in the unknown Oriente!

At almost the beginning of his eighteen months in the jungle, fifteen out of his seventeen Indian porters deserted him at 14,000 feet as he was trying to cross the Andes. Then he watched another Indian topple off a sharp shoulder and flatten out on the rocks of a river-bed a few thousand feet below. Getting around these untraveled spurs of the Andes, this Englishman told me, was one of the most terrible experiences of his life. Yet either he had to do that or lose height—go down several thousand feet, and exhaust the whole party by trying to win back height again. I have a pretty good idea why the Indians deserted him; he is known as "a hard man in the field." The one Indian left to him was too frightened to desert. He knew he was in a hostile Indian country, and he thought it was best to stick to the one man who might get him safely home. Then that Indian fell off a cliff. He caught some bushes, and the Englishman climbed down and rescued him. Then—climax—the Englishman fell off a cliff himself and broke all his right ribs at the back near the spine.

It was a month or so before he could travel again— and then he pushed on into the unknown Oriente. Tenacity such as this usually gets some reward; and it got a queer one now. Because of the slow marches he could make with only one Indian, because of his broken ribs, the Englishman happened to turn up at the junction of two rivers a few days after an Ecuadorian prospector had found these gold nuggets and unbelievable fish-hooks at the foot of a rapid.

"Señor," said the Ecuadorian, "as an Englishman and leader of the Andes-Amazon Expedition you have an official position in Quito. I am no one. If I try to prove my claim, some smart official will probably get it away from me. Become partner with me and I will go halves."

In the National Bank of Ecuador I held these gold nuggets and fish-hooks in my hands. They are about $1,800 worth, brought back as samples. The fish-hooks could not have held anything bigger than a minnow. They were without barbs. But they are unquestionably fish-hooks. When Pizarro murdered Atahualpa, probably not believing the Inca's promise that, if the Spaniards would free him, he would fill a large room full of gold, gold was at that very moment being brought to Cuzco by Indians on trails running in from all parts of the Andes. When these Indians, through their runners, heard that the Inca had been murdered they simply threw the gold down ravines or hid it in places where they knew the Conquistadores would never find it.

The Spaniards never did. It is possible that the English captain might have stumbled on some of it.

✓ ✓ ✓

A dark-haired young American who was with us that night is now a well-known Quito bullfighter. He studied the art of fighting bulls out on the *hacienda* of a wealthy friend. One of his instructors was the Spanish bullfighter I had seen gored months before at the village bullfight behind Cartagena. The American was gored once or twice in training, but not badly enough to shake his nerve. In fact, like many a flyer's crash—when you haven't got too far to drop and time to think it over—he had experienced the one thing most to be feared in his profession and found he could "take it." Under the tutelage of the old Spanish matador the young American reached a point where he was considered good enough to fight professionally in Quito's arena of blood and sand.

"After his first *corrida*," wrote a Quito bullfight *aficionado* in the Press, "he was showered with flowers, romantic red carnations, from the balconies by dark-eyed señoritas, and the bullfighting public gave him the name —as they always do give a name to a new matador—'the man without a soul.'"

I sat in the hotel bedroom of the English explorer one morning while the young American bullfighter, taking a napkin from the breakfast-tray, showed me the fine points of the dangerous game. Gracefully he demonstrated how "you kill the bull with the cape"—not moving your feet—by drawing the bull past you so that you can lean over and drive home the curved sword.

Spectator of this exhibition was a large, white-billed toucan which the English captain kept in his bedroom. He was a silly bird. He sat there with an olive in his bill, debating whether he would eat it or not. And he had made an awful mess of the room. So had two dic-dic birds the Englishman had brought back from the Oriente. Strange rail-like creatures with flaps on their feet—so lightning quick that they can run across short patches of water. They added their untidy habits to the mess which the wretched hotel proprietor insisted the English captain liked to live in. The toucan slept on one side of his bed on a piece of wrapping-paper; the dic-dics had a basket on the other side. They were looked after by a little Indian boy, an orphan the English captain had also brought back from the jungle. And they all seemed very fond of each other.

✓   ✓   ✓

Most melodramatic among the Quito foreign colony was a Chicago taxi-cab driver. He had come down to Ecuador to kill a lion. He was going to kill it with a sword. And he had an armored suit he had made for himself which made him look like a porcupine. It was full of nails, sticking out from a monkey-suit of thick canvas. He also wore a flying-helmet with a large spike sticking out of the top.

"But there aren't any lions in South America!" the bullfighter told him. "You can kill a jaguar, if you want to."

"No, what I come down here for to kill was a *lion*."

He would not take anything else. Neither could he be brought to believe there was no such thing as a lion in South America. He is still looking for a lion.

"Gee!" said the bullfighter to me. "He sure was the nuttiest squirrel I ever saw!"

✓   ✓   ✓

Taciturn member of the colony, a man seldom seen in Quito, was a quiet, distinguished-looking American who had been successfully operating a gold-mine in southern Ecuador for twenty-three years. And that, said cocktail conversation at the Hermitage, was as much of a feat as killing a lion with a sword.

I hated to leave these charming people. If I could never feel that I was getting quite enough breath in Quito, if I did not appreciate the "eternal spring" of its climate, and the way its streets suddenly bent upwards so that you had to get down almost on hands and knees to get up them, I found others there who will not exchange Quito for any other city in the world.

One of these is the American woman who had seen the shell explode in her street the day the Calderon Regiment mutinied. I had tea in the rose-garden behind her house. She was playing bridge here on that hectic day. She went to her balcony just at the moment when the shell exploded in her street. She was too horrified to leave the sight. So she got a hand-mirror, and lay down on the floor and watched what was going on in the street through this home-made periscope.

Then she went back to the rose-garden on her terrace. The four foreigners in that house played bridge through-out the rest of that uncertain afternoon. Whoever was dummy lay on the floor, with the hand-mirror, to report the progress of revolution.

Chapter XXX

SERFS OF THE ANDES

THE SADNESS of the Indians hangs like a mist in the valleys of the Andes. That 800-mile strip between Popayan in Colombia and across Ecuador down to Guayaquil on the Pacific is certainly one of the most unreal, monstrous parts of the world I ever hope to travel. But it will not be the sight of its snow-capped volcanoes, standing in a row, that I shall remember; nor the fantastic roof of Ecuador, where not even an Indian can live, and the faint valleys of the Andes are covered with nothing except a weird silver cactus; nor that antediluvian desert of black volcanic sand below Quito itself. The one figure that will remain in my mind from now on is that sullen, squat enigma of the landscape—the Indian of the Andes.

"They get on my nerves!" I told a Spaniard down at Riobamba. "I don't know whether it's just me, but they all have such a reproachful look. They depress me. The untouchables I saw out in India were positively gay by comparison."

"They are sad," he said. "They are slaves."

✐   ✐   ✐

The "slavery" he talked about is the peon system under which most of the Indians of the Andes have to eke out their wretched lives. It is much the same as the old peon rule in Yucatan, exposure of which so shocked the world several years ago. To see how it is possible it must first be realized that in a country like Ecuador the whites number less than 10 per cent of the population; and in Peru they are less than 15 per cent. Next realize that this thin strip of whites, who pride themselves on the amount of undiluted Spanish blood in their pedigrees, are the ruling class—exploiters is the more correct word—over this great bulk of Andean Indians, very few of whom can even read or write. Official statistics themselves give the amount of illiteracy in Ecuador as 75 per cent. Peru admits to 70 per cent. And official statistics in South America are always vaguely optimistic. Theoretically, as only literates have a right to vote (male only, in Peru), this great mass of Indians have no say whatever in the affairs of these countries. Realize the final outstanding truth—that very few Indians within the reach of Government rule have any land of their own in South America—and you have the peon system as it now prevails in Peru and Ecuador.

The system is this: The farm-owner gives the Indian an acre or so of land to work for himself, and a nominal wage, in some cases, of a few cents a day. In return for this the Indian agrees to work free for his master anywhere from one to six days a week. The landlord in many cases also owns the local store. In nearly every case the Indian feels obliged to go on working for him, either because he is chronically in debt to his master, or because, working under this system, he never has enough money to own land himself; and he might as well work for this landlord as any other one. The Indian land laborer has no alternative. There are laws made to protect the Indian; he can appeal to them—if he has ever heard of them, and if he can get any Government official to listen to his complaint. But the big landlords of Ecuador and Peru are very powerful; and you only have to go short distances out from the capitals in South America to find yourself in districts as remote from Government "interference" as were the plains of the American West during the days of the forty-niners.

"The law!" said this Ecuadorian of straight Spanish blood. "Such *haciendas* are beyond the law. When one of those local kings orders his peons to be beaten, they are beaten."

I quote such extreme abuses because this was a remark I had made frequently to me in the Andes—and I do not wish to use it as evidence. Call it hearsay. I only use it to re-emphasize a fact which is not hearsay—that is, that under the peon system which prevails on the majority of the farms in the Andes the Indians are sold, like cattle, with the land when it changes hands.

"Give an Indian a straight wage," almost any farm-owner in the Andes will declare to you, "and you will ruin him. He will only work until he gets enough to eat, then he will spend the rest on *chicha* and go off on a good drunk. You can't get any work out of him."

⟍   ⟍   ⟍

Riobamba is a good public spot to prove my point. It is a rich farming district, at 9,200 feet, half-way down along the railway line from Quito to Guayaquil. Even in South America, nobody could say that Riobamba was beyond the reach of the watchful Government. Yet when I was there the chief topic of discussion at the moment was the recent action of a German woman who owned a large farm in that district, and who had just introduced the hideous innovation of paying her Indian farm laborers a straight daily wage. She gave them no land, as there are Indian villages at Riobamba, but gave them 1.20 sucres a day. This is about fivepence. But the Indians seemed to be able to get along on that; and the experiment, according to my Spaniard friend, was acknowledged a success by them. But the German woman was then the target for all the rest of the landowners in the district, who were furiously declaring that she had ruined the market.

Riobamba, it might be mentioned, is always the center of Indian discontent in Ecuador. And just before I arrived several Indian leaders had been arrested for what the Government alleged was a "Communist" uprising.

✓ ✓ ✓

This question of the mistreatment of the Indian has considerably more in it than merely the question of his miserable plight. It is the reason for that "rawness" that a sensitive foreigner finally comes to take as the essential characteristic of South American life. This comes from the fact that there is no indigenous civilization. Four hundred years of misrule have filled the Indian with suspicion. He has shut himself up within himself, retreated into his own mind. With a strange unanimity, from the valleys between the Cordilleras of Colombia, over the high Andes, all the way down through the burning deserts of Peru to the borders of Chile, the Indian has tenaciously clung to his native dress. Even in the main streets of Quito, where the Indians are the street laborers, you will see at six o'clock any morning a mad rush of Indians trotting off to their work; the men barefooted, in red ponchos, wearing their hair plaited in pigtails down their backs; and their Indian women trotting after them. It is hard to tell men from women, except that nearly all of the women have young babies tied on their backs. In their hands are picks and shovels.

There are places in the Andes, such as Otavala in Ecuador, where the Indians do have some land of their own and live in "communities." They merely serve to emphasize the others' plight. Their dignity and pride are so different from the rest of the Indians that even a passer-by cannot fail to notice it. At Otavala you see the Indian women with strings of glass beads around their necks—some look as if they were made of gold—that are counterparts of the gold torn from the necks of their ancestors by Pizarro's Conquistadores four hundred years ago. Here a faint shadow of the Incas still seems to linger.

Throughout the Andes the landowners will tell you that they would much rather have a Negro to work for them, or a mestizo, than an Indian. They say the Indians are all weak from drink. And they do have some peculiar physical characteristics. The Ecuadorian Indian is pro-verbially weak in the arms. He cannot lift anywhere near as much as a white man can. Yet he can trot uphill with a grand piano on his back.

The Indian taking my baggage down from the fourth floor of a primitive hotel in Quito asked me to lift up my trunk and put it on his back. Then he asked for the rest of the bags. He walked downstairs, and I watched him trot happily up the street with a perfect mountain on his back. He was happy because any Indian who is lucky enough to be allowed to hang around a hotel doorway can make more in one load of baggage than his pack-train brother could make in a week on Ecuador's dusty roads.

On the road between Pasto and Quito I passed a long succession of these Indians trotting—they never walk— with freight-loads on their backs that would have strained a strong horse. In fact, no one in the upper Andes would ever think of employing a horse if an Indian were about. Which he always is. They trot, bent over, holding the loads with head-straps. It is said that they put themselves into a haze by chewing coco-leaves coated with lime. Chewing this, they get cocaine. The cocaine increases their endurance and, it is said, gives them even increased strength. At any rate, it must help to deaden thought and pain. And in every Indian market in the Andes you will see vendors sitting behind little piles of coco-leaves and cones of lime.

✦   ✦   ✦

These Andean Indians, their vast numbers and their vast ignorance, present a political problem that almost excuses the Governments for not doing more to attempt to solve it. It is so appalling. Theoretically, they should provide fertile ground for Communist propaganda. But, as I have pointed out, their vast ignorance makes them just as much a puzzle for the Communist as it does for the Government.

✦   ✦   ✦

In Chile, things are different. The Spanish Conquistadores never conquered the Araucanian Indians. About 100,000 of them still remain in the region of Temuco,

where they have their feasts of horseflesh and their ancient dances. But if the Conquistadores never conquered
the Araucanian Indians, the early sheep-ranchers (mostly
British or Scotch) practically annihilated the Indians with
whom they came into contact in southern Chile. I have
talked with sheep-ranchers who had ranched in Patagonia
who knew men who told them that "in the old days" they
regularly paid $10 for a pair of Indian's ears. "Had to,
my dear chap; if you didn't shoot them, they shot you."
All that has stopped, of course; but it provides one reason
why the Indians in that part of the world are now spoken
of as "a vanishing race." The present-day Indians in Chile
are the farm laborers for Chilean or German landlords,
given a certain amount of land where they can graze sheep
or goats, and about five pesos—tenpence—a day. Riding
horseback home at dusk one night from a fishing expedition in the German colony of southern Chile, I came on
two drunken Indians on the road. The Frenchman with
me translated what he heard one moan to the other.

"I would like to kill the whole German population,"
he said.

*   *   *

But you seldom hear an Indian speak. At Popayan, in
Colombia, I came on a Jap who was pursuing the strange
profession of mending broken typewriters in the Andes. I
called him in to mend mine. He was the usual inscrutable
little Jap. But he was Latin in his abandon compared to
the Indians around me. In Chile, the Indian unconquered
by the Spaniard is a fine upstanding human being. On a
horse, with huge roweled spurs lashed to his bare feet, he

is even a commanding figure. But in Ecuador or Peru he is a mute, silent, flat-faced enigma on the landscape. And no one knows what he is thinking about. You never hear an Indian child cry. And this silence, this unexpressed sorrow, drenches the Andes.

Chapter XXXI

"WHITE MAN'S GRAVE"

IT WAS the rainy season in Guayaquil. My typewriter ribbon was a wet rag. The sweat dripping off my forearms had made the carbon run. My pajamas were sausage-skins; and they were the third pair I had put on that morning; and downstairs some unperturbed Ecuadorians were eating alligator-pears and olive oil, a white fish from the Pacific, a tournedos of beef, French fried potatoes, heads of lettuce salad, ice-cream, and cheese. I had watched them eating precisely that same menu for the last seven days. I was waiting for a boat to get away.

My thoughts fluttered, and then fell down like damp moths. Noguchi? Ah, yes, that was the Jap; the Japanese army doctor who had helped the Rockefeller Foundation to drive the bubonic plague and the yellow fever from Guayaquil. What a pity. Fine chap. As the Ecuadorians have no generals in their army, the highest honor they could confer on him was to make him a colonel. Went out to Africa afterwards, inoculated himself with some fever he was trying to combat—and died for science.

Guayaquil—mud and rats and mosquitoes and flying cockroaches two inches long. They used to call it "The Pest-Hole of the Pacific." The mosquitoes carried the yellow fever and the rats carried the plague; and the Rockefeller Foundation and Colonel Noguchi mopped them up. But they hadn't mopped up the termites that shed their wings and fell down my pajama-neck when I was idiotic enough to try and read in bed. Nor had they done much against the flying cockroaches. How that American official had jumped when one banged against the awning that kept the rain off our heads.

"They're poisonous," he said. "Don't let them sting you. A flying cockroach is no joke."

I had never found them very funny when on the ground. The previous night, when I had lifted up the screen over my window to see what all the screaming was about, a flying cockroach hit me straight in the eye. He killed himself.

The screaming was from the fire department's siren directly across the street. Part of the clean-up of Guayaquil was helped by a fire that razed the city about forty years ago. It burnt down nearly all the wooden buildings that used to house the rats. When they rebuilt their city the Guayaquilians made the streets so wide that even a prairie fire could not leap across. They brought down modern fire-fighting equipment from the United States, and have been adding to it, so that today the hook-and-ladders of Guayaquil are old rickety Model T Fords and the fire-engine is a belching Mack that has only just been unloaded from New York.

Then they divided their city into zones, each one with its own siren signal. If fire happens to break out in Zone 5, the siren gives five screams; if it is Zone 20, it gives twenty screams. It must have broken out in a very obscure zone the night before; for that fire department siren screamed steadily for a good fifteen minutes. And I was fascinated by the 3 A.M. apparition of prehistoric Fords careening through the rain under hooks and ladders, also screaming; and toots of glee from the red roadsters of the fire chiefs left them behind. Vision terminated by a flying cockroach in my eye.

✱   ✱   ✱

I took off my pajamas and hung them up on a pair of wire coat-hangers with the hope that they would not rust but dry, and took up my position under the shower-bath. It was very little different either in temperature or intensity from the hot rain that was splashing the empty streets. Everybody walks under the arcades in Guayaquil. If you can run fast enough, you need not carry an umbrella: you can dash across street intersections and be under the arcades again.

Then I put on the last unwrinkled drill suit I had that was still white and went down to eat. I had been invited by an American automobile salesman who had just been discovered by an old college friend.

"Well, well, well," said this passing tourist, "good old Bill! To think of finding you here—down in old Guayaquil. Have another drink."

"No, thanks, Joe. I've got some work to do this afternoon. Can't drink in this climate like you can back home."

"Don't I know it! Say, what's that disease you get coming down from high altitudes? *Puno,* that's it. Well, I've got it."

This American, a most amusing card, gave us a horrid description of how the *puno* tied him up in knots. How, for instance, the cramps brought all of his toes up in hard, taut ridges, and, when he tried to push them down with his other foot, that also got tied in knots.

"Honest to God, Bill, last night I thought I never would get straightened out. And coming down from Quito, down that damn' zigzag that only comes down from the Andes twice a week—well, I thought I never was going to get here. If it hadn't 'a' been for a bottle of Scotch I had with me I think I'd have died."

"Damn' wonder you didn't. Only way you can keep alive in this climate is by keeping a strict grip on yourself."

"Aw, apple-sauce. Come on, just for old time's sake; and let's have a real one this time. I've got another bottle."

"Oh, all right; but it means I'm finished with work for the rest of the day. Go on, make it snappy. I'm simply dying for a drink."

"And," said my automobile friend as the other went up to his room, "that's just the hell of it. That's why we all push the boat out so much down here. It's the loneliness. I always do this when a friend comes to town."

⸓ ⸓ ⸓

Back in my room, I changed into the least soggy of my three pajama suits and sat down before my typewriter again. The conversation of the American automobile salesman had brought up a very interesting topic. And that was: the days of the Tropical Tramp, the Beachcomber, the men so beloved by O. Henry in *Cabbages and Kings*, are over.

"Even a tough nut like one of Richard Harding Davis's

characters couldn't make one of these countries give him a living these days. The cards are just stacked against him."

He spoke of the new laws, arising out of the new-found South American self-consciousness, limiting the number of its own nationals any foreign concern could employ, and of the £50 deposits that some of the Republics in Central and South America make a foreigner put down, unless he can show financial evidence of his ability to take care of himself. But, as he talked, my thoughts were fluttering— as they always did in Guayaquil. I thought of:

WANTED: *Earl Snyder. Escaped 1930 from State Prison, Jackson, Michigan.*

I thought: Well, Earl Snyder, where are you now? When I saw your picture it was under a notice in the Cartagena jail: "CARE YOUR PERSONS—THESE VERMIN ARE IN THIS COUNTRY."

I wondered then if you really were still in the Republic of Colombia. While I looked at your photograph I was having my own fingerprints taken—all ten of them—so that I might get a little pass with my photo on it, and right thumb-print, allowing me to remain in the country. In addition to my passport, I had to show this card to the police at any place where I stayed more than four days. And without that ugly "Certificate of Identity" I could not even leave the Republic of Colombia.

Earl Snyder, I thought, have you always been on the move? Are you trying to lie up in some of those wretched Negro huts built on stilts over the jungle mud? No police will ever come near you if you do. But what a place for a hide-out! And are you sorry now you came to the tropics? Not what you'd thought you would find, are they! Wav-

ing palm trees, and lazy beaches, and obliging native girls.
. . . No, they are not like that.

✓ ✓ ✓

The next day I went aboard my ship as soon as she
dropped her anchor in Guayas River mud. I wanted to get
back to, at any rate, a floating section of my own land again.
She was full of tourists on a long South American cruise.
They had all rushed ashore to see the sights. This, from
what they said on their return, was: "How many postcards
did you buy, Arthur? Twenty-five? Well, that's not
enough; we've got twice that number of people to write
to."

The ship lay an extra three hours off Guayaquil waiting
for a lighter to come out to take off an American motor-
truck chassis. For a new fire-engine, I suppose. A seven-
mile flood tide was sweeping back an incessant stream of
bobbing jungle growth up the Guayas River. Most of it
was long strings of water-hyacinths from some hot swamp
up above. They had been floating back and forth on the
tides until, one day, they would be swept into the Pacific
Ocean. The green leaves of the lilies had air-bubbles in
them to keep them afloat. They caught against our anchor
chain. Beautiful, but—well, when you have seen where
these plants grow you never want to see a water-hyacinth
again.

And it was while I was sitting like this on a lonely corner of the deck that a mestizo sidled up to me and tried
to sell me a crude model of the German Dornier Wal
seaplane made of feathery-light *balsa* wood; then he tried
to make me buy an Indian bow-and-arrow; then he tried
to sell me a human head.

Chapter XXXII

THE MAN WHO LOST HIS HEAD

At Popayan, at the foot of the 500-mile road that climbs over the Andes into Ecuador, I was offered three human heads. They were about the size of oranges, black, with long strings of hair dangling from them. Their lips had been sewn up with a white fiber of some sort; and they were all frowning. I was shown them by the local druggist. He had bought them in Quito; and I could have my pick for $25.

"They are made by the Jivaro Indians over in the Oriente," he said. "Whether they killed the owners to get them or not, I can't say. The chances are that they did. It's a custom of theirs. They are still wild over there; there's a tribe called the Phantom Indians which no white man has ever seen. These heads might have died a natural death—on the other hand, señor, a point that makes them more valuable—they might not. Anyway, the Ecuadorian Government will fine you $400 if you are found in possession of one of these valuable heads. I smuggled these out."

The secret of how these heads are shrunk is still kept from the white man. Nose, ears, and all the facial planes are all shrunk symmetrically. The likeness is preserved; holding one in your hand is just like looking at somebody's face through the reverse end of a telescope. Scientists in South America are always speculating how it can be done.

How do they get the bones out without cutting the flesh over the skull? How, for instance, is it possible to shrink a human ear until it is about the size of an almond? The Indians will not speak; and the silent heads still keep coming out of the steaming jungle on the eastern side of the Ecuadorian Andes.

At the Hermitage cabaret in Quito I was offered a head that very nearly overcame my scruples about possessing such a gruesome souvenir. It was that of a young girl, her eyes closed peacefully as if in quiet sleep. He lips were not sewn up. The expression of that head was complete repose. It slept in its pillow of long black silky hair. The hair had a soothing texture as I handled it. It was too life-like. I knew that head would get on my nerves if I carried it about with me. I put it away from me. It was also very expensive. The unpleasant creature trying to sell it to me would not take less than $35.

A friend of mine told me that when she was lying ill with fever in the hotel across the street, and left her door unlocked as she was too unwell to get up and open it, she was awakened three times one night to find one of these ghastly human heads being thrust into her face—the would-be vendors in their bare feet had come into her room so silently.

The Japs, with their genius for copying anything, have now gone into this business. They stretch skin over un-born lambs' skulls. They sell them to unsuspecting tour-ists. I saw three of these human heads in a display case of a Hindu shop on Front Street at Colon, in the Canal Zone.

But the secret of how the Indians shrink the human head is still undiscovered.

There is a story that you hear all up and down the west coast of South America of a German scientist who was determined to find it. He was an old chap, bald as an egg, with a Kaiser Wilhelm mustache. His greatest friend was the manager of one of the coastal shipping lines, an Englishman who had actually retired but who liked to cruise up and down the old familiar coast in the ships he had once managed. Whenever he wanted to, the old German could have a free passage with him. On one trip the German scientist waved him farewell and said he was going over into the Oriente. He got off at Callao and headed for Iquitos—and for a couple of years no more was heard of him.

One day, when the old Englishman was sitting on one of his ships in the harbor of Callao, a boy came aboard with a note. It was from the old German who keeps the curiosity shop in Callao: Would the Englishman please call at the shop before he left Callao? The Englishman very reluctantly did so.

"Well," said the old German, "here he is."

The Englishman held the head of his old friend in his hand. It was unmistakable. While it had no hair on its crown, it was practically all mustache. The Jivaros can't go as far as to shrink human hair.

"How much will you give me for it?" asked the old curiosity man.

"Good God!"

The Englishman went back on board ship and told the steward to put a fresh bottle of whiskey in his cabin— immediately.

✶　✶　✶

While I was in Guayaquil there was a head that had recently been offered that was still causing a lot of talk. Some believed it to be the head of a courier for the German Embassy who had started from Iquitos for Lima the year before. He had expressed a curiosity as to just how these Jivaro heads are made. And he had just vanished. Two men who had been offered the head and had held it in their hands said that it was not the courier. It had red hair, a bald patch, and a clipped red mustache.

"Obviously an Englishman."

Both believed the head to be genuine.

Chapter XXXIII

A SAILOR'S HUSBAND

"Me?" said O'Leary. "All I ever seen of this lousy world is through a bleedin' porthole."

Staring at the eye-scorching west coast of South America, I told him I did not think he was being deprived of so much. After the green steaming jungles of Colombia and Ecuador the coastline is just one long burning desert from Guayaquil to Valparaiso. And it takes twelve days in a fast ship to get there. For just twice the time it takes to cross from New York to London the big ship pounds down along a shore that is either a monotonous line drawn along the sky, like northern Peru, or sweeps of sandy shore mountains. During the hot day the sun fills these cliffs with deep violet shadows; at sunset, when the red ball slides down across the Pacific, for a few seconds the high shore glows a bright flamingo pink. Behind may lie fertile valleys; occasionally a hazy silhouette inland or the blissful sight of snows shining in the sky betoken the Andes. But this coast is a leafless land. There is not a palm tree with the courage to grow there. I believe there are one or two river mouths with green around them—but we must have passed them in the night.

Steamers lie off-shore, sometimes a full mile, and send their cargo and passengers in on lighters and tugs. The passengers, a bit taken aback by the coast they have two weeks to stare at, go ashore on any provocation. They are,

258

in fact, literally dragged ashore by the local South Americans. If you have ever seen a tug-load of local Peruvians scrambling up a steamer's side to get at the passengers at the same time that an outgoing boatful is fighting to get down, then you know what chaos is. There are occasions when a ship is in a hurry, and her captain doesn't want his passengers to leave the boat. In this case one has to repel the South Americans.

At Paita, in northern Peru, a few years ago an American skipper ordered the hose turned on some up-charging Peruvians. It repulsed them. But they pushed off a few feet from the ship in their bumboats and hurled everything loose they had in them at her black, imperturbable sides. The Peruvian Government followed up their indignation by refusing to let any ship be accepted at a port in Peru— if that particular captain was in command. For eight months his New York company had to put him on the San Francisco run until they made peace with the Peruvians.

We had 900 tons of tin and steel pipes to be swung overside into lighters at Talara, the top port in Peru. Talara is an Anglo-Saxon oil concession—an artificial town of board shacks and tanks lying at the foot of a cement-colored clay plateau. The only color, when I was there, was a red-and-white Peruvian flag waving over a wooden church, and two black oil-tankers loading at the end of a long pier. Some speckled pelicans were also diving for fish or else skimming in gloomy meditation in long flights along the waves.

The British, with that tenacity that marks the Englishman in foreign parts, had managed to get some grass to grow around their tennis-court and screened bungalows on the top of the plateau—a cliff washed by the cool green and white surf of the Pacific, which, owing to the Humboldt Current, was just as frigid for a bathing-beach as the top of the plateau was frying. But, so far as the "native" town was concerned, the only color at Talara was this waving red-and-white flag.

The passengers were astonished to be told that at Talara that day it was Carnival-time.

"And that means," yelled down our gloomy chief officer to a man on a lighter, "that we've got to lie here all day?"

"Sure," yelled back the white boss of the Peruvian stevedores on the lighter. "These people got to live and eat and play just the same as you do, don't they?"

We all hoped that our chief would shout "No!" But it is a rule of these steamships working the west coast that all relations with South Americans must be amicable. So our Wallace Beery merely sighed and turned away.

Which brings me back to O'Leary.

*   *   *

O'Leary belonged to that class on a ship about which very little is ever written. He was neither crew nor passenger; he was a table-and-cabin steward, alternating in those two capacities from 5 A.M. until around an hour short of midnight. Somewhere down below, along that greasy steel alleyway beside the stokehold, there was a berth in a cabin for O'Leary.

But from when he began polishing brass portholes at five until nearly twelve he was at the beck and call of "his" passengers. They might be passengers who had servants of their own and knew how to treat them. Or they might, like the Man-with-the-face at the center table, have had a rough time in this life and were now taking it out of every menial they met—just to show their authority.

"Did yeh just hear him this mornin'?" said O'Leary as he was placing some fresh towels in my cabin off Talara. "Yelling at me again. 'YOU—you git me some WAFFLES.' Orders everything on the menu twice—just because he thinks he's paid for it. Dat's what it means when you come down in life—having to be polite to So-and-So's like dat. I'd like to take a crack at him."

I knew the man; everyone on board the ship knew him —although we all tried hard not to.

✓   ✓   ✓

Now, one of the things that made O'Leary's life so bitter was that his wife had deserted him and gone to sea. What is more, O'Leary thought she had taken some good honest man's job away from him. Probably O'Leary's. On these palatial cool ships built for the tropics the company which owns the most splendid among them has done away with male table stewards. You are waited on by a nice, clean, fresh girl—definitely a lady. And these girls sleep in real comfortable cabins, like the lady passengers. They don't have to follow the traditions of the sea and sleep in a Turkish bath of a bunk down near the stoke-hold, like male O'Learys. Even more unbearable, from what O'Leary said to me, was the fact that these girls go ashore in the big ports, just like the lady passengers; and when the ship stops at Antofagasta to take on a load of

Andean copper, the girls go to the racecourse. They have their own flutter at roulette out at Viña del Mar, the Chilean Monte Carlo. They even run up to Lima and Santiago. In fact, these young women (many who are quite too perfect young ladies) went wherever the passengers went. Whereas O'Leary, face scarred from following the male traditions of the sea—particularly in bars ashore— wouldn't be allowed in many of these places. The Casino at Viña del Mar would quite definitely shut its nickeled plate-glass doors against him.

So there he was—a sailor's husband—and she hadn't written to him since she first went to sea.

"For all I know she's dancing down in Santiago now. Dis is the kind of dump where I'm welcome ashore. Sure, any bar, so long's my money lasts. Well, I'm going ashore today and I'm going to get stinking drunk. Dat's a promise."

✔ ✔ ✔

I would not waste a word on the carnival at Talara— except for one thing. The Talara band! The Latin-Americans at Talara, the oil-well workers, were not going to be outdone by the Anglo-Saxons in showing how *they* could conquer the barren monotony of the desert. When a cannonade of fire-crackers drew us ashore we found Talara's one cement street lined with carnival floats. Some extremely pretty South American girls were in them. Standing up with paper crowns on their heads as the Queen of Joy, and other things. There were children with paper wings to represent angels. They were interesting—but the band at their head was just unbelievable.

In that uniform such as only a romantic South American

can invent for special occasions, clasping horns, flutes, drums, and bassoons almost as big as themselves, there was a cluster of these decorative figures, all in a lumbering 15-ton motor-lorry, all standing up, packed as tight as a bunch of asparagus. In this *mélange* of gold lace and brass they came past at the head of the carnival. And in that position someone tossed a 2½-lb. "dynamite" fire-cracker into them.

That band simply rose up into the air and exploded in all directions like a colored rocket.

As I said, there was not much color at Talara. But there was color in all directions for the next few minutes during which the terrible infants of the Talara population walked up and threw rubber balloons full of water in our faces, and one girl—saved from death by her beauty—went about with a "stink-squirt" whose spray was something only a skunk could envy. The Talara carnival was a distinct success.

So was the blind of O'Leary.

There was no question where O'Leary had spent the Talara carnival. Any native *cantina* welcomes a red-headed *Americano* with plenty of money in his pocket. O'Leary was swaying like a Japanese doll on the landing lighter. He waved his arms wildly and fell back towards the seas. Then some miraculous heave of the lighter brought him upright again. When a wave washed the lighter away from the ship, O'Leary looked down into the gap and prepared to dive into it. He was saved from that by the chief table steward.

"I'll log him!" shouted down the chief officer from the

top of the gangway. "I'll log him two days' pay—so help me I will!"

And as O'Leary was led into the side of the ship his open shirt displayed a stomach tattooed with female designs that would also have barred him from any respectable bathing-beach.

✓ ✓ ✓

"He's a danger to the ship," declared the bar steward. The bar steward was contending with a coterie of white-clad port officials who were clamoring for the usual free drinks and American cigarettes. They demand hospitality. And the big steamship companies are prodigal hosts to the white-clad officialdom of South American ports—otherwise you might not get your papers passed.

"Let 'em wait," said the bar steward. "They'll get it all right, or they'd let out a yell you could hear from here to Valparaiso. They can wait till dinner-time—when they gets their free meal."

He deliberately attended to another passenger's order and then came back to me.

"This serving of free meals is a problem," he went on. "We used to feed dozens of 'em—any time of the day they wanted it, too. Well, the chief of one ship I was on was a bit too fast for 'em. One night, when a crowd comes aboard, he walks up to the head of them and he says: 'Tell me, sir, just how many of these people are distinguished enough to eat with you?' The big fellow draws himself up and looks around at his pals. 'Three,' says he. And that's all we ever give free feeds to at *that* port any more."

✓ ✓ ✓

O'Leary in the meantime was undergoing a miraculous cure in the Turkish-bath atmosphere of his little cabin down by the stokehold. As we passed in to dinner we saw him, a little the worse for wear; but it was obvious that the terrific heat must have sweated it out of him. He came in with the other stewards in a jacket of spotless white. The fact that he had forgotten to button it at the neck was perhaps the only giveaway.

"Hey—YOU!" said the pest at the center table. "I want some sweet pickles, see? . . . And the tunny fish . . . and some sardines and celery . . . and . . . well, you might as well just bring me the lot." Then the pest made the joke which always convulsed him at meals: "Bring 'em *today*—see?"

"Yessir," said O'Leary. And no menial could have looked more solemn or respectful as he went towards the pantry. He came back bearing a tray-load of all the dishes on the long list of *hors d'œuvres*. He balanced himself to meet the sway of the ship, and began to put them down.

"Sw-eet smilin' faces . . . passing to and fro. . . ." O'Leary put down a dish of pickles, and his rich Irish voice filled the cabin. . . . "Change here for Thurles . . . Limerick and Mayo. . . . Sweet smilin' faces . . ."

By this time the chief steward had reached O'Leary's side. Shaking his head puzzledly, he was led from the room. There was a sudden burst of laughter—from everyone except the Man-with-the-face at the center table. He scowled at the *hors d'œuvres* as if he were a personal enemy of every one of them.

O'Leary was logged. I read it:

*Terence O'Leary . . . for being under the influence of
drink and unable to perform his duties. . . .*

But the pay he was docked was more than made up by
the tips from sundry other males in that dining saloon.
From all except one man.

Chapter XXXIV

PORTRAIT OF A DICTATOR

THIS is the portrait of a dictator. The most important thing about it, as a lesson in South American politics, is how he came to be there. The picture of the man himself is of secondary importance. General Oscar R. Benavides of Peru did not seize power like Hitler or Mussolini. He heads no political creed such as National Socialism or Fascism. He is the product of chaos. He was elected to fill out the unexpired term of office of an assassinated President. Then there were to be new elections.

Yet when the next elections were held—and Benavides saw that the other candidate, a Socialist, had won hands down—he annulled the elections. A docile Constituent Assembly prolonged his term of office for another three years; Congress obediently dissolved itself; and General Oscar R. Benavides now rules Peru by decree.

His Cabinet, when I talked with him, consisted of four Army generals, three colonels, and two regular Navy captains.

When I asked him in the Government Palace at Lima, within a few feet of where the great Pizarro was assassinated, whether a military dictator was *ever* justifiable, he evaded a direct reply, but finally said:

"A strong man was needed."

First: an introduction to the picture of a strong man. In 1910, as an unknown lieutenant, Benavides was on the Peruvian border over in the Oriente, that steaming unmapped jungle east of the Andes, where the Jivaro headhunters will remove your skull and shrink it; and where Colombia, Peru, and Ecuador are still arguing (and occasionally fighting) over boundary-lines covering a territory larger than most of Europe. Benavides discovered an outpost of Colombians on Peruvian territory and fought them so well that he was given command of the regiment on that frontier. At the age of only thirty he was made Chief of the Peruvian General Staff. He was President of Peru in 1914. Not a bad four-year record even in the fireworks of South American politics.

Benavides served two years and then went as Minister to Italy in 1915 and—mark the date—remained in Europe until 1920.

While Benavides was away another President, unimportant in this story, held office four years. Then, for a second time, came the famous ill-starred President Augusto B. Leguia. He could have regained office peacefully; but he seized it by revolt. Leguia, the man who has done more for modern Peru than anyone else, the man who got Wall Street to loan Peru $100,000,000 ($85,-000,000 of which got into circulation—good average, considering the usual South American rake-off); Leguia, who was to serve three more terms (by means of altering the Constitution and making himself dictator) and then die, practically put to death, in the most horrible circumstances.

*   *   *

When Leguia seized the presidency at the end of 1919, Benavides resigned his post as Minister, resigned his commission as a general in the Army, and returned to Peru as a private citizen, hoping to persuade Leguia to form a Coalition Government.

Leguia immediately deported him. He put Benavides, and the previous President, on a boat bound for Australia, a destination for which Benavides never forgave him. Usually it is over the Andes into the Argentine, or some adjacent country, from which the exiles immediately make for Paris. Benavides and ex-President Pardo had the same intention. They waited until the ship got out to sea, then they went below and overcame the scruples of the crew. Then they marched up on the captain's bridge to "persuade" him to turn his ship around and land them at Costa Rica. The captain was persuaded. Benavides finally got to Paris—where he remained a long, long time.

✓ ✓ ✓

These were the boom years when Leguia was getting the millions from Wall Street and building the parks and boulevards that now make Lima one of the most beautiful cities in South America—boulevards by the red brick prison in which he was to lie in agony for two years. With Leguia in office, and everything coming his way, Benavides did not dare come home. He took a villa at Nice. During the boom years, President Leguia could have anything he wanted from the Peruvians—even the death of Benavides.

But then came the slump. The New York loans stopped. Cotton crashed, copper: Peru's chief exports. And Leguia

—unfortunate man—could not pay the Army. That, in the politics of Peru, Ecuador, and Chile, means the end. There was a revolt.

⚡ ⚡ ⚡

The revolt was led by a certain Colonel Sanchez Cerro. He persuaded two regiments to mutiny over at Arequipa. Himself, he climbed into an aeroplane and flew to the environs of Lima. The 'plane landed outside the city. Sanchez Cerro jumped on a horse and galloped to Lima. When he reached the city he rode through the streets and tore his shirt open. "Look!" he shouted to the excited mob. "See the blood I have shed for Peru!"

The fact that they were some old wounds he had received in Spanish Morocco did not matter. The crowd did not know that, nor did it care. The streets of Lima went mad. Sanchez Cerro did not get the presidency immediately. In the South American chaos that followed there were something like five Presidents in five days—then he got it. Colonel, now General, Sanchez Cerro was made President of Peru.

⚡ ⚡ ⚡

Sanchez Cerro, mixture of Spaniard and Indian, was a cold-blooded brute. He was the man who, when the Aprista party staged an abortive revolution at Trujillo, sent in two regiments and slaughtered 3,000 people. If the soldiers did not catch a man with a rifle in his hands, they ripped open his shirt to see if there was any bruise to show that he had been firing a rifle. If his shoulder showed anything like a bruise, he was lined up against a wall and shot. I have seen that adobe wall, with its rim of cactus, out near Chan Chan, the ruins of the Chimu, pre-Inca Indians.

President Leguia resigned the moment Sanchez Cerro rode into Lima. It is customary in the game of South American politics to let the resigned or deposed President make a graceful get-away; take a train or boat and leave the country. Leguia tried it. Sanchez Cerro sent a destroyer after his ship and brought him back. He threw him into Lima prison, that sinister red-brick building, made more macabre by its position, occupying one whole block by the parks and boulevards Leguia built with the boom-year Wall Street millions. And there poor old Leguia—for he was old now—was to lie in agony for two years. He had a prostate gland. People who brought him fresh clothes every week said that he could not even attend to himself. His condition was so pitiable that protests came in on all sides from the Diplomatic Corps. I know one Ambassador who went to Sanchez Cerro and said:

"If you value your own reputation abroad—or the reputation of Peru—let that old man out of the country to get some decent medical treatment. He will die if he is kept there."

"If he dies, he dies," said Sanchez Cerro.

It was an American doctor who finally raised such a hell that Sanchez Cerro, made a little nervous now by the disgust with which the Diplomatic Corps regarded him, allowed the American doctor to operate on Leguia in the Peruvian Naval Hospital at Callao. The American doctor said it was a hundred to one chance, and Leguia lost; he died in the prison hospital.

Then Sanchez Cerro was assassinated. The brother of

one of the victims of Trujillo stood in the crowd that watched the pompous President General Sanchez Cerro ride out of the Hippodrome, the Lima racetrack, after holding a review of the Army. He shot Sanchez Cerro.

In the chaos, Sanchez Cerro's troop of guards shot fifty bystanders—and put several more bullets by mistake into the dying Sanchez Cerro as well. He was plenty dead.

"I was lying in hospital," said a woman friend of mine, "and I heard the bells begin to toll. 'Is it for Sanchez Cerro?' I asked my husband, who came running into the room.

" 'It is.'

" 'Thank God!' I said."

✦   ✦   ✦

The wheel turns around. During the Sanchez Cerro regime Benavides, who had resigned his post as Minister to the Court of St. James's, had returned to Peru and was again fighting over in the Oriente against the Colombians. The Peruvian Congress immediately sent for him when Sanchez Cerro was shot and General Oscar R. Benavides became President of Peru again.

"I am a Peruvian patriot," he said with great reason when I sat with him among the marble columns and gold mirrors of Government Palace—most ornate of all South American presidential abodes. "I am a soldier. I place my country above all party politics."

This was when I asked him why, when he saw he had lost, he had arbitrarily canceled the last election results instead of letting the other candidate take his legally acquired office. He always insists he is a constitutional President.

"Because they are *assassins!*" The general actually hissed the last word. He was a small, stocky man, the only officer in a gilded palace glittering with officers who was not in uniform. Swinging one dapper foot over the other, white-mustached, continually chain-smoking aromatic cigarettes, he looked like a Parisian *boulevardier*. The story told about him that when a balky Cabinet would not give him a decision he wanted he summoned them to the Palace, put his back against the door, and said, "You won't get your dinner until you give it to me," seemed quite far-fetched of this plump little figure. Yet a parrot's voice is seductive compared to his harsh croak—and that *flair* that the Spaniards have for sheer manhood made General Oscar R. Benavides think there was no reason why his inches should prevent him from treating other generals, admirals, and political blusterers like naughty boys. He got that unanimous Cabinet decision within less than an hour.

The "assassins" are Peruvian Leftists. And anyone who knows anything about South American politics knows that if free elections were held in Peru—or Chile—the Leftists would be in the next minute. In Chile, the Rightist Coalition buys the votes—and the Leftists are so wretchedly poor that they take the money. In Peru, General Benavides simply cancels the votes. Which, if less orthodox, is more economical. But the real reason is that while both countries have plenty of reasons for a Leftist revolution, the Peruvians have the strongest, most appealing, probably most "native" Left-Wing movement in South America. It is not imported European ideology.

This is the Apra. And its leader, Raoul Haya de la Torre, is spoken of by his followers as the New Messiah. His main aim is to awaken and mobilize an Indo-American consciousness. He wants South American civilization to be "Indian." As out of the Peruvian population of six millions there are probably less than 400,000 who are *not* Indians, it can be seen that he has many followers. As only males over twenty-one who can read and write are eligible for a vote in Peru, very few of these five million odd Indians will be found on the voting register. But a Leftist victory in Peru will not be decided at the polls. It will be something bloody—like the Trujillo massacre.

Raoul Haya de la Torre is a young intellectual of good family who in 1921 founded the Gonzales Prada Popular University, initiated and maintained entirely by the students. Its leaders are said to have obtained the complete confidence of the laboring classes. The Peruvian Rightists try to pin the badge of Communism on the Aprista movement. But Haya de la Torre has been the guest of Moscow —and came back saying he did not believe Communism was the answer to the South American problem. And— most dramatic difference between the Apra movement and Soviet or Hitlerian doctrines—Haya de la Torre wants the Church to remain as a spiritual force in the civilization he wishes to create from the South American Indians.

It can be seen that, with the Indians and Labor behind him, and the Church—provided he looks like winning— not against him, young Raoul Haya de la Torre is a constant source of danger to General Oscar R. Benavides and

his Rightists. It was the Aprista movement which actually
elected a Socialist President of Peru at the last elections—
the election so summarily canceled bv General Benavides.

✦   ✦   ✦

Some idea of the official attitude toward Labor may be
gained from a little handbook called *Peru in Your Pocket*.
It was given me by the Government's official propagandist.
It says:

*Speaking generally, Labor in Peru is not possessed of
even elementary notions of economics, and being tempera-
mentally open to the influence of oratory, is easily persuaded to unreasonable action by interested propagandists.*

✦   ✦   ✦

Haya de la Torre was in hiding when I tried to see him
in Lima. Perhaps I was given the right reason when I was
told he would not see me because he was afraid the police
would follow me. Incident that might have had some
bearing on his caution was that the night I drove up from
Callao two dead Apristas had been found in the park. The
Government gave out an official explanation that they had
been killed by their own Apristas. Reason being that they
had been selected to murder Benavides—and lost their
nerve.

This gruesome explanation was given to me in the mar-
bled foyer of the Hotel Bolivar, in which at that moment
was a party of young Spanish girls from a finishing-school.
I say Spanish, although they were actually Peruvian, because these delicious creatures with their lovely eyes and

laughing lips were the daughters of the Spanish class that
rules Peru. It was their fathers who were the generals,
the naval captains, the bankers, the Cabinet Ministers, the
great *hacendados*. And to this group of gay beauties also
belonged young Haya de la Torre. He was of the same
blood, the same breed, the same traditions—and he was
hiding.

"Yes," said a Scandinavian who was with me, "there
they are—the clans. Lima is a city that still echoes with
the thunder from Pizarro. You have seen him—of course
you have—lying in his glass case under his gold lion over
in the Cathedral. Spaniards, Spaniards. Yes, and the Spaniards are still exploiting the Indians even as they did in
the old days of the Conquistadores. That's Peru.

"Let me tell you a story. When Venizelos, the great
Greek, came out here, he wanted to see Cuzco. An aristocratic young friend of mine was deputed to take him up.
That night, when he had shown the old man the capital
of the Incas, and they began to talk about what he had
seen in Peru, he said: 'Now, do be quite frank with me.
Tell me, just what do you think of the way we are governing this country?'

" 'My friend,' said Venizelos, 'you know less about your
own countrymen than you know about me.' "

✓   ✓   ✓

These were some of the things that I thought about
when I sat with "President" General Oscar Benavides:
that less than 15 per cent of the people he was governing
were white; that 70 per cent were illiterate; that Ameri-

cans owned her copper, and British and Americans between them owned her petroleum; that the Germans are supposed to have large agricultural interests; that the retail shops—as largely evinced in the streets—were run by either Japanese, Chinese, or Italians—and Peru owed the American bankers so much money that to pay it would take at least half the national budget.

In Europe or the United States the political intellectuals speak of the Fascist or Communist movements in South America. Benavides is a perfect example of how off the mark this is. This is what Benavides is up against; it was written in the *South American Journal*, September 16th, 1933; and it says Peru is:

A large and struggling area sparsely inhabited, with a small ruling class, and a large number of more or less docile Indians easily led and dragooned by generals momentarily in control, and difficult to hold in check by the central authorities in Lima. The task of the President has been no sinecure. Add to all this the plotting for power of those in opposition and seeking to obtain for themselves and friends the spoils of office, it is wonderful to find, not that there have been so many changes of government, but that there have been sufficient daring Peruvians to seek and plot for such temporary power as they could hope to obtain.

✦ ✦ ✦

And there he sat—with elections two years overdue—with his Cabinet of four generals, three colonels, and two navy captains.

"Tell me, sir," I asked, "for the safety of Peru, do you

think it would be wise to hold elections for some time to come?"

Put that way, General Benavides answered it.

"I am a Peruvian patriot," he croaked in his guttural French. "I am a soldier. There will not be elections in Peru for some time to come."

It was the answer of a dictator—South American species.

Chapter XXXV

TWO EXILES

I HAD the unique experience of talking to two South American Presidents—both of whom have exiled each other.

I saw the present President of Chile, Don Arturo Alessandri, in the summer palace overlooking the Pacific at Viña del Mar, outside of Valparaiso. I found General Carlos Ibañez, former occupant of that Presidential Palace, living in two rooms in a flat on the outskirts of Buenos Aires. One of his first acts was to open a little mahogany box on his desk and take out two passports.

"Mine and my wife's," he said with a philosophical smile. "I applied for leave to go back to Chile two days ago. The Chilean Consul sent them back to me. I cannot go home." He pointed to a photograph hanging on the wall of three children. "Mine," he said. "They are in Chile. I cannot bring them here. The exchange is against us. I am too poor."

I had to admit that it was a predicament. Ibañez really was ruined when he was deported from Chile. He has nothing but his general's pension to live on now.

The contrast was sensational, both in the circumstances under which I had seen the two men and in the two men themselves. Viña del Mar, with its glittering casino, roulette tables, racecourse, and vast Hotel O'Higgens (which is exactly like a fashion plate from *Harper's Bazaar*), is the smart Chilean watering-place. In fact, it is the Monte Carlo of the west coast of South America. The mauve Presidential Palace rests on a green cliff overlooking the settlement of stucco pseudo-Spanish villas surrounding the casino. Its gates, guarded by soldiers, opened out to a broad lawn surrounded by flower-gardens. There was a bulldog strolling across this lawn when I took the long walk along the pebbled drive-way to the presidential portals. "Grrrr!" he said. "Nice doggie," I said—but made no attempt to pat him. At the door of the Palace an aide-de-camp saluted me and led me into an ante-room. Here I was left alone for some minutes.

While I was standing there, looking out of the window at the bulldog, I was nearly shoved through the window-pane. Clutching the sill, I looked round. It was a Great Dane this time—about four feet high. The biggest dog I have even seen in my life! He was friendly—too friendly; I couldn't keep him away from me. Finally the aide-de-camp returned and bowed. "You can see the President," he said.

When I started for the door, the Great Dane came with me. My intention to make a dignified entrance was frustrated by a violent push from behind; it was the Great Dane trying to get in to see his beloved master—and thus we entered.

Don Arturo Alessandri is seventy years old, yet he has copious hair as black as an Indian's, pulled down in a bang over his right forehead like an old-fashioned actor's. General Ibañez put him on a train for Buenos Aires in 1928 with some detectives to see that he got there; and Don

Arturo lived in Paris until 1932—when the Socialists recalled him and he was, with their vote, elected President.
He came in as a man of the Left. Many people have forgotten that; and so, say some unkind people, has Don
Arturo Alessandri. At any rate, in the Congressional elections that were to follow a few days after this interview,
the Left parties were fighting Don Arturo and his crowd
for all they were worth.

"Are you still a man of the Left?" I asked him.

"Of course," he said, "I am still for the people. Have
you not seen our Labor laws?"

"Yes," I said, "I have seen them. On paper, they seem
the most progressive Labor laws in the world."

Don Arturo smiled. The Great Dane took another paw
at me. I could not, under the circumstances, point out to
Don Arturo that they seemed only on paper—that I had
seen more ragged people in the streets of Valparaiso than
in any other city on earth. I asked him about the huge
loans Chile owes the United States.

Now Chile, the most sporting country in South America, is an amazing country in the most unexpected respects
—one of them, as I have said, is that they have never
defaulted on a foreign debt. And they do not intend to de-
fault on this one. They are the frankest, most straightfor-
ward people, and you can't help but like them—tremen-
dously! Don Arturo, the minute this debt question was
mentioned, leaned forward in his chair. It was then that
he told me how he had wired Mr. X of the XYZ Bank
of New York and begged him not to make those loans to
Chile that Ibañez was getting.

"But you will repay them?" I asked.

"Of course we will. It will take time—but Chile will pay those loans."

✦　✦　✦

I repeated this statement to a New York banker. He said: "If morals have anything to do with it, the Americans holding Chilean bonds have a better chance of getting their money back than from any other South American country."

✦　✦　✦

I thought of this as I faced General Ibañez in one of the two rooms in his flat in Buenos Aires. Ibañez is tough; the sides of his head go straight up to a crisp crust of curly black hair. A Rightist. It is said of Ibañez that when he had arrested a quantity of Communist, or alleged Communist, agitators, he put them on barges to be towed by destroyers to Easter Island. "Tow them under!" Ibañez is reported to have ordered. No Communist ever reached Easter Island.

Ibañez, when he deported Don Arturo to Buenos Aires in 1928, also deported his son and several other prominent Chileans to Easter Island, two thousand miles off in the Pacific. These distinguished people did get there; and they stayed there for years. One of them was Vicumza Fuentes, Professor of the University of Chile, one of the most learned men in the country. Easter Island, with its giant monoliths of unknown origin, is, if nothing else, remote. A boat from Valparaiso goes out there once a year. Apart from these political exiles there is no one on Easter Island except some Kanakas, raising sheep. I know a sheep-rancher who was allowed to land there to bring back some sheep to Chile. It was three years after the exiles had been sent there.

"Bless my soul," said the sheep-rancher, "those exiles had changed the whole style of life on Easter Island. When I was out there before, the Kanakas were running around dressed in anything—nothing. This time I found the Kanaka girls in short skirts, silk stockings—and they had been using lipstick!"

✓ ✓ ✓

Alessandri had the unique experience of being deported by the Army, then recalled from Paris by an army *junta* and again made President, again deserted by the Army and deported to Paris, again recalled to be made President—this time with the Leftists supporting him.

Despite the fact that the Leftists now oppose him, Alessandri is generally conceded to have been the strongest force for good in Chilean politics for over twenty years.

✓ ✓ ✓

I asked Ibañez if force had been used to deport him from Chile; had soldiers taken him out of his home and put him on a train? He said:

"No; the President wrote me a letter saying it would be better for Chile if I left the country. So I left."

Chapter XXXVI

A DUCK SHOOT

THIS was a Diplomatic Corps shoot. A certain Cabinet Minister, knowing what no one else did—that he was going to resign after the forthcoming elections—remembered a promise he had made years before to two Ambassadors. Being a man of his word, nothing could stop him—not even the fact that it was fifteen days before the duck season opened. What was a duck to a man who had helped kick a previous President over the Andes?

When the Corps got the invitations, certain sporting members rubbed their eyes, looked at the date, and debated whether they ought to call up and see if there had not been some mistake. Instead of that, they called up each other and found all dates tallied. So that was all right.

But, then, the shoot was fixed for the leisurely hour of nine o'clock—and ducks, as everyone knows, rise with the dawn. Surely that must be a mistake? No; more telephoning between the Corps confirmed the date and hour exactly.

Well, it was all very queer.

The Ruritanian Naval Attaché, who was a passionate duck-shot, and I (as I was lucky enough to be invited), waited in the hotel lobby for the Ruritanian Ambassador. There were very few things the Ruritanian Ambassador has not shot in this world. Finally His Excellency did step out of the elevator, followed by his man carrying a twin-gun case. The lean greyhound type with that waving hair that it seems only an Ambassador can acquire, he was not to be hurried.

*   *   *

"Make your will," whispered the Naval Attaché as we waited on the lake-shore for the launches to take us to our blinds. He nodded towards two members of the Corps who were already loading their guns. They wore neat little kid mittens—in case the barrels got hot. They saw him looking at them and waved delightedly. Simultaneously, they let their guns point directly into our stomachs. Said the Ruritanian Naval Attaché: "We'll be lucky if it's only ducks we get today."

*   *   *

It had been many, many years since a gun had been fired on that lake—being, as it was, the sacred reservoir for a big city's water supply. Flocks of flamingoes had rested for years undisturbed along its marshy water-edge. They had come to think that they owned the place. With a resentful flick of their black hooked beaks they took the air—a motion like the first steps of a tango dance—and undulated their pink bodies to where a fringe of green eucalyptus decorated the blue mountains that held the lake. Then, thinking there must be some mistake about this invasion of their sanctuary, they undulated back, and one of the two diplomats with loaded guns raised his gun to shoot at them. No, he was told, that was not etiquette; we must wait until everyone was in his blind, and the Cabinet Minister gave the signal for the shoot to start.

"Oh," he said regretfully, looking at the flamingoes.

✓   ✓   ✓

While the Ambassador from Ruritania and his Naval Attaché, in the two blinds above me, were firing as if the new world war had begun, I never had a duck come within two hundred yards of me. I could not understand it. They always sheered off. Then I discovered that a little boy had been put in the blind without my noticing it, and had been walking up and down like Mickey Mouse—in full view! —behind me.

I pulled him in, sat on him, and managed to get a few unwary ducks before lunch-time. When the launch came to take me out of the blind, I looked anxiously at the two diplomats who had wanted to shoot a flamingo—and one had got one!

The Ruritanian Ambassador and his Naval Attaché were the last to be collected. We gave His Excellency the comfortable rear seat in the launch and his Naval Attaché sat beside him. One of the two diplomats who wanted a flamingo—I suppose the one who hadn't got this one— was standing up in the boat with his gun cocked. There was nothing we could do about it. Just sit there. Suddenly—he saw a duck on the lake! Quick as a flash, he fired. The Ruritanian Naval Attaché's hat came off. He picked it up and held his singing ear, almost deafened by the concussion of having a gun discharged within six inches of his head. He gave his *confrère* the sweetest smile.

"Missed," he said.

Chapter XXXVII

CHILEAN REFLECTIONS

"Yes, he's dead all right," said the night-nurse in hospital; "the poor old man. The devilish things you men will do to yourselves!"

"It was hospitality, Sister—the horseraces at Antofagasta, the copper men at Chanaral who come down from the Portrerillos mine; good men, those; you know, they shoot ducks up there at 11,000 feet. Chuquicamata, Coquimbo . . ." I ran off the names along the interminable Chilean coast; ports that were just railheads for the interior nitrate *pampa* or high copper-mines—most of them just a collection of roofs lying like turtles on the side of sandy mountains—ports where Americans and Englishmen had collected purposely to come out on board ships, have a good gab, and wash the dust out of their throats. There are 2,000 miles of this between Callao and Valparaiso. And what a lot of dust there was in some of those throats!

"That's what killed him, Sister."

"Ah, yes, we get a lot of 'em. But you should have read the dear old man's letters. The manager had to read them, you know; somebody has, before they get sent back home—and they were all from his *sister*. Apparently he was a single man—and those two were writing to each other just like a pair of blooming children—she, of course, telling the things he ought to see, and he, of course, writ-

287

ing back he'd seen them all, an' just what they looked like. The old Irishman just cried when he read some of those notes—said they struck him all of a heap. Ah, you men! I'm fed up with the lot of you—you and your throats."

It is true that our steamer going down the west coast of South America was a good deal like a traveling bar—especially when the captain was so popular. Also, she was a floating bit of home again. Close on the heels of the horde of port officials who were first up the ladder came mining engineers and their wives who had been living for years at elevations of anywhere from 11,000 to 14,000 feet. They came for company, and they got it; and with them, in hardly less of a holiday mood, came the traders and shipping men from the port itself. The two grinning Filipinos in the bar ran a continual relay race with drinks, saying, "Hello, Missr Thompson; how are you today?"—although it had been three months since that ship had touched that port on her run to New York and back, and Mr. Tompkins had been blasting copper out of a volcano all the time.

So you can see that the men who board the boat at these ports are interesting. And they should not be maligned with the intimation that they are too keen on drink. It is just the gala spirit of being down for a few days on the coast; although in the good old nitrate days (before that rude German invented the process whereby you could take it out of the sky—and nearly sank Chile, as a consequence) the great British companies used to induce sporting young Englishmen to remain up on the god-forsaken nitrate *pampa* by giving them free champagne and polo-ponies—and the English dressed for dinner.

"It's a grand old coast," said our captain, "but you've got to watch your step on it."

✦   ✦   ✦

It was night when the Sister sat on the foot of my bed and we talked about life so profoundly, and the lights of Valparaiso still went up into the sky as I had first seen them from the Pacific; a yellow bowl beneath the stars. They were significant of the savage contrasts of the country, for when those lights went out and the dawn came up I saw some of the most ragged people in the streets of Valparaiso that I have ever seen in my life—toughest days in Soviet Russia not excepted.

Rags so fantastic that it looked as if the tatterdemalions must have done it for a joke. Suits in which literally there was not a square foot of cloth of the same color, texture, age, or pattern. And I saw these, of all places, on the main business street, the Calle Prat, squatting before *El Mercurio*, the leading newspaper office. Not that I did not see them everywhere in Chile. The last person I fished with in Chile, down in the snow-tipped volcano region before I crossed the Andes into Patagonia, was a Chilean peasant, so fuzzy in his suit of rags that he looked like a Teddy bear. And I have never seen such wretched human beings in all my life as I have among the lower depths of Chile's city workers.

And yet—on paper—Chile has probably the most progressive program of social services in South America. Workmen's insurance, with sick benefit and free medical attendance; unemployment insurance schemes; laws regulating the increase of pay of the lower workers to meet increasing cost of life.

"But do we get it?" a Chilean worker demanded of me. "Like hell we do! You're sick, see, and you don't get any money for ten days. You don't think we've got a bank account, do you? And what are we going to do during those ten days? When you're *sick!*" He was alluding to the fact that sick benefit begins after ten days' illness.

The worker spat on the sidewalk. "What's the use of talking about things that don't exist? You can't even get the *doctor* to come and see you. The whole thing's just written down on paper."

His English came from his life as a sailor and stevedore, twenty years up and down the coast, attending English and American ships. And these stevedores showed some of the appalling illiteracy of the Chilean workmen. Most of them sign the pay-roll with their thumb.

On one steamship's pay-roll for unloading a cargo at Valparaiso, on one sheet 11 out of 20 signed with their thumbs; next sheet, 12 out of 20; the third sheet was 17 out of 20!

One thumb-print was opposite the picturesque name of Santiago Macdonald!

✒ ✒ ✒

Some illiterate Chileans (for voting purposes) have learned to sign their names, although they don't know what the letters mean. They make a scroll with their signature, however, a grand flourish—*and they know that by heart*. That's how they sign the voting register as "literates" at election time—and get twenty-five days' wages as a bribe for their vote. If anyone attempts to change one curve of that scroll, they can spot it instantly. These scrolls are as hard to forge as an orthodox signature.

✔ ✔ ✔

There was an election in Chile when I was there. They had the streets sanded in Valparaiso—so that the mounted carabineers could charge. This national constabulary of Chile is one of the finest, most patient body of police in the world. Both sides throw stones at the carabineers during election day. They carried bamboo lances, with red and white pennants fluttering from below the sharp steel tips. A naval brigade was also marching through the streets. The Army was guarding the polling-booths.

The Popular Front was making a strong drive to get in.

✔ ✔ ✔

The present combination of Conservatives in office was paying 200 pesos for a vote in the morning of election day—twenty-five days' wages for a vote. By five o'clock they were paying, in some districts where they were hard pressed, 400 pesos. Fifty working days. No wonder a ragged workman said to me:

"Two years from now is going to be a good year for all of us, because there will be *two* elections!"

I talked with a man in the country who was naïve enough to tell me that he had been paying 80 pesos all day for votes.

"But how do you know you get them? Suppose they vote another ticket after they get into the booth?"

"Ah, no. Most of our Chileans can't read or write.

The ballots are given out beforehand. We mark them
for them and then they go in and drop them into the
box. In some parts of Chile, where they think the men
might be too foxy, they fold the ballots like little paper
boats. That is very clever—because it takes force to push
them into the ballot-box—usually two hands. And we
stand outside to watch them do it."

Climax of naïveté was when at cocktail time he told
me he had drawn all of the funds he had been expend-
ing that day so liberally among the peons from the Conservative Party headquarters.

"The Minister of —— gave 4,000,000 pesos!"

❧ ❧ ❧

"Money!" growled a tattered-collared Chilean door
porter. "They buy our own souls from us!"

Nevertheless, the Popular Front did make some slight
gains that day. If it had gained a victory sufficient to
throw out the Government, the Army and Navy would
very likely have assumed control.

"But don't let them forget," said the door porter. "We
are working there. What if the soldiers and sailors won't
march against us?"

❧ ❧ ❧

In such an event there is another force in Chile which
will come into operation—the White Guard. This is com-
posed chiefly of the foreign residents in the country and
Chileans of British descent. In Valparaiso they numbered
about 5,000. I am using the past tense, because that force
is not in being at the moment. But before the elections of

1931 it was hurriedly assembled and armed against an expected Communist uprising. Every block of city streets was made a unit, every White Guard in that street had his post, and every White Guard's house had its arsenal. I know one man who had thirty-two rifles in his house.

For two weeks during 1931 a Chilean Radical, with the poetical name of Marmaduke Grove, was President of Chile—for Chile still persists in going through the form of legal elections. During these two weeks Marmaduke Grove went the limit in Radical oratory. On the night in which he advocated over the radio that the Communists and workers of Chile should confiscate all private property, the White Guard got out its revolvers.

A friend of mine, when the alarm was sent out, seized his two revolvers and ran to his post. It was behind a culvert directly below his flat window. He lay down behind that and placed some extra ammunition in a row on the culvert before him. He was a young Scotsman, in fact, and very methodical.

"I stood all the revolver bullets in a row," he said. "My wife was looking down at me. 'Shall I fire from here?' she said. I said: 'For God's sake don't shoot!' She'd have probably killed me. And there we sat . . . for hours . . . waitin' for the Communists. But they didn't come. Neither did my support—the rest of my group of White Guards were all at the movies."

✓ ✓ ✓

No better comment on the social situation in Chile could be found than merely the existence of this White Guard. When the workers become so desperate in their bondage that foreigners in a country feel they have to arm themselves against them, something is wrong with the way the workers are treated—despite all Chile's social services on paper.

Marmaduke Grove, incidentally, was re-elected to the Chilean Senate at the last elections.

✓   ✓   ✓

The Spanish civil war played a large part in these last elections. Franco was the hero of the Right; Miaja of the Left. The Right had its "Carlistas" and "Falangistas"; the Left had its Red Guard and "milicias." And, with no female suffrage and only literates eligible—theoretically —less than one-tenth of the adult population was entitled to a vote.

Chapter *XXXVIII*

LANDSCAPE WITH FISH

As THE two tough movie men said at Guayaquil, the
Andes get you. They had just been "shooting" South
America, and said it was the toughest job they ever had.
We all agreed that it was not merely the physical strain,
rapid changes of altitude, and living for weeks at heights
around 10,000 or 12,000 feet; it was your mind that went.
Your eyes facing that cruel chaos of volcanoes and valleys and jungle and snow and that antediluvian emptiness
below Quito where the world is nothing but sweeps of
black sand. We discussed this in a steamship office beside
the muddy Guayas River, with miles of purple water-
hyacinths floating by and catching in the anchor cables of
the ships. They were buying their tickets home after a
year in South America.

"The camera's got some of it," they said, "but, my
God!"

Well, the Andes got me all right. And I can say quite
definitely that I will never get over South America; it
has left a mark on me for the rest of my life. It is like
a tattoo. And it was while I was lying up for a bit to
get on with the job that two men walked into my room.

One said: "You're coming out to my farm—and you're
going to stay there as long as you like. It's yours."

The other said: "When you get through with him, I

am going to give you some fishing that will take the hair off your head."

I had never seen either of these two men before. They were typical of life in Chile. One was an Irishman who had begun sheep-ranching in Patagonia not long after those days when the sheep men down there, mostly Scots, were paying professional "Indian hunters" ten dollars for every pair of Indian's ears. He had hunted deer with the Indians, using a bow and arrow himself. This man had a ranch that ran from the surf of the Pacific to some foothills of the Cordilleras.

The other was a Scot—but he was the third generation of his family to be born in Chile, and was therefore a Chilean. He was an officer in the British artillery during most of the World War, and had been to a very posh English public school. He was reputed to be one of the best fishermen in Chile.

"The fishing he will give you," said the Ruritanian Naval Attaché, "*will* take your hair off! I don't dare tell people back home that the first three rainbow trout I got in Chile averaged five pounds each."

Then the Ruritanian Naval Attaché gave me some flies and the Ruritanian Ambassador gave me five Silver Doctors, which in that part of the world cost about $1.25 each. The story is still told in Chile of the rainbow trout that took this elderly diplomat a mile down a river full of nothing but rapids and volcanic rocks. "He weighed seven and a half pounds," said the Ambassador.

✓ ✓ ✓

The ranch was sanctuary. Long, only one room high, the ranch-house ran along three sides of a patio filled with a cool green grape arbor—so that the clusters of grapes hung just over our heads. Its dining-room had a long refectory table about which shooting-parties would soon sit long over their evening wine. And among other things that that excellent country, Chile, produces is a hock which is not much inferior to the wines of the Moselle or Rhine.

The sheep were away, grazing over in the Argentine; some 30,000 Merinos which had been taken over a snow-flanked pass 12,000 feet high in the Cordilleras. Only the cattle-men remained. Little centaurs, with silver spurs as large as butter-plates, and tight-fitting black leather *chaps*, and flat black hats which they held on with a strap under their noses. The big Irishman looked like a giant among them; and they took off their hats when they spoke to him and called him "Patron." He loved them.

"It doesn't make much difference what you pay these chaps," he said, "as long as you give them a horse—a good horse."

He had sent for his foreman to show me how a Chilean can handle a horse. A shy, embarrassed little man, simply dying to get off the veranda and back into the safety of his saddle again. When we went out into the farmyard he shot out into the ranch beyond it and then, turning, he raced back at full speed along the wire fence until he reached the gates, through which he brought the horse in a sharp right-angle turn. Both leaned over sharply as they took it. Then the Irishman told me to draw a line in the sand and walk back fifteen feet. I set up my camera there, and through its finder watched a horse charging at me until, in a cloud of sand, I saw that I was looking at its belly. From full speed it had come to a dead stop—directly on the line.

It is said that when the Conquistadores first landed in the west coast of South America, bringing the first horse after the prehistoric horse to that continent, the Indians thought that the man and the horse were one piece. This was some monster. It was not until the first Spaniard was knocked off his horse that the Indians lost some of their terror. And as I watched this little Chilean I also could easily believe that he and the horse were of one piece and of one mind.

He didn't do any tricks; it was just the way he and the horse maneuvered before us. They were as agile as a cat. When I reached up to shake hands with him he broke into an embarrassed grin, and even the horse seemed to smile with pride.

"Ah, that's grand stuff," said the Irishman, unable to keep the tremor of emotion out of his voice. "By God, it's a grand life to be working with fellows like that."

And that comradeship is the life of a rancher in Chile.

✠   ✠   ✠

A few nights later the Scot and I were on a train going down from Santiago to the Laja River. Twenty-five years ago there were no trout in Chile. But as the English and the Irish and the Americans will take their sport with them, some rainbow were imported. Today the Laja and some of the swift rivers down in the lake district are some of the finest trout rivers in the world. And the beauty of it all is, there is hardly anybody on them.

My first fish was a six-pound rainbow. He was caught

at the foot of a swift rapid in the Laja, with Chillan, an active volcano, shooting its sulphurous jet 2,000 feet into the sky at regular ten-minute intervals. I don't know any fish that ever gave me so much thrill. It might have been the weird wild scene, the blue silhouette of the Andes, and the volcanic country; but for half an hour that fish took me down the river in a state of absolute frenzy. I was so afraid I would lose him. I had merely a light Hardy rod, the same one I use whenever I get a chance in the streams of Somerset—and here was a big brute who in one rush had stripped me down to my last ten feet of backing, and me stumbling along among the boulders trying to win some line back from him.

The trouble is, these rivers of lower Chile are full of crayfish, and the rainbow are as healthy as prizefighters before a match. Frankly, after a few days, I was glad to get away from that fishing. That sound of the reel screaming was beginning to get on my nerves. They always made the same first, swift rush—and I always began to tremble. It's a terrible strain on the nerves. And it is on the legs. Whoever said that fishing is a gentle sport has not fished for rainbow.

With the Scot came an English naval officer who had at one time been a spy during the war—and an English girl. An ironic creature, she did not like fishing, much less talk about fishing; and she was brutally rude to both of them on the train.

"It all sounds such a damn' *bore*," she drawled.

"*Bore!*" Both of their eyes opened like saucers.

They held their fire admirably. But in the little village where we all had to stop, about a two-hour drive from the desolate Laja River, they solved their problem. They went without their dinners. The Englishman, very neatly, explained that after the fishing he had driven over to see a chap on another ranch. The Scot was more dour. He drove home with me, but, when we arrived at the hotel in the darkness, he strode into the little arbored patio and simply vanished. No amount of search could unearth him. A little puzzled, I ate a lonely dinner. The solution, of course, rested upon the fact that the English girl always had her breakfast in bed—so we talked over the day's fishing when we three met the next morning at breakfast-time.

"This place is getting too crowded," said the Scot. He was incensed because he had heard someone had been on the river about ten miles below us. At that moment, spitted on hooks in the kitchen, were a dozen rainbow, among which were two four-pounders of mine. We were eating them boiled, cold, for breakfast. "That's the trouble," continued the Scot. "Find a good river, go back to Santiago, and just *mention* what you've caught on it—and they come down after you like a flock of damn' gulls."

They had intended to put up a shack on this lonely stretch of Laja; essentially a horse country of arrogant Chileans with their hats held on by nose straps, and young girls, even old hags, riding through the scrub on side-saddles as their ancestors had done for hundreds of years. About as barren and barbaric a bit of country as one could wish.

"But now," said the Scot, "we are going to try further up. After you go, Jack and I are going to try another river I know of in the Andes."

And so I left them, they going off across the scrub towards where Chillan was shooting its yellow jet into the cloudless sky. I, to go down to the snow-capped volcanoes of the lake country, cross a pass into Patagonia, go up to Buenos Aires, and end my South American days.

I had made up my mind that Chile would be the end of them. Once I got over into the Argentine I was just going to take the train, boat, or anything I could, home. I wouldn't even look.

Chapter XXXIX

ANTONIO AND ERIC

Down in southern Chile I was walking with a Scotsman across his ranch. It was the end of summer, an unusually dry summer, and the burnt earth was waist deep in dead thistles. As we walked in search of a dove to shoot, he struck matches and threw them into this brittle scrub. Instantly the thistles crackled into flames. "Aren't you afraid of starting a fire?" I asked.

He shook his head and pointed to where a red road ran across the hills leading up to Santiago. "That'll stop it," he said, "with the wind where it is."

We got no doves, as one might expect under such circumstances; and then we walked back along the meadow made by a stream to see if there were any ducks lying under the willows. He had planted most of the trees on this ranch himself, turned a desert into a spot that was year by year becoming more inhabitable. One of his dreams was to re-forest a large section of ranch with eucalyptus-trees. He had just started this, and it was with pride that he showed me his young forest, now already some twenty feet high. "It'll be fine—to have that where a man can see it every day," he said.

Otherwise, it must be admitted, the ranch was a dusty solitude. That afternoon he drove north in his motor-car along the red sandy roads that lead to Santiago. The rest of us lolled around the veranda of worn, soft-red bricks, until in the cool of the evening it was time to go in and get into some fresh clothes for dinner. While I was washing some of the red dust off me, I heard Eric's brother-in-law come trotting into the yard on his horse. The Scotsman, like so many Britishers in Chile, had married a beautiful Chilean girl. During the summer her young brother (a handsome-looking brute) came out and helped run the ranch. I heard him call out something in Spanish to his sister as he passed her window; then I heard his spurs on the veranda.

"Phew!" he smiled, jabbing his fingers through his thick black hair as he came into my room. "There's a fire on."

"Yes, I know. I was with Eric when he started it."

"You were, were you? Well, why didn't you stop him?"

"It's his ranch."

"Yes—and it's his eucalyptus-trees it's moving towards. Well . . . I'm going to get into some clean clothes."

"What about the fire?"

"Oh, I've got to go and put that out."

Twenty minutes later I saw him standing in the drawing-room with the cocktail-shaker. His sister in a light evening gown was draped along a sofa. "There's a fire," she said, "moving towards Eric's trees."

"It is," said Antonio seriously. "And Eric—I know him —he loves those trees!"

"Yes," I said. "He seemed very proud of them."

"Oh, he is; Eric loves those trees."

"Have a cigarette," said Antonio. He really was a handsome man. He told me he got tired of being taken for a gigolo by aged American tourist women at Viña del Mar casino. "One of them tried to give me a tip!"

The maid came in and announced that dinner was served. We had conger eel soup, which is made with cream and a touch of tomato, a touch of flaked Parmesan, some special herbs, and the conger put into it at the very last minute. A delicious dish. "Really, Nita, you have excelled yourself," said proud Antonio. "How do you like Chilean dishes?" I answered that question by taking all the conger there was left. "About that fire . . ." I asked. "It's a frightful nuisance," said Antonio, buttering a rusk. "Eric *does* love those trees."

Then we had a roast sucking-pig split in half. The crackling carved beautifully, the way Antonio handled the knife. "Poor little pig," he said, "and you were alive only a few hours ago!"

I thought of poor Eric, bumping along those rutted roads on the long night drive to Santiago—and his precious nursery going up in flames behind that dour, unsuspecting head of his. He might have been an ass to start the fire, but it was the custom to burn thistles on the ranch at this time. And here was Antonio, with all the *mozos* at his command. All he had to do was give an order. "Maybe the flames aren't going towards that stand of eucalyptus?" I said hopefully. "Eric said they wouldn't."

"Well, he was wrong," said Antonio. "Eric is always so positive about things. That's the only fault I've got to find with Eric. He'll never admit he's wrong."

The dessert was very elaborate: a rich pastry with sugared blackberries and cream, that could not be poured out of a jug, from Eric's contented cattle. The cheese, which was very pungent, was also made by Eric's hands. In fact, except for the conger eel, which had been removed from among its rocks in the Humboldt Current, everything in that delightful meal came from Eric's steady Scots brain. He was making a great success of his farm. It was a very model of efficiency—when Eric was around. Too efficient, said Antonio, who accused Eric of bullying him.

"Sometimes," said Antonio, as he twisted the knob of the radio after dinner, "we can get Moscow. Want to hear your friends, the Bolshies?"

I nodded. But, twisting, Antonio got the Argentine—Buenos Aires, where the El Ta-bar-is Cabaret was sending out a tango which two members of the Silver Ballet were dancing.

"Mmmmmm!" said Antonio, biting his lower lip. "Isn't that *mar*-velous!"

He took his sister's coffee-cup away from her and seized her by the wrist. With a grace entirely different from the Anglo-Saxon acrobatic interpretation of the tango, Antonio and his sister, the world forgotten, moved until a chorus of applause from Buenos Aires told us that the dance had stopped.

"That's better than Moscow, isn't it?" demanded Antonio, baring those perfect teeth of his.

Decidedly. But I wish he could have got through to Santiago and told poor Eric to hurry back home because his trees were burning.

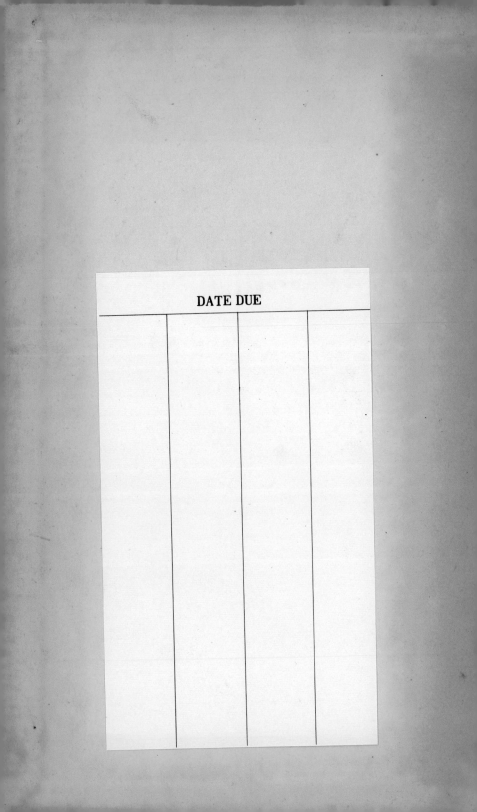

DATE DUE